FAST LANE

DREAM CARS

FAST LANE

DREAM CARS

Edited by Peter Dron

HAMLYN

CONTENTS

6 INTRODUCTION

10 ASTON MARTIN VANTAGE

14 ASTON MARTIN VIRAGE

18 ASTON MARTIN ZAGATO

22 AUDI QUATTRO

26 BENTLEY TURBO R

30 BMW ALPINA B12

34 BMW 850i

38 BMW M3

42 BMW M5

46 BMW Z1

50 CALLAWAY CORVETTE
   TWIN TURBO

54 CHEVROLET CORVETTE ZR-1

58 DE TOMASO PANTERA GT5

62 FERRARI 328

66 FERRARI 348

70 FERRARI 412

74 FERRARI F40

78 FERRARI TESTAROSSA

82 FORD SAPPHIRE RS COSWORTH

86 FORD TAURUS SHO

90 FORD THUNDERBIRD
   SUPER COUPÉ

94 HONDA NS-X

98 ISDERA IMPERATOR 108i

102 LAMBORGHINI COUNTACH

106 LAMBORGHINI DIABLO

110 LAMBORGHINI JALPA

114 LAMBORGHINI LM002

118 LANCIA 8.32

122 LANCIA DELTA INTEGRALE 16V

126 LISTER LE MANS

130 LOTUS ESPRIT TURBO

134 AMG MERCEDES HAMMER

138 MERCEDES 500SL

142 MVS VENTURI

146 NISSAN 300ZX

150 PANTHER SOLO

154 PLYMOUTH LASER

158 PORSCHE 911 CARRERA 4

162 PORSCHE 911 CARRERA CLUB SPORT

166 PORSCHE 928 S4GT

170 PORSCHE 944 TURBO

174 PORSCHE 959

178 RENAULT GTA V6 TURBO

182 TOYOTA SUPRA TURBO

186 TVR 420 SEAC

190 VECTOR W2

First Published in 1990 by
The Hamlyn Publishing Group Limited
a division of The Octopus Publishing Group,
Michelin House, 81 Fulham Road, London SW3 6RB

ISBN 0 600 57014 2

Produced by Mandarin Offset
Printed and bound in Hong Kong

INTRODUCTION

The modern motor car is a remarkable technological achievement; comfortable, quiet, extremely safe within its high design limitations, and convenient. In fact, today's cars are so good in so many ways that it is a shame to use them merely to get from home to work and back again.

The cars in this book are designed for much more than that. They are the stuff that schoolboys' dreams are made of: Ferraris, Lamborghinis, Aston Martins, Chevrolets, Porsches and BMWs. Together they represent the very best in terms of design, engineering, and sheer speed, from the classic high-performance supercars of the 1980s to the pre-production models of the 1990s.

At *Fast Lane* we have a constant stream of these vehicles passing through our hands in the course of a year. We drive them, measure their performance at the test track, photograph them, and then they are taken away again.

Without the financial burden or the emotional ties of ownership ('I've bought it so it *must* be good, even if it does break down every now and again, and the flat spot in the power curve isn't so bad really . . . '), we are able to judge all these cars dispassionately and

objectively. Indeed, there is a danger that road testers can too easily become blasé about cars, which can blind them to the virtues of a flawed masterpiece such as an Aston Martin Vantage. We always try to approach every car we get into without prejudice, however difficult this may be at times.

Every car in this book can really be called a dream car, selected from the top end of those we cover monthly in *Fast Lane*. In making the selection I initially thought of imposing arbitary rules, such that eligible cars would only have two doors; but I soon abandoned this because it would eliminate interesting models such as the BMW M5. In the end I simply chose as many interesting cars as possible, in terms of variety of price, rarity, size, nationality etc. Where several versions of a car have been available, I have

chosen the one I consider to be the most interesting; for example, the Porsche 911 Club Sport rather than the Carrera 2 or earlier versions.

Road tests appearing in a monthly magazine are inevitably somewhat ephemeral in that they freeze a model at a particular point in its development. Manufacturers constantly introduce modifications, often minor, but with the cumulative potential to cause a radical change in the nature of the car, even though it may look exactly the same. Technology moves at such a rate these days that standards also must be adjusted from time to time.

For those reasons, different judgements may be made of a particular car by the same writer, from one year to the next. For example, those who drove the new Chevrolet Corvette in 1983 will remember it as a car which handled satisfactorily on a smooth-surfaced race track, but which was almost undriveable on bumpy surfaces. Three years later, it was visually unchanged but intensive chassis development had cured it of its worst tendencies. In a book such as this, based on actual driving experiences, it is not always possible to clarify all such subtleties.

Naturally, one of the parameters by which cars are judged is value for money. But times and manufacturers' pricing policies change; last year's bargain can be over-priced this year, or vice versa. For this reason most references to money have been excised from the text.

It seems probable that, for all the wrong reasons, the kind of motoring many enthusiasts enjoy will not be possible in a few years' time. It is not just a question of arbitrary speed limits and other unintelligible laws, but the destruction of the environment. Eventually everywhere will look like city suburbs, and there may come a day when you will simply programme your destination into your car's satellite navigation system. You may retain a measure of control in that you will actually steer the car out into the unending stream of traffic but the fun will have gone.

That day has not yet arrived, and it is not yet a crime to admit that you enjoy driving. The cars featured in this book provide the most exciting experiences you can have on four wheels on the public highway, and they are assessed dispassionately by *Fast Lane*'s experts.

Peter Dron

ASTON MARTIN

VANTAGE

Some pundits argue that the last real Ferrari was the Daytona, and that the modern range of cars bearing the Prancing Horse emblem is little more than an expensive collection of upmarket Fiats. This is not only unfair, but untrue. But the Daytona was the last representative of a particular type of Ferrari, immensely powerful and fast, but also fragile and temperamental.

The last examples of this type of car – with large-capacity engines bristling with twin-choke Webers – disappeared after long production runs in early 1990. They were the Lamborghini Countach and the Aston Martin Vantage. Both companies which produced these splendid leviathans have been absorbed in recent years by large multi-national companies, Lamborghini by Chrysler and Aston Martin by Ford.

The most significant engineering change in the replacements is that the stacks of carbureters are replaced by the most modern multi-point fuel injection systems. They will not slip out of tune so easily, and they will be easier to start, but a little of the magic will have disappeared.

All Vantages require slightly different techniques to persuade them to start working, and a different procedure is necessary depending upon whether the engine is cold or hot. In the latter case, it is considerably harder, and unless it fires on the initial churn of the starter motor, and gets, three, two, four, five, three, and then all eight humming away at the first attempt, there may be a long wait before this expensive motor car will entertain further overtures. This could provoke discontent in a wealthy owner (not that there is any other kind!) used to the obedient behaviour of a Porsche or, these days, a Ferrari. With greater familiarity, though, a combination of improved technique and a brief prayer will pay dividends.

Peak power output for the final standard 580X version of the Vantage was 405 bhp at 6,250 rpm, with maximum torque of 390 lb ft developed at 5,000 rpm. Aston has consistently developed the V8, and the 580X engine had modified cylinder heads, new cam profiles, and a simplified oil flow system.

The Zagato-specification engine (with at least 434 bhp) was not an option in the Vantage, but it was possible to obtain a yet more powerful version, with a further 30 bhp (peaking 50 rpm earlier) and slightly increased maximum torque.

The car borrowed for these impressions was the personal property of Aston boss Victor Gauntlett. Since it had only 600 miles on the odometer when we took it over, it was not possible to extract performance figures from it. The factory claims a maximum speed of '162-174 mph', and experience suggests that this is a fair estimate; a few years ago a German magazine achieved 168 mph.

The claimed 0-60 mph time of 5.2 sec also rings true but, impressive though that is – especially in a car weighing just over 4000 lb – it is only part of the story.

The sound of the engine is wonderful, ranging from the characteristic V8 rumble at low rpm to an aggressive growl which makes the hairs on the back of your neck stand on end as the revs rise. There is a vast reserve of torque, almost regardless of which gear is engaged, and the car

ASTON MARTIN VANTAGE

ENGINE

Cylinders: V8 (90-degree), in-line, front-mounted.

Capacity: 5,341 cc (320 cu in).

Bore/stroke: 100/85 mm (3.94/3.35 in).

Valve gear: sohc per bank, chain driven, 16 valves.

Compression ratio: 10.2:1.

Fuel system: four downdraught twin-choke Weber 48 IDF 3/150 carbureters.

Maximum power: 405bhp/6,250 rpm.

Maximum torque: 390 lb ft (529 Nm)/5,000 rpm.

TRANSMISSION

Type: 5-speed manual, rear-wheel drive, limited-slip differential.

Mph/kph per 1,000 rpm in top gear: 25.2 /40.5.

SUSPENSION, WHEELS

Front: independent, by double wishbones, coil springs, anti-roll bar.

Rear: de Dion axle, Watts linkage, trailing arms, coil springs.

Steering: power-assisted rack and pinion.

Brakes: (Front) ventilated discs/(Rear) ventilated discs, servo assisted.

Tyres/wheels: 255/50 VR 16 - 8J.

DIMENSIONS

Length: 183.7 in (466.5 cm).

Width: 74.4 in (189 cm).

Height: 52.2 in (132.5 cm).

Wheelbase: 102.8 in (261 cm).

Front/rear track: 59.1/59.1 in (150/150 cm).

Weight: 4,077 lbs (1,850 kg).

Fuel tank: 23.0 gallons (104.5 litres).

PERFORMANCE *

Maximum speed: 174 mph (280 kph).

Acceleration: 0-60mph (96.5kph) 5.2 sec, 0-100 mph (161 kph) 12.2sec.

Fuel consumption (average): 13.4 mpg (21 litres/100 km).

*Factory figures

---

responds astoundingly to the application of full throttle even at 120 mph; in this respect, the Vantage is reminiscent of the Daytona.

An engine of this nature requires a gearbox of strength, and the Vantage's ZF is well up to the task. A slick, fingertip touch is not to be expected, and it is not what you get. But the change is absolutely positive, and with practice acceptably fast changes are possible. The clutch is heavy in traffic, but fine on the open road. Towards the end of the production run, it was possible to buy a Vantage fitted with the Chrysler Torqueflite three-speed automatic; but that was hardly a device to please enthusiasts!

Information gleaned from Zagato development was applied to the standard Vantage. This included the use of lower-profile (255/50) Goodyear Eagle tyres on 16 in rims with revised

offsets. There was also a touch more castor to add to steering feel, and some more negative camber to keep the tyres flat on the road during cornering roll. Dual-rate coil springs with Koni dampers were among further changes.

At low speeds, the Adwest steering is only modestly assisted, and the lock is poor, so in tight spaces the car feels ponderous. Once beyond parking speeds, the steering lightens sufficiently to take the effort out of changing direction.

The chassis responds in a similar way to the Zagato, though it is not quite the same: the wheelbase is identical, but the Zagato's track is wider, spring and damper settings are slightly different, and some 330 lb has been pared from the weight, all of which makes the Italian-bodied car feel a shade nimbler when pushed hard. Even

so, the standard Vantage has outstanding damping control at speed, soaking up most bumps with ease, and a purity of response matched by few rivals.

In most circumstances, the Vantage behaves in a neutral manner, with a tendency towards understeer which can be adjusted either by adding to or subtracting from throttle opening.

Even on wet surfaces, traction from the de Dion rear end and limited-slip differential is impeccable.

If necessary, it is possible to close the throttle and come back hard on it again just before the apex of a bend, and you can then exit in what looks like a lurid tail slide but which is actually quite easy for a moderately skilled driver to control. This sort of behaviour is not recommended on public roads, but it does illustrate the forgiving nature of the chassis. If you lose control of a Vantage, it is more than likely that you have not been listening to the messages it has been sending you, gently at first but with increasing insistence.

No other supercar capable of matching the Vantage's performance in a straight line and on twisting roads combines that ability with the extravagant exuberance of the traditional British luxury-car interior: polished walnut facia and door inserts, tightly bound Connolly leather, and deep-pile Wilton carpets. The paint finish on the voluptuously curving aluminium exterior panels goes a long way towards justifying the car's high price.

The Vantage is effectively only a two-seater, but it is very comfortable as such, especially for tall drivers. Even before the Ford takeover, the interior had been tidied up, with much improved stalks and switches.

The Virage Vantage will be a very different car, even apart from its new bodywork. With programmed fuel injection, integrated ignition, and four valves per cylinder, it will fire up instantly on all eight cylinders, hot or cold, it will never oil its plugs, or object to trickling along in traffic. It will not be so loud, its service intervals will be at least 12,000 miles, and it will consume less fuel. The clutch will be lighter, and the brakes will have an anti-lock system. It will be an easier car to drive and to live with, but some of the intangible magic will have gone.

13

ASTON MARTIN VIRAGE

O nly a few years ago, Aston Martins seemed to be the last of the dinosaurs. A few financial crises later, and after a welcomed takeover by Ford, we are now looking at the Virage, 'the Aston Martin for the 21st Century'.

The Virage is *not* the slightly less expensive car which Aston chairman Victor Gauntlett so dearly wants to build; that will follow, probably in 1993. Instead it is a replacement for the entire existing range of cars, apart from the Lagonda.

The styling of the Virage is the most obvious change. However, although in principle the car is the same type of animal as before (the 5.4-litre V8 attached to a separate chassis, with aluminium body panels, and suspension by wishbones at the front and a de Dion rear axle), this is much more than a simple reskin. It is a radical evolution.

The Virage appeared first in Fixed Head Coupé form (equivalent to the previous V8 'saloon'), followed by the Volante convertible (probably in late 1990), and the high-powered Vantage, with Weber carbureters replaced by fuel injection.

One day, then, there will be a Virage Volante Vantage, if the badges will fit.

The all-alloy V8 always had twin overhead camshafts per bank, but now they actuate four valves per cylinder, the new heads having been developed by Aston with Callaway Engineering of Connecticut. This takes the power output up from 305 bhp to approximately 330 bhp and peak torque from 320 to 350 lb ft.

Twenty years and a few facelifts on, William Town's DBS shape was still recognizable in the outgoing Astons. This car is handsome in a brutal manner, but a little dated in one or two details. The new body is the work of John Heffernan and Ken Greenley. The sense of aggression may have been softened, but the car is purposeful and some of the elegance of the DB4GT has been (consciously) recaptured, in the elliptical plan shape of the cockpit.

As ever, the aluminium body panels are hand beaten by skilled craftsmen. Beneath the front bumper, there is an aerodynamic undertray similar to that on the Vantage Zagato; that and the shaping of the tail surface result in zero lift at each end. Flush glazing is used all round.

As before, there is a separate steel chassis. Input from Cranfield Institute of Technology helps to ensure that this is torsionally stiffer, lighter and simpler. The wheelbase is as before, though overall length is increased by 2.8 in and width by 1 in. The car is 65 lb lighter, but that is a small percentage of the 3940 lb weight.

Redesigned double wishbones are used at the front, and the de Dion rear end is now entirely in aluminium, for stiffness, strength and reduced road noise. Bilstein worked with Aston to develop dampers specially for the car and, as before, dual-rate springs are used, with location by Watts linkage.

The wheels for the standard car are a size larger than previously, 16 in in diameter, fitted with Avon 255/60 VR tyres. Rim width is 8 in. The Vantage will again run on the Goodyear Eagles which suit it well.

The Aston saloon had ventilated discs all round, the rears mounted inboard; the Virage's plain rear discs are outboard. There is no sign yet of anti-lock brakes.

'It's completely different, but the signals are there,' says Gauntlett of the Virage's interior. 'You open the door and smell the Connolly leather, and that goes through to the old subliminal. Then you get in and see the wood and the carpets. So it's traditional, but more like a cockpit.

'The interior is a compromise between what stylists would like and what is practicable when you are hand trimming. The original design was much more suited to some sort of modern process rather than the way we do it.

'The new car, like the old one, is designed so

that big people can actually be comfortable. I can even sit in the back.' (He is about 6 ft 4 in tall, and powerfully built.) 'We've increased the head-room and legroom slightly, and there's a lot more luggage space.

'I think they (Heffernan and Greenley) have done a super job. They've done what we asked them to – it's properly modern yet still clearly an Aston.'

The Virage should be an easier car to build than its predecessor. In some areas (such as the de Dion casting) more expensive components are used, while others are simpler.

The factory claims a maximum speed of 155 mph, and acceleration figures (for the three-speed automatic version) of 0-60 mph in 6 sec, 0-100 mph in 15 sec. This is all substantially improved, and it is now achieved on unleaded fuel. More efficient combustion should lower the consumption rate, and tank capacity has been increased to 24.8 gallons.

Aston's prime objective with the Virage was to have a motor car that met all legislative requirements. One thinks of all the direct marketing reasons for making the new car with its new shape, but everything is subsidiary to the

fact that the current car would not meet the regulations.

'Another important point is that many of the parts associated with the current car will become unavailable,' continues Gauntlett. 'We've had to spend much of our engineering time each year resourcing components. With a car that's 20 years old, you're bound to have that problem, especially with our volumes, of certain elements falling out of the supply chain and having to be replaced.

'It would not have been efficient to have kept the current car alive. Anyway, there is the desire

ASTON MARTIN VIRAGE

ENGINE

Cylinders: V8 (90-degree), in-line, front-mounted.

Capacity: 5,341 cc (320 cu in).

Bore/stroke: 100/85 mm (3.94/3.35 in).

Valve gear: dohc per bank, chain driven, 32 valves.

Compression ratio: 9.5:1.

Fuel system: Weber-Marelli electronic fuel injection.

Maximum power: 335bhp/5,300 rpm.

Maximum torque: 364 lb ft (494 Nm)/4,000 rpm.

TRANSMISSION

Type: 5-speed manual (or three-speed auto), rear-wheel drive, limited-slip differential.

Mph/kph per 1,000 rpm in top gear: 26.7/43.0

SUSPENSION, WHEELS

Front: independent, by double wishbones, coil springs, anti-roll bar.

Rear: de Dion axle, Watts linkage, trailing arms, coil springs.

Steering: power-assisted rack and pinion.

Brakes: (Front) ventilated discs/(Rear) ventilated discs, servo assisted.

Tyres/wheels: 255/60 VR 16 - 8J.

DIMENSIONS

Length: 186.4 in (473.5 cm).

Width: 73.0 in (185.5m).

Height: 52.0 in (132 cm).

Wheelbase: 102.8 in (261 cm).

Front/rear track: 59.1/59.1 in (150/150 cm).

Weight: 3,942 lbs (1,790 kg).

Fuel tank: 24.9 gallons (113 litres).

PERFORMANCE*

Maximum speed: 155 mph (250 kph).

Acceleration: 0-60 mph (96.5 kph) 6 sec.

Fuel consumption (average): 15.7 mpg (18 litres/100 km).

*Factory figures for automatic version

to show that one is alive and kicking, so obviously a new motor car is needed. People say "Ah, the current car's doing so well. Why don't you just keep doing that?" That is where the enthusiast in you would be allowed to run riot. We can't introduce new models that often, but we've certainly got to do it. A new Aston is something pretty significant.

'The Ford connection has had very little effect on this car, because they came in at such a late stage, and the die was cast. When we enter the American market, they will be more involved, especially with things like passive restraint. 'The good thing is that they didn't come in and say

"Hold everything", go through the whole project and ask "Could you please do this . . ." and so on. It would have been impossible, and we would not have had the car for two years.

'They've managed to restrain themselves, which must be quite difficult if you think about it. The natural reactions when you've bought something is to leap in through the door and put your stamp on it. It's jolly helpful from our point of view that they didn't.

'They recognize that, however frustrating it might be, the project was so far down the road that it was proper to let us get on with it. One could have got into styling committees so easily.'

The first Virages were delivered in early 1990, around the time that Victor Gauntlett was forced to close down his racing team, just when it seemed on the brink of success in world sports car racing. The official reasons were uncertainty over Le Mans and lack of an engine for a changed formula. Many observers, however, took the view that Ford disapproved of two of its divisions (Jaguar and Aston Martin) racing against each other.

It is too early to speculate on the Virage's prospects, but if waiting lists and resale values are useful indicators, it is well placed to succeed.

ASTON MARTIN

ZAGATO

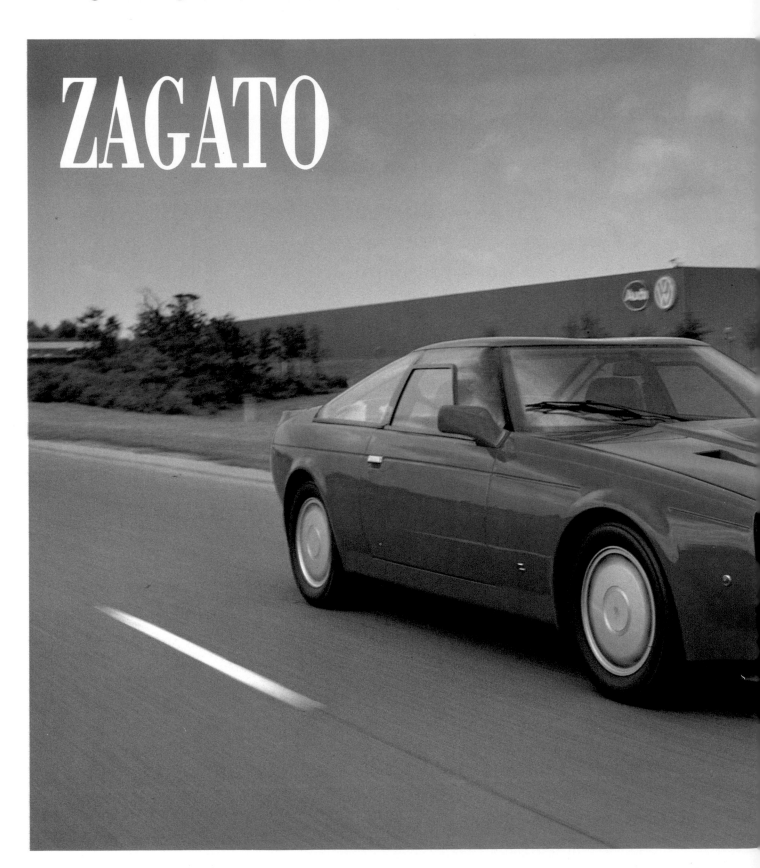

It does not matter much whether or not you like the shape of Aston Martin's Zagato, or Vantage Zagato to give it its full name. All 50 were sold, 30 going rather surprisingly to British customers. This was the best answer to critics of its shape.

Aston Martin gave a selected group of journalists a chance to drive one of the first Zagatos off the line. It is evident in the Zagato that Aston Martin has lost none of its long-renowned skills in developing and sorting chassis, and it bodes well for the future that engineers were able to make such substantial improvements to a chassis that was highly regarded even in standard form.

As for the shape, though it looked much better out in the open air – especially on the move – than in the artificial surroundings of a motor show stand, and the aerodynamic add-ons also improved it.

We did not have the opportunity to check the claimed top speed of almost 186 mph, but it seems credible. The car will fly up to 140 mph in a very short distance, and it is definitely quicker than the Vantage, by an appreciable margin, even though it has the classic Aston characteristic of feeling as if it is travelling about 20 per cent slower than is actually the case, always a sign of a well-engineered chassis.

There are two reasons why the car was so much quicker. The first is that the power of the 5.3-litre V8 had been increased to 438 bhp. The second was that the aerodynamics of the body were much better than those of the Towns-designed (and since much modified in detail) shape dating from the late 1960s.

Not only was the frontal area reduced and the efficiency of the airflow over the body substantially better, but the underside was also very clean. After the 1986 Geneva Show, when the Zagato made its first public appearance, the front end gained a small 'bib' spoiler, while at the rear, there was an aerofoil (which in production versions was blended into the boot and rear wings combined) with a lower valance spoiler to take the underbody air out beneficially.

Aston claim a 0–60 mph time of 'under 5.0 sec', which may be difficult to achieve. It is always easier to remove weight from the rear end of a front-engined car, and this inevitably happened here. The spare wheel is one of those motor cycle-type get-you-home devices, mounted upright in a special recess in the luggage space, under whose glass fibre floor is a special lightweight battery. So while the grip of the tyres was excellent in normal driving, and the acceleration from low speed exhilaratingly impressive, it seemed likely that really rapid standing starts would be hampered by difficulty in putting all the 432 bhp down on to the tarmac in the crucial first few yards. That is a mere technical difficulty, and trivial in the extreme unless one is attempting to set records.

Once the complete rolling chassis was built, it was shipped out to Italy for the body and interior to be attached to it. In this rolling chassis form, it looked a very tempting proposition simply to bolt on a couple of seats, pull on some goggles, and charge away into the sunset. It also looked absolutely standard – standard Vantage, that is. But in fact quite a few changes were built in, which made a significant difference to the ride and handling.

Fixed-rate springs are used on the standard Vantage, with 225 lb/in at the front and 175 at the rear. For the Zagato, greater stiffness in the front suspension was desired for high-speed stability, but not at the expense of ride comfort around town. The answer, clearly, was to use dual-rate coils.

Until three-quarters of an inch of travel – up or down – is exceeded, the front spring rate is 160, but above that it is stepped up sharply to 250; at the rear, the respective figures are 100 and 160. In high-speed driving, aerodynamic downforce is sufficient to compress the springs that initial distance. To marry with this change in springing action, the standard dampers also had to be

changed, to progressive-rate. The car has a slightly lower ride height than that of the standard Vantage.

Aston also decided to change the geometry of the front suspension, so that there is not so much castor. While developing these complexities, a decision had to be made about which rubber to use on the car. While Pirelli's P7 is magnificent, it has never (especially in the massive 275/55 VR1 15 size fitted to some Vantages) been an ideal match for the Aston chassis. In contrast to the late-lamented CN12, which gave excellent handling qualities and reasonably good grip, the P7 on the Vantage, while giving superb roadholding in the dry, not only sacrificed a lot of the car's almost uncanny 'feel', but also incurred unpleasant tendencies to aquaplane.

Aston Martin's engineers went back to first principles, inviting many manufacturers to supply suitable tyres. It was stipulated that the wheel diameter was to be increased to 16 in. The various types were thrashed around the test track, and the winner of the contest was the Goodyear Eagle (size 255/50), which became *the* supercar tyre of the late 1980s. Apparently where it scores over the P7, and the P700 for that matter, as far as the Aston is concerned (and although the Zagato is about 10 per cent lighter than the standard Vantage, it still weighs a hefty 3,600 lb plus) is in its resistance to squirming around on the road surface. The Pirelli's nylon sidewalls distort as heat builds up, while the Goodyear's rayon walls do not.

Whether or not the Eagle can match the P7's ultimate roadholding on a dry track it put the magic back in the chassis; in fact it is there to a greater extent than ever before. Trundle around town, and it is remarkable how absorbent the car is over potholes and raised surfaces, the normal jiggling sensation having been eliminated.

Head out on to the open road and there is that superb and reassuring feeling of balance through curves which distinguished the Vantage, from its introduction, as a very special car: on paper it appeared to be overweight but its extraordinary nimbleness meant that it could be chucked smoothly around like a little sports car. It was, if you like, an Elan for big boys with fat wallets. It was one of the truly great cars of all time.

With the Zagato, all this was restored, and more. Where the Aston's body starts to roll gently when settled into a curve (not like a Deux Chevaux, but to an appreciable extent), the Zagato is considerably tauter.

Out on the road, the practical results of all the changes are quite surprising. For example, the car generally feels less bulky than in the standard Vantage, even though perceived weight through the steering, the identical (and excellent) Adwest assisted system, is actually higher. This is perhaps due to the reduced castor, but may also be a function of the smaller-diameter wheel. Steering precision is, if any different, better than ever.

Give the Zagato a run at a series of very high-speed S-bends and it becomes really impressive. As ever the shift in loading can be sensed very well through the chassis, but the roll angles have been considerably reduced. It is more satisfying as well as inherently better, a tricky combination to achieve.

The brakes are standard, which means heavy in action but very powerful and well up to the job. In fact, because of the changes to the suspension and the fitting of Eagles, they feel even more reassuring. On a bumpy surface from high speed, the Vantage tends to move around a bit under heavy braking, not to an alarming extent, and the driver is probably more aware of it than his passenger. The Zagato simply loses speed efficiently.

One aspect of the styling that is truly remarkable is that the car looks so much smaller than the Vantage, yet the track and wheelbase are identical. From the inside, the car also feels much less bulky and has a greatly increased glass area. Even tall drivers feel dwarfed inside the Vantage, but that is not the case in the Zagato, perhaps because of the relatively low facia.

The interior design was highly attractive, especially the colour combination in the test car of beige, tan and black, although the softer Italian leather, possibly does not wear quite as well as the more traditional firmly padded seats with tight stitching found in other Astons (except the Lagonda).

The instruments and switchgear were neatly blended into the facia, most of them recognizable from the contemporary Astons, but for some reason they look more modern in the Zagato. The major controls were unchanged, and the driving position does not feel any different, but the seat gives better lateral support. It feels as if it would be just as comfortable on a long run.

All-round visibility was excellent on production models with two door mirrors, but even with just the one, in combination with the interior mirror, there was a better view of the road behind than there is in a normal Vantage. The frame of the wind-down section of the windows does not impair visibility, either, and the window itself is considerably more practical than the letterbox slot in the Countach.

As a whole, the car was very practical indeed; with no rear seats, there was a substantial platform for luggage, even if normal luggage space was not voluminous.

It may not be beautiful but it has to go straight into the list as one of the truly great high performance cars of all time. It may be that the most significant achievement in its creation is not its creation per se, but its effect on existing and future models in the Aston range.

ASTON MARTIN ZAGATO

ENGINE

Cylinders: V8 (90-degree), in-line, front-mounted.

Capacity: 5,341 cc (320 cu in).

Bore/stroke: 100/85 mm (3.94/3.35 in).

Valve gear: sohc per bank, chain driven, 16 valves.

Compression ratio: 9.3:1.

Fuel system: four downdraught twin-choke Weber 48 IDF 3/150 carbureters.

Maximum power: 438bhp/6,200 rpm.

Maximum torque: 395 lb ft (536 Nm)/5,100 rpm.

TRANSMISSION

Type: 5-speed manual, rear-wheel drive, limited-slip differential.

Mph/kph per 1,000 rpm in top gear: 29.2/47.0

SUSPENSION, WHEELS

Front: independent, by double wishbones, coil springs, anti-roll bar.

Rear: de Dion axle, Watts linkage, trailing arms, coil springs.

Steering: power-assisted rack and pinion.

Brakes: (Front) ventilated discs/(Rear) ventilated discs, servo assisted.

Tyres/wheels: 255/50 VR 16 – 8J.

*Factory figures

DIMENSIONS

Length: 172.8 in (439 cm).

Width: 73.2 in (186 cm).

Height: 51.0 in (129.5 cm).

Wheelbase: 102.7 in (261 cm).

Front/rear track: 59.8/60.6 in (152/154 cm).

Weight: 3,640 lbs (1,650 kg).

Fuel tank: 23.0 gallons (104.5 litres).

PERFORMANCE*

Maximum speed: 186 mph (300 kph).

Acceleration: 0–60 mph (96.5 kph) 5.0 sec.

Fuel consumption (average): 12.3 mpg (23 litres/100 km).

AUDI QUATTRO

This is the car which began a small revolution, and which played a major role in the building of Audi's image as the manufacturer at the cutting edge of modern technology.

In recent years, for a variety of reasons, things have not gone so well for Audi, but the Quattro, which in its initial form was quite a beast when the limits of its exceptional roadholding were reached, has been refined into an outstanding road car. The 20-valve engine is the best yet (though it lacks the exciting exhaust warble of the previous model, which made it sound identical to the rally cars) and it remains in production thanks to continuing demand from customers.

The power increase is undramatic and so is the torque – up from 210 to 228 lb ft. but what *is* significant is that peak torque comes down from 3,500 rpm to only 1,950.

Audi says it has adopted 20-valve technology not primarily to boost top-end power, but to offer minimum resistance to the air delivered from the turbocharger at all engine speeds. The four-valve-per-cylinder configuration is also intended to improve combustion efficiency, reduce exhaust emissions, reduce fuel consumption and provide an opportunity to run a higher compres-

sion ratio – in this case 9.3:1, surprisingly high for a turbocharged engine.

But whatever the intention, the most significant result of the engine development work has been the virtual total elimination of turbo lag. On the move, the 20-valve Quattro is nothing short of astonishing: it offers breathtaking performance, particularly in the mid-range, which in turn means that overtaking manoeuvres can safely be

executed in situations that would be lunatic in normal machines.

Minor revisions have been made to the gear ratios but, ideally, second is still too low. However, third is a splendid ratio for cross-country travel – flooring the throttle provides an instant, neck-snapping response and running all the way to the 7,000 rpm red-line in that gear takes the car close to of 100 mph. The Quattro behaves just like an immensely powerful, normally aspirated unit. According to Audi's own figures, the top speed of the 20-valve Quattro is 143 mph, while the sprint from 0–60 mph takes 5.9 sec.

The 20-valve engine is far smoother and sweeter than the earlier version. All the way to the red line, there is no harshness, simply an increase in noise levels to warn of an increasing lack of mechanical sympathy. More noticeable than increased engine noise at higher speeds is a rapid increase in wind noise levels – perhaps inevitable in a bodyshell that was conceived more than 10 years ago.

In traffic, and at lower engine speeds, the 20-valve Quattro is quiet, relaxed and refined and can be driven gently and easily. On open roads, the sheer sophistication of Audi's permanent four-wheel-drive chassis becomes clear. In normal conditions the Torsen differential linking the front and rear axles provides a 50/50 torque split. But when wheel grip varies, so does the power transmission ratio, from 72/25 to 25/75, to favour whichever axle has the most grip.

What is best about the Quattro is the way it puts down its available power, with no wheelspin. In the tightest bends, it is better to go in relatively slowly to avoid a touch of understeer and then power out, revelling in the grip that the Torsen differential ensures always remains at the optimum level. Other than in very tight or very slippery bends, the Quattro's cornering limits are not going to be found by anyone whose brain is in gear.

In off road driving what becomes clear is that the Quattro is far more tractable and amenable than early models. If understeer makes itself felt,

it is only necessary to lift off slightly to get the nose to tuck in; if the rear breaks away, a modicum of opposite lock sorts it out. With the Torsen differential providing its helping hand, the Quattro is now really quite user friendly. Nevertheless the laws of physics still apply, which is when one can be grateful for the standard anti-lock braking.

The latest Audi Quattro fulfils the expectations of its loyal customers. The combination of its instant throttle response, stunning performance, rock-steady handling and high levels of grip make it an exciting car. Furthermore, its ride is preferable to that of compatible vehicles though transverse bumps in the road and cats eyes make themselves quite severely felt in the cabin.

AUDI QUATTRO

ENGINE

Cylinders: straight, in-line, front-mounted.
Capacity: 2,226 cc (133.5 cu in).
Bore/stroke: 81/86.4 mm (3.19/3.40 in).
Valve gear: dohc, driven by toothed belt, 20 valves.
Compression ratio: 9.3:1.
Fuel system: Bosch K-jetronic/Motronic, KKK turbocharger with air/air intercooler.
Maximum power: 220 bhp/5,800 rpm.
Maximum torque: 228 lb ft (309 Nm)/1,950 rpm.

TRANSMISSION

Type: 5-speed manual, four-wheel drive.
Mph/kph per 1,000 rpm in top gear: 22.2/35.7.

SUSPENSION, WHEELS

Front: independent, by Macpherson struts, lower wishbones, anti-roll bar.
Rear: independent, by Macpherson struts, lower wishbones, anti-roll bar.
Steering: power-assisted rack and pinion.
Brakes: (Front) ventilated discs/(Rear) plain discs, servo assisted, ABS.
Tyres/wheels: 215/50 VR 15 - 8J.

DIMENSIONS

Length: 173.4 in (440.5 cm).
Width: 67.9 in (172.5 cm).
Height: 53.0 in (134.5 cm).
Wheelbase: 252.5 in (99.4 cm).
Front/rear track: 57.5/58.9 in (146/149.5 cm).
Weight: 3,875 lbs (1,760 kg).
Fuel tank: 19.8 gallons (90 litres).

PERFORMANCE

Maximum speed: 143 mph (230 kph).
Acceleration: 0-60 mph (96.5 kph) 5.9 sec.
Fuel consumption (average): 28.3 mpg (10.0 litres/100 km).

BENTLEY TURBO R

Bentley's Turbo R has presence, or star quality. It is not pretty (in many ways it is very old-fashioned), and it has several elements which are irritating, yet it has a charm which only a driver without any sensitivity could resist.

Its most surprising qualities, to anyone who has not previously driven the 'R' version of this car, are in its dynamics: before the chassis was properly sorted a couple of years ago, the Mulsanne Turbo was simply a big lump of luxury car propelled by a big lump of an engine. It rolled, it wallowed, its damping was unable to cope with a combination of high speed and an uneven surface. It was amusing for a while, but before long one wanted to get back to driving *real* cars.

With even more power and torque since the adoption of Bosch KE-jetronic fuel injection at the end of 1986, the Bentley's performance is remarkable, and at no disadvantage compared with other very fast luxury cars. Its top speed of 145.8 mph and acceleration from rest to 60 mph in 6.3 sec (and on to 100 mph in 17.5 sec) are more than respectable, and taking the car's weight into account, astounding. It simply leaps away from the line, with no hesitation, and its overtaking ability is matched by few saloons.

But it is the manner by which this is achieved which is most impressive. Though the engine is actually 'oversquare' by a few millimetres, though it delivers its gigantic 'grunt' within a relatively narrow rev band (the red line is at 4,500 rpm!), it has that pleasantly lazy quality of American engines of the late 1960s. There is the characteristic, attractively deep rumble of the V8, audibly giving no hint of serious exertion while the scenery is fairly zipping past the side windows.

There is none of the dreaded turbocharger 'lag'. Floor the throttle at any speed and full kickdown gives an instant response, the nose rises gently and you simply take off into the distance, to the bewilderment of toiling hot-hatchback drivers. Before the suspension modifications, the Mulsanne Turbo used to squat so much in these circumstances that it felt in danger of hitting the rear bumpstops.

At 'high' rpm, the Bentley's engine begins to slide off the end of its power curve, but it gives the car tremendous overtaking ability. It would be unreasonable to expect a V8 to be quite as smooth as a 12, but the Turbo R is not far off. The car gently rocks at tickover (which means about 400 rpm), trembling in a meaningful way when the throttle is blipped, and thereafter the engine is impressively smooth.

With so much engine propelling so much weight, fuel economy is not going to be a major virtue. But the Bentley returned 12.3 mpg, despite being driven hard. The 23.8-gallon tank allows a range of up to 350 miles.

It was not so long ago that the first four-speed automatic gearbox went into production, and soon we will have five or even six ratios at our disposal in two-pedal cars. The Bentley needs no more than the three it has now, and the manual change is almost redundant. Upward changes are a little jerky under full-throttle acceleration, but otherwise smooth.

For such a big car, the Bentley is not only very nimble, but also rarely feels unwieldy. This is partly due to the relatively high driving position, which gives an excellent view of the car's extremities, but also is aided by the precise handling.

The steering, in particular, is a revelation: pleasantly weighted so that the sting is taken out of low-speed manoeuvres, but giving just the right amount of resistance on the move. Unfortunately, there is rather too much kick-back over bumps. Turn-in ability is outstanding and the Bentley tends most of the time towards gentle understeer, gradually converting into neutrality. It is possible to provoke the tail out of line and hold it there. Under this kind of ruffian provocation it will also spin an inside rear wheel – Bentley does not see the need for a limited-slip differential.

You can still specify Pirelli P7s (275/55 VR 15) for your Turbo R, but the advantage in outright dry-road grip over the Avon GR2 Turbospeeds (255/65) is small, and outweighed by a tendency to aquaplane, a faster wear rate and some deterioration in ride quality. The Avons look old-fashioned, but they are ideal for this car.

With a car of this weight and performance a reassuringly powerful braking system is essen-

tial, and Bentley certainly has one. Required pedal weight, firm but not enough to induce cramp, is just right, and the progressive response is excellent. Fade is unlikely to be encountered on the road, and even on a demanding race circuit it takes some time and effort before it manifests itself. Just as the car no longer squats as much as it used to, neither does it pitch severely. The action of the ABS system is discreet and as always of great benefit.

Since the car is much more firmly damped than previously, one might expect a heavy penalty to

as jumbled is too flattering. It all looks lovely, as you sit on cowhide, your feet on lambswool and lovely pieces of polished wood all around, but some cars built in the 1920s displayed a sounder grasp of ergonomics.

The instruments are clear enough except when exposed to sunshine or darkness (the rheostat ranges from dim to blank), while playing tunes on the air conditioning system at first appears no simpler than attempting to master the controls of a Hammond organ.

Mind you, once you realize that there are more

be paid in low-speed ride comfort. However, although the bodyshell shakes a little in response to surface irregularities at below 20 mph or so, it never jars badly, while damping control at higher speeds is exemplary. The Turbo R is now fitted with electronically controlled damping, as is the entire Rolls-Royce range.

Considering its size, the Bentley's accommodation is no better than fair. There is plenty of legroom in the front, and good headroom all round, but although rear legroom is adequate and access via the big, heavy doors easy enough, there is not as much space in the back as might be expected.

There is voluminous luggage space, with a low level lip. Internal stowage, despite the rather shallow door pockets, is pretty good, with two lockable boxes.

The new seats give very good support, especially laterally, which was a problem with the previous design. The driving position is good as far as the relationship between the steering wheel, seats and pedals is concerned, but to describe the arrangement of the minor controls

controls to the air conditioning than might at first be guessed, and you learn what each of them does, the system emerges as by far the best in the world, with (for it is written) enough heat to warm a house and the cooling power of 30 refrigerators. It reacts quickly too, if required the climate can be altered from Sahara to Alaska in a very short space of time. Best of all is the ability, simultaneously, to melt your shoes and freeze the tip of your nose, or any combination in between.

'The only noise you hear is the ticking of the clock.' Well, not quite, and the Bentley is certainly less quiet than a Jaguar XJ12. But, overall, it is very refined, with a bit of intrusive wind roar in blustery conditions, rather a lot of tyre whine over some surfaces, but little else apart from the distant warbling of the engine when given lots of throttle.

The Turbo R does not have the precision-fit appearance of German luxury cars, but it does give a feeling of old-fashioned hand-crafted quality, and as one might say of a pair of handmade shoes, I should think so, at that price.

BENTLEY TURBO R

ENGINE

Cylinders: V8 (90-degree), in-line, front-mounted.

Capacity: 6,750cc (405 cu in).

Bore/stroke: 104/99 mm (4.09/3.90 in).

Valve gear: single camshaft, gear-driven, pushrod ohv, 16 valves.

Compression ratio: 8.0:1.

Fuel system: Bosch KE-jetronic fuel injection, Garrett TO4B turbocharger with air/air intercooler.

Maximum power: 330 bhp/4,300 rpm.

Maximum torque: 443 lb ft (327 Nm)/2,500 rpm.

TRANSMISSION

Type: 3-speed automatic, rear-wheel drive.

Mph/kph per 1,000 rpm in top gear: 35.6/57.3.

SUSPENSION, WHEELS

Front: independent, by lower wishbones and upper links, coil springs, anti-roll bar.

Rear: independent, by semi-trailing arms, hydraulic self-levelling, coil springs, anti-roll bar.

Steering: power-assisted rack and pinion.

Brakes: (Front) ventilated discs/(Rear) plain discs, servo assisted, ABS.

Tyres/wheels: 255/55 VR 15 - 7.5J.

DIMENSIONS

Length: 209 in (531 cm).

Width: 74 in (188 cm).

Height: 58.5 in (149 cm).

Wheelbase: 121 in (307 cm).

Front/rear track: 60.5/60.5 in (154/154 cm).

Weight: 4,861 lbs (2,205 kg).

Fuel tank: 23.7 gallons (108 litres).

PERFORMANCE

Maximum speed: 145.8 mph (234.6 kph).

Acceleration: 0-60 mph (96.5 kph) 6.3 sec, 0-100 mph (161 kph) 17.5 sec.

Kickdown: 30-50 mph (48-80.5 kph) 2.4 sec, 50-70 mph (80.5-113 kph) 3.8 sec.

Fuel consumption (average): 17.0 mpg (16.5 litres/100 km).

BMW ALPINA B12

Owning a top-model BMW is beyond the means of most people. But for some, possession is only the start of a crazy dream. For those who are never satisfied – who always crave for more – specialists such as Alpina and Hartge have the solutions. Each carries on where the car maker leaves off, adding muscle and beauty until their creation is unique. Their targets may differ, but not their quests for perfection.

Alpina consider themselves car manufacturers, preferring to sell fully modified BMWs built to order, whereas Hartge's operation is more flexible: like AMG with Mercedes-Benz, they supply a range of engine tuning and body parts to suit means and taste.

Alpina's 'flagship' is the B12, based on the 750i, which you might think represents the pinnacle of BMW's achievement. Alpina thinks not: instead it is regarded as merely the starting point from which the B12 is built. When they have finished, the result is a subtly altered 7-series, whose only real giveaway is the enormity of its rear tyres: 265/40 ZR 17s.

With raised compression, bigger valves and cam lobes, and a carefully doctored Bosch engine management system, the tuned 12 turns out 350 bhp, 50 bhp up on standard. It is also catalyst equipped and stripped of the governor that holds the standard car to 155 mph. Fast? You bet it is. Even with automatic transmission, the B12 is claimed to go beyond 170 mph.

When BMW launched the new 12-cylinder engine, they claimed that 'smoothness and low noise levels are to a standard never before achieved in automobile engineering.' We beg to differ: even though it is beautifully 'dressed' and compact, it cannot match the silkiness of Jaguar's elderly V12. Alpina makes it more efficient and more tuneful – and just a shade more vocal. Gone is the flat and soulless sound of the stock 750i, instead, a gentle hum gives way to a muted wail under assault, but it's never loud enough to offend. It sings a glorious tune. And it idles as smoothly as an electric motor, glued to a rock-steady 600 rpm by Bosch Motronic engine management. The loudest sound is the whirring electric fuel pump.

Amazingly, the engine's crankshaft seems to have no inertia, such is the way it responds to a touch of the throttle. But there is a sense of disappointment in the acceleration. The car's quietness doesn't help: it fools the senses into thinking that not much is happening. Neither does its weight of over 4,000 lbs, or a bottom gear good for nearly 60 mph.

The truth is, the B12 doesn't feel that much quicker than a run-of-the mill 750i, though a stopwatch would confirm the extra 50 bhp. It is

claimed to reach 100 kph in 6.9 sec (approximately 6.4 sec to 60 mph) compared with 7.4 sec for a 750i.

It is quite different once the car is rolling, almost as if the energy is being conserved for greater things higher up the speed range. Like an aircraft on take-off, the B12 gives the impression of linear acceleration, unhindered by upward gearshifts. It passes 100 mph barely into its stride – and only just into third gear – and will cruise at an easy 140 mph when conditions allow.

Few roadgoing manual gearboxes can handle

the torque that this engine produces. Automatic transmission suits the car so well that Alpina judges unjustifiable the costly and complex re-engineering which a manual option would require.

The traction of the Alpina cannot easily be broken. For a start, the car is fitted with Automatic Stability Control (ASC), which shuts down the engine as soon as there is any sign of slip – it's easily accomplished, since the cable-less throttle linkage lends itself to modulation. But even if you override the ASC – by pressing a button on the facia – those enormous rear tyres are more than equal to the torque on tap, as long as the road is dry. You get the feeling that the B12 has been engineered to stay on the road, irrespective of the driver's ability.

Having fatter tyres at the back than at the front (where 235/45s are fitted) cures any waywardness brought about by the extra power. Even so, there's enough attitude movement to let you know when cornering grip is fading. The tail will edge out long before a full-blooded slide develops, so the driver can feel exactly what the car is going to do before it happens.

Handling balance feels neutral, with no tendency towards excessive understeer or premature oversteer: what the car does is largely up to the driver. An unwanted downshift while powering round a greasy bend might upset the equation . . .

At parking speeds, the BMW's steering is almost finger light, but Alpina has altered the Servotronic assistance to firm up more quickly as speed builds. It works well, since the extra perceived weight coaxes smoother and more deliberate in-

puts from the driver.

At the time of our test, Alpina had yet to decide on suspension settings for the B12. The car we drove was the first right-hand-drive version, and it had German-specification Alpina dampers which UK importer Frank Sytner considers too firm for British roads. British B12s may retain the standard 750i's electronically-controlled dampers, which allow two quite different settings – though in our experience neither would be ideal. We prefer the tauter set-up, since it better complements the B12's sporting nature. It keeps you in touch with the action, yet it's never really uncomfortable.

Opulence is the only word to describe a 750i's interior. In the B12, the walnut and leather trim is inherited from the standard car, the only change being that the test car was fitted with BMW's excellent sports seat option. There's some texture and colour difference between leather and plastic, but the wood veneer tastefully lifts the interior without dominating it.

Enthusiasts might bemoan the lack of instruments, for the binnacle contains no more dials than you would find in a Sierra. But there can be no complaints about the control layout, the fully-linked heating/air conditioning, or the equipment supplied. The only Alpina hallmark is – or should have been – a facia-mounted plaque showing the car's serial number.

The B12 increases the already high price of a short-wheelbase 750i by more than 40 per cent, and by any standards that's a lot to pay for fancy wheels, an extra 50 bhp and some careful tuning of the gearbox and suspension characteristics. But it is a superbly honed sports saloon, more appealing and more driveable than the car on which it is based. It impressed us for its refinement and civilized ways – it just happens to be one of the world's fastest big saloons as well. And it is very exclusive, especially in Britain, where Sytner's of Nottingham assemble about 120 Alpinas per year, few of these being the flagship B12.

BMW ALPINA B12

ENGINE

Cylinders: V12 (60 degree), in-line, front-mounted.

Capacity: 4,998 cc (300 cu in).

Bore/stroke: 84/75mm (3.31/2.95 in)

Valve gear: sohc per bank, chain-driven, two valves per cylinder.

Compression ratio: 9.5:1.

Fuel system: Bosch Motronic injection/engine management.

Maximum power: 350 bhp/5,300 rpm.

Maximum torque: 347 lb ft (470 Nm)/4,000 rpm.

TRANSMISSION

Type: 4-speed automatic, rear-wheel drive, limited-slip differential.

Mph/kph per 1,000 rpm in top gear: 32.0/51.2

SUSPENSION, WHEELS

Front: independent, by double-joint spring strut axle, coil springs, anti-roll bar.

Rear: independent, by semi-trailing arms, coil springs, anti-roll bar.

Steering: assisted recirculating ball.

Brakes: (Front) ventilated discs/(Rear) ventilated discs, servo-assisted, ABS.

Tyres/wheels: front 235/45 ZR 17 - 8.5J, rear 265/40 ZR 17 - 10J.

DIMENSIONS

Length: 193.3 in (491 cm).

Width: 72.6 in (184 cm).

Height: 54.8 in (139 cm).

Wheelbase: 111.5 in (283 cm).

Front/rear track: 60.6/60.4 in (154/153 cm).

Weight: 4,099 lbs (1,859 kg).

Fuel tank: 22.4 gallons (102 litres).

PERFORMANCE

Maximum speed: 152.1 mph (244.7 kph)

Acceleration: 0-62 mph (100 kph) 6.9 sec, 0-100 mph (161 kph) 15.8 sec.

Kickdown: 50-70 mph (80.5-113 kph) 2.9 sec, 30-50 mph (48-80.5 kph) 2.7 sec

Fuel consumption (average): 21.9 mpg

BMW 850i

By creating a new 8-series and naming its new coupé 850i, rather than following the tradition of the 6-series, as has always been the case with other models, BMW wants to emphasize that the new car towers at the top of its range. This is also why the Bavarian manufacturer does not intend to offer it with anything less than its five-litre V12 engine, as also used in the top version of the 7-series models.

Apart from the engine (and gearbox in the case of the automatic) and the structural part ahead of the front bulkhead, the coupé is a completely new design and does not pretend to be anything but a 2-plus-2 (albeit a rather comfortable one). Interior space is about the same as in the now discontinued 634 CSi and the new car is 1.5 in shorter, but – thanks to its wider track and even wider tyres (235/50 ZR 16) – 5in wider than its predecessor.

Great care has been taken to combine a traditional BMW shape with low drag, and the drag coefficient figure of 0.29 is exceptionally good considering those big tyres and the handicap of the cooling requirements of the 304 bhp engine. Lift has not been eliminated entirely, but the 0.12 factor is divided equally between front and rear.

If a sports car can be defined as a car in which non-essential, luxury items have been sacrificed in pursuit of performance, then the 850i is not a sports car, but – like the Mercedes 500 SL – rather a Grand Touring car, as almost every imaginable accessory is on the list of standard equipment.

Even the steering column is electrically adjusted and, whenever the driver's door is opened, the column is raised to facilitate exit and entry. Its memory returns it to its original position when the door is closed, and also controls the position of the heated, external mirrors as well as the driver's seat.

The electrically operated windows and central locking system hardly require mention, and the same goes for the multiple front seat adjustment. The remote control of the central locking system also controls the windows, which close automatically when the doors are locked and can also be opened by means of the remote control unit, to allow fresh air to circulate and reduce the inside temperature when the car has been exposed to the sun. As in the 7-series, the windscreen wiper blade pressure is automatically increased as road speed rises.

Automatic air conditioning is standard and can

BMW 850i

ENGINE

Cylinders: V8 (90-degree), in-line, front-mounted.

Capacity: 4,988 cc (299 cu in).

Bore/stroke: 84/75 mm (3.31/2.95 in).

Valve gear: sohc per bank, chain-driven, 16 valves.

Compression ratio: 8.8:1.

Fuel system: one Bosch Motronic injection ignition system per bank.

Maximum power: 304 bhp/5,200 rpm.

Maximum torque: 332 lb ft (450 Nm)/4,100 rpm.

TRANSMISSION

Type: 6-speed manual (or four-speed automatic), rear-wheel drive.

Mph/kph per 1,000 rpm in top gear: 30.7/49.4.

SUSPENSION, WHEELS

Front: independent, by MacPherson struts, coil springs, with anti-dive geometry, anti-roll bar.

Rear: independent, by five-link suspension, coil springs, anti-roll bar.

Steering: power assisted recirculating ball.

Brakes: (Front) ventilated discs/(Rear) ventilated discs, servo-assisted, ABS.

Tyres/wheels: 235/50 ZR 16 - 7.5J.

DIMENSIONS

Length: 188.1 in (478 cm).

Width: 73.0 in (185.5 cm).

Height: 52.8in (134 cm).

Wheelbase: 105.5in (268 cm).

Front/rear track: 61.0/61.4 in (155/156 cm).

Weight: 3,942 lbs (1,790 kg).

Fuel tank: 20.0 gallons (90 litres).

PERFORMANCE*

Maximum speed: 156 mph (251 kph).

Acceleration: 0-62 mph (100 kph) 6.8 sec.

Standing km: 26.3 sec.

Kickdown: 50-70 mph (80.5-113 kph) 4.6 sec.

Fuel consumption (average): 19.2 mpg (14.7 litres/100 km).

*Factory figures for manual version

optionally be completed by a device which switches the system to recirculation whenever abnormally polluted atmosphere is sensed.

Weight saving and simplicity are built into the elaborate check control system in which a variety of information is transmitted down a single line of the multiplex electric cable.

A further development of the electronic damper system used in the latest version of the 635 CSi is standard and is supplemented by an automatic ride height governor. Anti-slip control (ASC) is also standard, as is ABS, the wheel speed sensors being common to the two. ASC can be switched off, but the ABS is full-time. A

tyre pressure and temperature monitor will be fitted from the end of 1990.

As in the new Mercedes SL, the front safety belts are integrated in the seats, which means that the tensioned belt is always in the ideal position and also makes buckling up easier.

Inevitably, all this and more (pop-up headlights, impact-absorbing bumpers) leads to a lot of weight: 1,790 kg with a full 90-litre tank, over 300 kg more than the 635 CSi in its European version (but less than 200 kg more than the American 635 CSi).

Buyers of the 850i have the choice of either the excellent ZF four-speed automatic already standard in the 750i, or a completely new six-speed manual gear box, developed by BMW specifically for this car. In either case, the car's maximum speed is an electronically-limited 156 mph, and the acceleration to 62 mph is 6.8 sec for the manual version and 7.4 for the automatic.

While the front strut suspension with twin lower joints and recirculating ball steering is similar to the 7-series, at the rear there is an entirely new five-link system which BMW calls 'integral independent suspension'.

It provides anti-dive and anti-squat, considerable fore/aft compliance for a smooth low-speed ride and good road noise absorption without toe-in changes or other ill effects, avoids toe-out under braking and compensates for lift-off oversteer by turning both wheels a slight amount in the same direction as the front wheels when the driving torque changes from positive to negative. To achieve these effects, use is made of the suspension geometry and the resilience of the rubber bushes. Firmer settings will be standard in the manual, and optional in the auto.

Because of the long delay between the car's show debut and the press driving launch, it has not been possible to include driving impressions in this book.

BMW M3

Expressed in value for money terms, the BMW's accommodation and performance do not compare well with some rivals. Although it is based on the relatively light 3-Series shell, it has a comparatively low-capacity, unboosted engine. This oversquare, fuel-injected four cylinder engine has a swept volume of 2,302 cc, and produces its peak power of 200 bhp at 6,750 rpm, and few normally-aspirated engines (those of the Lamborghini Countach and Caterham 7 are among them) have a better bhp/litre ratio. Maximum torque is 176 lb ft at 4,750 rpm.

The performance resulting from this includes a top speed of 138 mph and 0-60 mph possible in 7.0 sec, figures which were once the preserve of only the fastest cars on the market. They still add up to a very rapid car, and the in-gear acceleration for fourth and top reflect not merely 'sprint' gearing but also a healthy spread of torque: 30-50 mph in fourth in 6.3 sec, 50-70 mph in top in 8.3 sec.

However, for only a little more money, you can get the BMW 535i with a higher top speed, similar acceleration, substantially more accommodation and (perhaps most important of all) considerably better refinement. It must be noted too, that the Sapphire Cosworth is quite a lot quicker than either of them, and costs less money.

The M3 that BMW loaned us had fat Michelin MXXs, 225/45 VR16 on 7J alloy wheels (a narrower type with reduced rim diameter, 205/55 VR15, is offered as standard).

Exceptionally high levels of grip on dry surfaces, with terrific traction, are aided by the 25 per cent limited-slip differential. Turn-in is crisp, but the low-geared steering demands a great deal of wheel twirling on twisty roads. Again in the dry, inducing tail slides is almost impossible, though understeer is not excessive. Especially when the M3's sporting connections are taken into account, there is more body roll than might be anticipated, but damping control over bumpy surfaces is admirable.

Even on wet roads there is much less of the heart-stopping snap oversteer for which the 3-Series used to be notorious; even the lesser versions these days are better behaved than in the past.

However, we came to the conclusion that it would be preferable to specify the standard rubberwear, which might reduce ultimate grip in the dry but which would almost certainly eliminate the unpleasant tendency to aquaplane in heavy rain. This behaviour is unwelcome in any circumstances, but above all when driving through mountain passes!

BMW M3

ENGINE*

Cylinders: four in line, in-line, front-mounted.

Capacity: 2,302 cc (138 cu in).

Bore/stroke: 93.4/84 mm (3.68/3.31 in).

Valve gear: dohc, chain driven, 24 valves.

Compression ratio: 10.5:1.

Fuel system: Bosch Motronic electronic fuel injection/ ignition.

Maximum power: 200 bhp/6,750 rpm.

Maximum torque: 176 lb ft/4,750 rpm. Evolution version as above, except:

Compression ratio: 11.0:1.

Maximum power: 220 bhp/6,750 rpm.

Maximum torque: 170 lb ft/4,750 rpm.

TRANSMISSION

Type: 5-speed manual, limited-slip differential, rear-wheel drive.

Mph/kph per 1,000 rpm in top gear: 21.3 34.3.

SUSPENSION, WHEELS

Front: independent, by Macpherson struts, lower track control arms, coil springs, anti-roll bar.

Rear: independent, by semi-trailing arms, coil springs, anti-roll bar.

Steering: power-assisted rack and pinion.

Brakes: (Front) ventilated discs/(Rear) ventilated discs, servo assisted, ABS.

Tyres/wheels: 225/45 VR 16.

DIMENSIONS

Length: 171.1 in (435 cm).

Width: 66.1 in (168 cm).

Height: 53.9 in (137 cm).

Wheelbase: 100.8 in (256 cm).

Front/rear track: 55.5/56.5 in (141/143.5 cm).

Weight: 2,643 lbs (1,199 kg).

Fuel tank: 15.4 gallons (70 litres).

PERFORMANCE

Maximum speed: 138.3 mph (222.5 kph).

Acceleration: 0-60 mph (96.5 kph) 7.0 sec, 0-100 mph (161 kph) 17.8 sec.

Fourth gear: 30-50 mph (48-80.5 kph) 6.3 sec

Fifth gear: 50-70 mph (80.5-113 kph) 8.3 sec.

Fuel consumption (average): 33.8 mpg (8.4 litres/100 km).

*non catalyst version

Overall the ride quality is not bad, but some ridges and potholes do induce a rather rigid response, jarring through the admirably rattle-free bodyshell.

In overall dynamic terms, though, the M3 is a joy to hustle through fast, winding roads, with its crisply defined gearbox gate matched by well-chosen ratios, and its powerful braking

system, fitted with a very good anti-lock system.

But is it the ideal BMW road car for the money? Ignoring the limited passenger space (it is really only a two-plus-two, though the luggage space is large enough), it simply lacks the silky refinement rightly associated with the Munich company. The engine is smooth enough and revs freely, but cannot match its six-cylinder stablemates for sweetness of sound and response. A beautifully finished interior, with leather trim, a perfect driving position and superb instruments do not amount to satisfactory compensation: you can get all that in any BMW. The only real advantage over the 535 is posing value.

Is it quick enough to match its racy image? Is it, on the other hand, refined enough to justify its price? It is in serious danger of falling between two stools, for all its fine qualities.

In fact, perhaps aware of this, BMW subsequently introduced several M3 variations, including faster 'Evolution' versions and a cabrio.

BMW M5

The M5 is the world's most discreet supercar, the antithesis of the 2 ft tall bespoilered monster sitting on grooved Grand Prix slicks and luggage space for two toothbrushes, a tube of toothpaste and two pairs of clean knickers.

The M5 looks like, and is, a perfectly normal, civilized, comfortable four-seater. It is special in that it is the only car built by BMW's Motorsport division. Thus, while the M3 had already exceeded 10,000 units by late 1988 the old M5 only reached just over 2,000 (of which some 200 were right-hand drive), and the reason is not only the high purchase price: Motorsport simply lacks the capacity to build more.

Though now completely re-engineered, the new M5 is identical to the old one in its character and purpose. Despite the use of a catalytic converter (for the first time in an M-car), the power output of the 24-valve straight six has been raised from 286 to 315 bhp, 400 rpm higher up the scale, at 6,900 rpm, while the torque peak has been lifted to 265 lb ft, again slightly higher at 4,750 rpm; more importantly, a depression in the torque curve has been virtually eradicated by the use of a 'resonance charge' intake system.

Complex changes have been made to the electronic management system; the exhaust manifold is a meeting of art and science, with equal-length pipes, and the stroke of the engine is lengthened to 86 mm, bore size remaining at 93.4, to give a swept volume of 3,535 cc (an increase of 82 cc). The compression ratio is up from 9.8 to 10.0:1, while other modifications have been made to the camshaft and flywheel.

Because of the greater weight of the new 5-series, the spring and damper rates have been substantially altered. A 50/50 front/rear weight distribution has been achieved, and the body sits 20 mm lower than the 535i. The M-Technic alloy wheels are of a fascinating design: incorporating a fan effect within the rim, they are designed to optimize brake cooling while remaining aerodynamically efficient. The M5's drag coefficient is 0.32, pretty good in view of the use of 235/45 ZR 17 tyres all round (either Michelin MXX or Pirelli P700).

Externally, apart from the little Motorsport badges, the 'M5' on the bootlid, and the subtly altered spoilers, it takes a keen eye to pick out the M5 from its less aggressive sisters, especially when it is moving. And it certainly moves.

As with the 750i, BMW has artificially restricted the maximum speed of the M5 to 155 mph. Even so, this is about 3 mph quicker than the old model could manage, and this M5 rockets up to high speed in a very short time, sprinting from rest to 100 kph (62 mph) in 6.3 sec according to BMW; this, given BMW's conservatism, should translate to a 0-60 mph time of around 5.5 sec, almost half a second quicker than the old car. The standing km time is said to be 26 sec, an improvement of more than 1 sec.

Apart from a trace of vibration at tickover, the engine is stunningly smooth throughout its wide range, and pulls with immense strength from low speeds, revving freely to its new 7,200 rpm limit. Third gear is remarkable on twisty roads, with the capability of propelling the car rapidly out of tight bends, yet with a maximum of over 100 mph. Once one has grown used to the clutch, the gearchange is probably the best in any high-performance car, and the gearing perfect for acceleration and high-speed cruising, which

is remarkably relaxing thanks to the refinement of the engine and the complete absence of wind noise.

The chassis is so well-developed that it takes a brutal application of power out of a tight bend to unstick the rear end, and there is a satisfying feeling of neutrality in most circumstances. Push a little too hard, and it will understeer, cor-

rectable simply by easing the right foot from the throttle pedal. Oversteer only results if this is done clumsily, at least on a dry surface.

We have not tried the car yet on Pirellis, but according to Thomas Ammerschlager, BMW Motorsport's Director of High Performance Vehicles (and one of the best chassis men in the business), there is little appreciable difference.

The M5 is such a *complete* car that it is difficult to find points to criticize. Maybe the ride quality at low speeds would feel harsher in some countries than it did on the billiard-table road surfaces of Bavaria (at high speed the car's damping control, especially in transient conditions in S-bends, is superb), and there also seems to be rather too much tyre roar

BMW M5

ENGINE

Cylinders: straight six, in-line, front-mounted.
Capacity: 3,535 cc (212 cu in).
Bore/stroke: 93.4/86 mm (3.68/3.39 in).
Valve gear: dohc, chain-driven, 24 valves.
Compression ratio: 10.0:1.
Fuel system: Bosch electronic injection/ignition.
Maximum power: 315 bhp/6,900 rpm.
Maximum torque: 265 lb ft (360 Nm)/4,750 rpm.

TRANSMISSION

Type: 5-speed manual, rear-wheel drive, limited-slip differential.
Mph/kph per 1,000 rpm in top gear: 23.3/37.5.

SUSPENSION, WHEELS

Front: independent, by Macpherson struts, twin lower links, double pivot, coil springs, anti-roll bar.
Rear: independent, by semi-trailing arms, auxiliary trailing arms, coil springs, anti-roll bar.
Steering: power-assisted recirculating ball.
Brakes: (Front) ventilated discs/(Rear) plain discs, servo assisted.
Tyres/wheels: front 235/45 ZR 17 -8J, rear 255/40 ZR 17 - 9J.

DIMENSIONS

Length: 185.8 in (472 cm).
Width: 68.9 in (175 cm).
Height: 54.7 in (139 cm).
Wheelbase: 108.7 in (276 cm).
Front/rear track: 57.9/58.9 in (147/149.5 cm).
Weight: 3,685 lbs (1,670 kg).
Fuel tank: 19.8 gallons (90 litres).

PERFORMANCE*

Maximum speed: 155 mph (250 kph).
Acceleration: 0-60 mph (96.5 kph) 6.5 sec, 0-100 mph (161 kph) 14.6 sec.
Fourth gear: 30-50 mph (48-80.5 kph) 6.5 sec.
Fifth gear: 50-70 mph (80.5-70 mph (80.5-113 kph) 8.7 sec.
Standing km: 26 sec.
Fuel consumption (average): 21.7 mpg (13 litres/100 km).

*Factory figures

BMW Z1

Few cars fascinate you with their doors. Anyone who didn't know might be forgiven for trying to get into the BMW Z1 as usual, reaching for the handle-like recess at the plastic door's top rear corner. It is a stylist's leg pull, as phoney as a dummy radiator cap, standing out all the more in such an otherwise very functional design; press what looks like the burglar alarm switch button in the car's flank just behind, and the door motors itself 'down'.

There is understandably quite a sill to step over, and a car-wide hoop behind the windscreen frame to hang on to, as you drop into the very neat, moulded plastic seat with its thin leather upholstery. Door-closing is done contrariwise, by pulling the normal-looking BMW door release.

Controls and dials are conventional German. The four small instruments (60-litre fuel guage, 240 kph speedometer with trip, 7,000 rpm revcounter and temperature gauge) go beyond BMW's excellent and long-held standards of clear marking and design into Porsche-like plainness.

On a technical and stylistic tour-de-force the seats tend to be last minute thoughts and neglected; not on the Z1, where the cut-down bucket itself gives very good lumbar support, and height plus enough longways adjustment to suit a 6ft driver.

Start up; the familiar ex-325i six bursts into silky life. Now begins the dynamically interesting bit. The Z1's running and direction gear is in several ways as fascinating as anything else on this remarkable and tantalizing car, and it is worth recalling as you drive.

The specification starts familiarly. Steering is from the 3-series, power-assisted rack and pinion to take the work out of twisting fat Pirelli P700-Z (225/45ZR16) rubber on 7.5 in rims. In view of the hydraulic assistance, Z1 designers puzzle that they did not put in higher gearing; 3.9 turns lock to lock sounds a bit low, although in combination with a wheelbase (96.3 in) a shade shorter than an Alfa Sprint coupé, it gives reasonably trim turning circles. Front suspension is 3-series coil and strut, with some positive offset and castor, plus anti-dive. For personal taste, it could have more castor, to give better feel of the straight-ahead position.

The first refreshing difference is the engine position. BMW talk nonsensically of the Z1 being a 'front mid-engined' car because the engine is mounted with its front just behind the line between the front wheels. But of course ever since automotive engineers pushed the engine forward between the front wheels, such a return to proper balance – with the rear-mounted battery's added help, the empty distribution is said to be 49/51 front/rear, which must change further to rear-heavy as load is added – does seem almost mid-engined, and it is an important part of the Z1's superb cornering behaviour.

The second novelty is the rear suspension, based around what BMW calls the Z-axle. It marks the company's long-delayed if not openly admitted acknowledgement that there are suspension linkages

which do not have to change camber excessively.

It is in effect a very narrow base coil-sprung double wishbone married to one of the purest trailing links imaginable; the link is aluminium-alloy cast in a near-S, so that its wheel end can pick up at the outermost top end of the upper wishbone (which is also a casting), while its body end swings outward to pivot from a point ahead of the wheel and very nearly in line with the centre of the tyre tread. The lower wishbone is made up of two steel tubes; the narrowness of the wishbone pivots plus suitable flexible bushing allows the geometrical quarrel between the conflicting radii of wishbones and trailing link

to be turned into a wheel location system that can border safely on the verges of toe-out at low cornering rates, but go into slight toe-in *in extremis*. The layout also provides anti-squat and anti-dive.

The result of all this does not impress too highly along an uneven straight road. Probably because of the inevitable steer effects of the front strut geometry, maybe (as one BMW man suggested) complicated by wide tyre effects and its low wheelbase to track ratio, the car bump-steers a little, so that although fundamentally stable – you can drive hands off and it does not go astray – it is constantly steering itself. It is on a hill road that it is very impressive.

First of all, there is this marvellous willingness to corner – a familiar BMW trait – but also, not so familiar, delightfully little understeer. Coupled with little roll, the Z1 begs you to have a go at every bend or corner. You become

braver, glorying in the superb (by road car standards) turn-in, and the very good grip on dry roads.

A wide safely-edged hairpin offers the chance to seek out lift-off-the-accelerator behaviour; hard into the bend, heel and toe down into first (pedal layout is ideal for this and the creamy smooth six is wonderfully willing to rev), chuck it round, then abruptly come off the throttle. Older BMWs would tail out violently under such treatment; current 3-series, even in M3 form, might slide the tail under wheelspin, but understeer is more the rule. The Z1 merely tightens its line. Try the same again but with maximum power in first, and you can spin the back into a slide – but not for long, since it is easily caught. There isn't enough poke to do so in higher gears, however.

This is quite simply the best balanced front-engine BMW chassis. It rides somewhat stiffly but acceptably, and brakes safely, helped with electronic anti-lock.

Z1's stout zinc-dipped pressed-steel perimeter frame chassis, and its very good cockpit side-intrusion and rollover protection, void of any

BMW Z1

ENGINE

Cylinders: straight six, in-line (20-degree), front-mounted.
Capacity: 2,494 cc (150 cu in).
Bore/stroke: 84/75 mm (3.31/2.95 in).
Valve gear: sohc, driven by toothed belt, 12 valves.
Compression ratio: 8.8:1.
Fuel system: Bosch Motronic fuel injection ignition.
Maximum power: 170 bhp/5,800 rpm.
Maximum torque: 164 lb ft (222 Nm)/4,300 rpm.

TRANSMISSION

Type: 5-speed manual, rear-wheel drive.
Mph/kph per 1,000 rpm in top gear: 23.4/37.7.

SUSPENSION, WHEELS

Front: independent, by Macpherson struts, lower track control arms, coil springs, anti-roll bar.

Rear: independent, by 'Z-axle' double wishbones, trailing links, coil springs, anti-roll bar.
Steering: power-assisted rack and pinion.
Brakes: (Front) ventilated discs/(Rear) plain discs, servo assisted, ABS.
Tyres/wheels: 225/45 VR 16.

DIMENSIONS

Length: 154.3 in (392 cm).
Width: 66.5 in (169 cm).
Height: 50.2 in (127.5 cm).
Wheelbase: 96.3 in (244.5 cm).
Front/rear track: 57.3/57.9 in (145.5/147 cm).
Weight: 3,214 lbs (1,460 kg).
Fuel tank: 12.8 gallons (58 litres).

PERFORMANCE*

Maximum speed: 140 mph (225 kph).
Acceleration: 0-62 mph (100 kph) 7.9 sec.
Standing km: 28.8 sec.
Fuel consumption (average): 28.0 mpg (10.1 litres/100 km).

*Factory figures

structural help from the separate bolt-on panels of its plastic skin, all co-operate to do an excellent job of resisting scuttle shake – there is just a trace. With the addition of an iron-block engine, it can't help being 4 per cent heavier than the 325i.

This car has the same power as its saloon cousin – 170 metric horses. At 19.7 sq ft there is less frontal area. With the handsomely rakish hood up, BMW claim a 0.36 drag coefficient (0.43 hood down), which includes the effect of a brilliantly neat way of avoiding graceless duck-tails – the near-flat underside curves up venturi-style at the back to duct air over the thick-wing-section crosswise final silencer to reduce rear lift.

The result is a very good maximum speed – 140 mph – and good acceleration – 0-60 in around 7.9 sec. This is ensured by fairly low intermediate gearing; the car is an exhilarating performer without being quite as quick as such a secure and responsive chassis deserves.

Driving with the doors down is fun at town speeds, if a little too windy further up the scale. It is like sitting in an exceptionally big bobsleigh. The door principle is the brainchild of engineering overlord Dr Wolfgang Reitzle who tells how impressed he was as a child by an uncle's Triumph TR6, low-sided enough for a cigarette to be stubbed out on the road. Only larger drivers will find this easy in the Z1, because it is quite a reach over the 9 in width of cockpit wall, and a fingertip stretch to touch the tarmac. A rival company's designer has described this door mechanism as 'an ingenious solution to a problem, the existence of which no one had previously realized.'

The car is not perfect, in several areas, but most of those who have driven a Z1 would love to own one – rather a forlorn hope when BMW makes only six a day.

CALLAWAY CORVETTE TWIN TURBO

I f the Chevrolet Corvette had been bodied in aluminium rather than plastic and had carried a different badge, smug Europeans would have heaped praise upon it for the purity and single-mindedness of its engineering, and for its dynamics, which are of the highest standard.

But it is American, and there is still a tendency to think of American cars as having an unhappy combination of attributes: no power in models produced since 1970, but outrageous fuel consumption, feeble brakes, roly-poly handling with no feel in the steering and dampers that run out of ideas when 60 mph is exceeded.

For several years, this was largely true, and the Corvette ('America's only sports car') of the late 1970s was hard pressed to see off a European hatchback in a straight line, never mind the corners. Company managements have now woken up, having found that their market was being carved up by imports, and American cars now are much better than they were a few years ago.

With the Corvette introduced in 1983, GM created a sports car that could stand comparison with the best Europeans. The engine may be

basically a crude old iron-block pushrod V8, but it does the business: top speed is above 150 mph and 0-60 mph takes less than 6 sec.

Early cars had a rock-hard ride and only handled well on totally smooth surfaces, but the potential was there. A few geometry changes later, after adjustments to the anti-roll bar diameters, the rates of the dampers and the unusual transverse composite springs, and here is a car with chassis engineering that would certainly not look out of place on a Porsche.

In the 35th year of Corvette production, 1988, the only thing that all models have had in common is the plastic body. The most produced in any one year was 50,000, and in the late 1980s it was closer to 35,000.

And then there is the Callaway, which is something else again. The Callaway Corvette Twin-Turbo is the first real American supercar, one of the very few cars in the world which combine virtual race-car performance with the suitability to be used for shopping. Average production of the Callaway Corvette Twin-Turbo is about six per week.

Reeves Callaway is an ex-racer for whom

excellence is only just good enough. He has a small but dedicated team at his little factory in Old Lyme, Connecticut, a beautiful part of New England. Callaway and his chief engineer, Tim Good, examined the Corvette carefully in its Z51 and Z52 (Sport Handling Package) form to see how they could make it better. They looked at springs, dampers, anti-roll bars, tyre and wheel sizes, and they did absolutely nothing.

From two men who started out as no great fans of the Corvette (most Americans do not realize how good the car is these days) that is quite a tribute.

The only chassis change in the Callaway car is the fitting of large front ventilated discs and a four-pot caliper system.

Otherwise, apart from a discreet badge here

and there and a different wheel style, the extra that Callaway charges his customers is all taken up by engine work. A Callaway Twin-Turbo still costs less in the USA than a Lotus Esprit Turbo, which it can comprehensively outgun.

Callaway's engine work is as beautiful externally as it is efficient internally. The Chevrolet power unit is a big old iron lump (though the heads are alloy) with pressed-steel trimmings, and you really are not meant to look at it because, apart from the fuel injection system instead of a Holley four-barrel, and one or two other giveaways, you could be looking at something from the late 1960s, not the end of the 1980s.

In the Callaway, you get pulleys which are cut and polished on the premises, and most of the original equipment which is retained around the surface of the engine is reworked cosmetically. But this is far from a simple job of bolting a Rotomaster and an inter-cooler on to each side of the block and hoping for the best.

The standard L98 engine (5,733 cc with 101.6 mm bore and 88.4 mm stroke) is stripped right down, cleaned, inspected for defects with the aid of Magnaflux, and machined to accept four-bolt bearing caps. The cylinders are finished for perfect alignment and the main journals are honed for straightness.

A forged race crank is used; the con-rods are also forged, and fitted with pistons from either Cosworth or Mahle.

Callaway uses the 'Wonder-bar' front cross-member as part of the air intake system. Getting sufficient cooling air to the turbos was a problem,

and until 1987 the tuned cars had NACA ducts on each side of the bonnet.

With the standard (0:68) top gear ratio, top speed is restricted to 172 mph. Convertible versions are slower, and Tim Good has calculated that since the standard convertible pulls 142 mph (compared with the auto's 150 mph), the Twin-Turbo convertible should be capable of 176 mph with the highest gearing.

With automatic versions, the plot thickens, because there are three possible axle ratios, giving top speeds of 178, 169 and 150 mph. That is with Callaway's overdrive, geared at 0.778:1.

With the high gearing, the Twin-Turbo has been timed at 4.7 sec for 0-60 mph, with a standing quarter-mile in 12.9 sec.

The end result of all these changes is that the

L98's quite respectable output figures (in a car that weighs less than 3,360 lb, which compares well with the 928 S4) of 245 bhp at 4,300 rpm and 340 lb ft at 3,200 rpm are made to look puny. The power output rises to 382 bhp at 4,250 rpm, but it is the torque output that is really staggering: 562 lb ft at 2,500 rpm!

The standard options for the Corvette are a four-speed manual gearbox with overdrive available on second, third and fourth, a rather strange arrangement, or the faithful old GM400 three-speed auto. The auto in the Callaway is taken a stage further, with a GKN overdrive built into it.

Well matched to the engine characteristics though it is, many drivers may still prefer the manual change, even with its unusual characteristics compared with a Getrag or a ZF. It is a typical American high-performance 'box, and the only way to make really fast changes is the application of scientific brutality. The clutch take-up, high in the pedal travel, does not help. It is almost impossible to miss a gear, though.

When considering gearing, the Callaway story gets very complicated, and has a crucial bearing on top speed and acceleration capabilities. The manual-gearbox cars are all fitted with a 3.07:1 final drive ratio, and with the optional 0.60 top gear overdrive, *Car* and *Driver* achieved 191.7 mph in a Twin-Turbo coupé.

That speed was achieved with an 'aero kit' consisting of front spoiler and side skirts, fitted to the car, worth only a couple of mph.

There is so much torque from low speeds in this car that the automatic version is at no disadvantage on a dry road.

It is expected that 80 per cent of Twin-Turbo buyers will continue to opt for the manual gearbox, whereas with the standard Corvette no more than 20 per cent go for three pedals.

It is hard to tell exactly what fuel consumption a Callaway Corvette would return in hard European driving. In fairly hard American driving, which is not the same thing, you can expect 13 to 17 mpg.

Engine noise in the Callaway car when cruising is about the same as in the standard car, possibly even a shade quieter thanks to the muffling effect of the turbochargers. When you give it lots of throttle, and wind up the boost scale, there is a distinctive whistling noise because Rotomaster's method of balancing is to shave off a piece of impeller.

Otherwise, the Corvette, with or without the turbos, is generally quiet in relation to its high performance. There is a fair amount of tyre noise and some wheel-generated clonks, but very little wind roar in either the hardtop model or the convertible with the top attached.

The Corvette has exceptionally good grip and traction with its Goodyear Eagle 275/40 ZR 17 rubber. The Callaway, like the standard car, has a tendency to understeer mildly in most circum-

stances, though flooring the throttle in medium-speed corners overcomes this most effectively, the tail swinging around smoothly. Oversteer can also be controlled by backing off and then flooring the throttle just before the apex.

Steering is by rack and pinion, and the assistance is just sufficient to take the chore out of low-speed manoeuvres, which are hampered by relatively poor lock.

Damping control at speed is of the highest road-car standards, with no float, and even though there is sometimes a minor sensation of overspringing, it does not reach the point of causing instability.

Although vertical shocks with the Z52 suspension are transmitted from the wheels to the shell, the car does not move off line in bumpy bends, though overall ride quality is firm.

In standard form, the Corvette has 12 in ventilated discs all round, with a very good anti-lock system. Callaway fits 13 in discs to the front. So great is the grip that activating the anti-lock on a dry surface is almost impossible.

Fade also seemed to be totally out of the equation, but with a couple of heavy decelerations from high speeds, a fair aroma of pad material wafts by.

The Corvette gives the driver as much leg room as is provided in the Porsche 928, with a wide range of possible adjustments. The pedals, in both manual and auto versions, are well sited,

and the gear lever is within easy reach. The minor switches are sometimes hard to identify but the stalks on the steering column are well laid out.

In designing the car, Chevrolet wisely opted for just two seats. It is a very good two-seater, with quite a lot of luggage space in the coupé, on a flat platform, and just about enough in the convertible. The latter has an efficient electrical system but rather fiddly catches for the soft top and luggage lid into which it locks. Again, luggage space is fair, but greatly diminished when running with the top down.

Forward visibility on the move is good. At parking speeds the Corvette is much like an E-type in that it is difficult to judge the forward extremity.

All-round visibility is also good on the move with the top down in the convertible but with it raised there is a 'three-quarters' blind spot; the B-post of the hardtop is narrower, so less problematic.

Corvette instruments are the all singing and dancing digital variety, with everything you need to know displayed, and much else besides. All this looks jolly good in the showroom, and is perfect for Callaway's development work, but for the customer it is an unnecessary mess.

Most of the functions in the centre can actually be switched off, reappearing (one hopes) in times of crisis, but the speedo (digital and electronic display analogue) and rev counter (bar graph) are both a bit of a joke. The display turns pale in direct sunlight, but is still just about readable.

The air conditioning controls are also theoretically clever, but in practice fiddly, and though the system is excellent in keeping the interior cool on a hot day, and heating up on a cold day, it is not very sophisticated.

The few flaws in the Callaway are inherited from the standard Corvette. By the same token, all the things that are right about the standard car, and they are many, also hold true for the Callaway.

CALLAWAY CORVETTE TWIN TURBO

ENGINE

Cylinders: V8 (90-degree), angled, front-mounted.

Capacity: 5,727 cc (344 cu in).

Bore/stroke: 99/93 mm (3.90/3.66 in).

Valve gear: single central camshaft, pushrod ohv, 16 valves.

Compression ratio: 7.5:1.

Fuel system: GM multi-point 'Tuned Port' fuel injection, twin Rotomaster turbochargers with air/air intercoolers.

Maximum power: 382 bhp/4,250 rpm.

Maximum torque: 562 lb ft (370 Nm)/2,500 rpm.

TRANSMISSION

Type: 4-speed manual (3-speed automatic with Callaway/GKn overdrive also available), rear-wheel drive, limited-slip differential.

Mph/kph per 1,000 rpm in top gear (manual): 40.3/64.8.

SUSPENSION, WHEELS

Front: independent, by double wishbones, transverse composite leaf spring, anti-roll bar.

Rear: upper and lower trailing arms, lateral arms, tie-bar, transverse leaf spring, anti-roll bar.

Steering: power-assisted rack and pinion .

Brakes: (Front) ventilated discs/(Rear) ventilated discs, servo-assisted.

Tyres/wheels: front and rear, 275/40 ZR 17 - 9.5J

DIMENSIONS

Length: 176.5 in (448 cm).

Width: 71.0 in (180 cm).

Height: 46.7 in (118.5 cm).

Wheelbase: 96.3 in (244.5 cm).

Front/rear track: 59.6/60.4 in (151.5/153.5cm).

Weight: 3,506 lbs (1,590 kg).

Fuel tank: 20.0 gallons (91 litres).

PERFORMANCE

Maximum speed: 191.7 mph (308.4 kph).

Acceleration: 0–60 mph (96.5 kph) 4.7 sec.

Fuel consumption (average): 15 mpg (18.8 litres/100 km).

CHEVROLET CORVETTE ZR-1

It has been dubbed the 'heartbeat of America'. For many years the Corvette, in its various forms, has been the USA's only real sports car. Some Corvettes have been very quick, some (especially in the 1970s) were so strangulated by emissions equipment that they couldn't keep up with a family hatchback in a straight line, never mind braking or cornering . . . So Dave McLellan, the Corvette project leader, decided that a version should be built to challenge the best that European sports car

manufacturers could offer. The car became known as 'the King of the Hill'.

At a glance, the ZR-1 looks very much like the standard Corvette, in the shape introduced in 1983, but a closer examination shows that the rear of the car is broader, that under the arches are wider tyres (P315/35 ZR 17s, though the standard front P275/40 ZR 17s are retained), and that the rear panel of the body is convex rather than concave, with a different design of tail lights and modified exhaust tail pipes.

In the standard L89 Corvette, the three-way damper control system, with its settings called 'Touring', 'Sport' and 'Performance', still in effect provides not much more than three different degrees of harshness, though much better than in early examples of these Corvettes which run on transverse composite springs.

In the ZR-1 these settings are much more successful in meeting different demands: 'Touring' is perfect for low-speed driving, and although the car still rides firmly, this at least does

not shake the fillings out of teeth around town. 'Performance' is perfect for driving on race tracks or at very high speeds – say, above 150 mph – while 'Sport' is suitable for all other circumstances, including fast road driving on twisting, undulating surfaces.

The ZR-1 engine is a V8 with a capacity of 5.7 litres. That much it shares with the L89, but in all other respects it is quite different. Developed with the help of Lotus, and built by Mercury Marine, this LT5 engine has 32 valves, is constructed entirely in aluminium (the L89 is all iron), and has a narrower bore and longer stroke. The compression ratio is 11.3:1, and there is one fuel injector for each of the 16 intake ports.

There are three induction stages: at idle (only 400 rpm) and at low speeds a narrow valve permits economical running; a power switch in the console (operated by a removable key) restricts power to 200 bhp by shutting off half the inlet ports; finally, there is the full complement of (allegedly) 380 bhp at 6,000 rpm, and 370 lb ft of torque at 4,000 rpm.

If ever there was an engine less in need of six gears, this is it, but it has that many so that Chevrolet will not have to pay the US 'gas guzzler' tax. Having six speeds certainly allows relaxed cruising – you can't get much more relaxed than 42.5 mph for every 1,000 rpm in sixth. That translates to just over 3,500 rpm at 150 mph, and it is no surprise that maximum speed (a little short of the claimed 180 mph) is achieved in fifth rather than top, which is *theoretically* geared to pull 306 mph!

To make life really difficult for the driver, less than a third of the throttle opening between 12 mph and 18 mph can be used, so that the lever slots obstinately into fourth in attempting to select second. It is possible to disarm this absurdity simply by detaching one wire.

GM claims acceleration for the car as 'zero-to-60 in the 4.2 second range'. Well, the car simply will not achieve that, especially two up, the way tests are conducted in Britain. But it should manage around the 5 sec mark, and that is with a catalytic converter fitted. More importantly, there is so much torque that it is really easy to exploit this wonderful chassis to the full.

It really is brilliant, and it is not just a question of those big, fat Goodyear Eagles giving lots of grip, though they certainly do that. It is the handling on, and especially beyond, the limit which is most impressive.

If you get everything right, there will be mild understeer, so mild that the attitude is virtually neutral. But push too hard into a bend, so that you need to back off, and the car tucks in gently and progressively. You can even apply the brakes if you need to shed a bit of speed, without getting

into the serious trouble such behaviour can cause in some cars. In tight curves, you can steer the car on the throttle and really put a grin on your face. This is high technology applied to the classic formula of the engine at the front driving the rear wheels.

Some people have criticized the steering, but it is hard to imagine why, since the gearing and weighting are virtually ideal in all circumstances.

Lapping Goodyear's test track at Mireval in southern France was tremendous fun. Even though the tyres and brakes went off after a couple of laps (that happens to any road car), it was an impressive demonstration of the car's capabilities.

All the European journalists who tested the ZR-1 in France felt that it was one of the world's few truly great sports cars. But these were pre-production examples: were they representative of the cars sold to the public? There have been suggestions that they were not, and that production versions do not handle as well.

CHEVROLET CORVETTE ZR-1

ENGINE

Cylinders: V8 (90-degrees), angled, front-mounted.

Capacity: 5,727 cc (344 cu in).

Bore/stroke: 99/93 mm (3.90/3.66 in).

Valve gear: Dohc per bank, chain-driven, 32 valves.

Compression ratio: 11.25:1.

Fuel system: electronic multi-point fuel injection.

Maximum power: 380 bhp/6,000 rpm.

Maximum torque: 370 lb ft (502 Nm)/4,000 rpm.

TRANSMISSION

Type: 6-speed manual, rear-wheel drive, limited-slip differential.

Mph/kph per 1,000 rpm in top gear: 42.5/68.4.

SUSPENSION, WHEELS

Front: independent, by double wishbones, transverse composite leaf spring, anti-roll bar.

Rear: upper and lower trailing arms, lateral arms, tie-bar, transverse leaf spring, anti-roll bar.

Steering: power-assisted rack and pinion .

Brakes: (Front) ventilated discs/(Rear) ventilated discs, servo-assisted.

Tyres/wheels: front 275/40 ZR 17 -9.5J, rear 315/35 ZR 17 - 11J.

DIMENSIONS

Length: 176.6 in (448.5 cm).

Width: 74.0 in (188 cm).

Height: 46.7 in (118.5 cm).

Wheelbase: 96.3 in (244.5 cm).

Front/rear track: 59.6/60.4 in (151.5 153.5cm).

Weight: 3,416 lbs (1,550 kg).

Fuel tank: 15.5 gallons (76 litres).

PERFORMANCE *

Maximum speed: 170 mph (274 kph).

Acceleration: 0-60 mph (96.5 kph) 5 sec.

Fuel consumption (average): 15.7 mpg (18 litres/100 km).

*Estimated

DE TOMASO
PANTERA GT5

A blend of unsubtle American pushrod grunt and Italian chassis and styling (a formula which was once more widely used than it is today), the Pantera is one of the great survivors among supercars: it was put into production back in 1972, yet even today it does not look outdated, although the big rear wing – identical to that of the Countach – does nothing for its aesthetics.

Exactly how it affects aerodynamic efficiency has been recorded: without the wing, the Pantera GT5 lapped the banked Millbrook test track at 151.7 mph; with it attached, this dropped by almost 3 mph, which was less than we expected (it takes 20 or 30 mph off the top end of a Countach, but that is a much faster car).

Motive power for the De Tomaso is provided by a very oversquare (101/89mm), all-iron, 5.7-litre Ford V8. It has only one camshaft, lurking in the centre of the vee, and the two

valves per cylinder are actuated by pushrods. There is no light alloy anywhere and above the pressed tin rocker covers there is a huge air cleaner which hides a squat four-barrel Holley carbureter.

No injection here, and the De Tomaso's unique appeal is that it is the simplest of all the world's mid-engined supercars. It has 350 bhp SAE at 6,000 rpm to push it along (that is 300 or so by the European DIN standard) and over 300 lb ft, but it does have more than 3,100 lb (unladen) to push through the air.

The wide spread of torque enables the Pantera to get off the line cleanly, where some rivals are, comparatively, struggling between the grip of fat tyres and the penalties of a narrow power band. It can reach 30 mph in two seconds dead, and goes on to 60 mph in 5.5 sec and 100 in 13.5. But it is in mid-range pulling power that it really excels, with a supremely muscular response

anywhere between 20 and 100 mph in either fourth or fifth gears.

American power is completely undemanding. In that range, it accelerates almost as quickly left in fourth with a foot planted, but shifting the ZF transaxle's ratios is a very pleasant and satisfying pastime. Savouring the rattling V8's racecar close rpm drop, as you snick the lever about its steel gate, is guaranteed to bring out the Walter Mitty in anyone. The gearbox on the end of the lever is a development of that fitted to the Le Mans GT40s of the 1960s, and its internals allow the short, spindly lever to move as fast as you like – the faster the better in fact.

The change is positive with a very short throw, but trying to move the lever slowly and economically does not work, and the synchros delay progress rather than help.

The whole lot *feels* indestructible, and the race car men tell us that it is. The ratios appear closer than the specifications suggest because of the engine's leisurely maximum, but the thunder of the bass drum exhaust still hardens as the revs rise, just as it does in those American car chases. Close you eyes and you could think it was a big Mustang – don't do it if you are driving . . .

Provided you can actually fit in it, and once you have become used to the hopeless rear

three-quarter visibility, the Pantera is one of the easiest supercars to drive. Rather less alive and demanding than some others, it nevertheless possesses enormous ability. It sits on giant 15 in light alloy rims, 11 in wide at the front and 13 in at the rear, clothed in similarly vast 285/40 and 345/45 profile Pirelli P7s. These are the sizes used on a Group C2 World Endurance sports car, and it is only now, in a switch to 17 in diameter rims, that bigger chunks of rubber are to be found at the corners of a few motor cars.

It is all but impossible to make the Pantera misbehave. Understeer builds gently as you try harder, and no amount of throttle will unstick the rear. Lifting off in the middle of a corner does not really tighten your line, it simply removes the push that the power had introduced.

Purely in the interests of science, we finally discovered the only means of upsetting the car was to prod the brakes in the middle of a fast corner. Then the steering proved accurate in retrieving the tail. However, it is heavy, and combined with the awkward seating, difficult to keep smooth. Nevertheless, there is no lurching – the body remains virtually flat at all times, and despite that, it rides well. It is a formidable package, even if it lacks a little subtlety.

Sadly, though, for anyone over 5 ft 10 in, the

DE TOMASO PANTERA GT5

ENGINE

Cylinders: V8 (90-degree), in-line, mid-mounted.
Capacity: 5,763 cc (346 cu in).
Bore/stroke: 101/88.9 mm (3.98/3.50 in).
Valve gear: single camshaft, chain-driven, pushrod ohv, 16 valves.
Compression ratio: 9.5:1.
Fuel system: Single downdraught four-barrel Holley carbureter.
Maximum power: 350 bhp/6,000 rpm.
Maximum torque: 325 lb ft (441 Nm) 3,500 rpm.

TRANSMISSION

Type: 5-speed manual, rear-wheel drive, limited-slip differential.
Mph/kph per 1,000 rpm in top gear: 26.4/42.5.

SUSPENSION, WHEELS

Front: independent, by double wishbones, coil springs, anti-roll bar.
Rear: independent, by double wishbones, coil springs, anti-roll bar.
Steering: unassisted rack and pinion.
Brakes: (Front) ventilated discs/(Rear) ventilated discs, servo assisted.
Tyres/wheels: front 285/40 VR 15 -10J, rear 345/35 VR 15 - 13J.

DIMENSIONS

Length: 175 in (444.5 cm).
Width: 77.5 in (197 cm).
Height: 43.0 in (109 cm).
Wheelbase: 99.0 in (251 cm).
Front/rear track: 57.5/61.8 in (146/157 cm).
Weight: 3,125 lbs (1,417 kg).
Fuel tank: 18.7 gallons (85 litres).

PERFORMANCE

Maximum speed: 149.1 mph (239.9 kph).
Acceleration: 0-60 mph (96.5 kph) 5.5 sec, 0-100 mph (161 kph) 13.5 sec.
Fourth gear: 30-50 mph (48-80.5 kph) 4.4 sec.
Fifth gear: 50-70mph (80.5-113 kph) 5.5 sec.
Fuel consumption (average, estimate): 15 mpg (18.8 litres/100 km).

Pantera is just not sensible. The seat is very close to the pedals, which are wildly offset to the left to miss the wheel arch. You sit with legs splayed, and keeping the throttle pressed on long journeys involves driving with the side of the foot, and makes the ankles ache after only a few miles. Despite the position of the seat, the wheel is still also a fair stretch, which is less than ideal with 11 in front rims. All this is a pity, because the car has astonishing traction (two seconds dead to 30 mph), tremendous composure and body control, and fantastic brakes in keeping with the style of the gear change. They require firm treatment, but they reward.

Not outstandingly agile, perhaps, but the Pantera is one of the safest of supercars, with a measure of gruff, workmanlike charm. It is as rare as the Countach and attracts as much attention, at considerably lower cost. And, if you are tall, at considerable pain.

FERRARI 328

The 328 was the final evolution of the 308, for despite considerable conceptual and mechanical similarities, the 348 is an all-new design.

The 328's V8 engine is an all-aluminium unit with twin belt-driven overhead camshafts per bank which operate four valves per cylinder. There is full Marelli Microplex electronic engine management, and Bosch K-jetronic fuel injection. The result of this complexity is 270 bhp at 7,000 rpm and 224 lb ft at 5,500 rpm, in a car that weighs in at around 2,800 lb.

Clean aerodynamics help push the 328 to a top speed of 158.5 mph. That was recorded at the Millbrook track, and suggests a genuine maximum of at least 5 mph more, which was a brilliant performance until the 348 came along.

Outright acceleration is very good, not helped by the combination of a relatively narrow effective power band (though the engine is admirably flexible throughout its range), with 0-60 mph in 5.5 sec, and 0-100 mph in 13.8.

The Ferrari's engine is pure racer, and it is wonderfully exciting. It does not sound like a V8, there is no uneven throb, instead there's a noise like a small Fiat to begin with, growing harsh as the revs rise, then opening out in a banshee wail as the induction chimes in. The red line is at 7,700 rpm, no less, and by then the crescendo is positively fearsome, but the driver needs to research these areas of the tacho to gain the car's real performance. For all that, the engine's power band is truly wide and low gearing allows the car to be muscular in the mid-range. Revmaster it may be, but the 328 shows no temperament.

The 328's gear change is precise but demands controlled brutality in order to avoid sullen non-engagement. It is not that you need to pump the gearshift with Herculean strength, more that you need to follow the path of the long chrome wand right up to the clack of the lever on the slotted aluminium gate. It will not just fall in with fingertip pressure in the manner of most modern saloons, and the throw is quite long, although this feels equally indestructible. The ratios are closely stacked so that swopping them becomes a rewarding part of the driving process, while to suit less adventurous moods the Ferrari will still allow pottering in fourth.

It takes a lot of effort to extract the best from a 328, but ultimately it is one of the most rewarding cars to drive, because of its purity and precision. These days, by comparison with some rivals it seems 'under-tyred' on 205/55 fronts and 225/50 rears (fitted to 16 in diameter rims, 7 in wide at the front and 8 in at the rear). The effort required is more mental than physical, because the controls are not heavy. The unassisted steering is light and direct via the elegant thin-rimmed wheel. Potholes will produce alarming kickback, but on smooth roads the car will turn in with absolute accuracy and no feeling of twitchiness from the rear. This is a mid-engined forte, because the masses are well within the wheelbase, and the Ferrari does it with style.

Try harder and the Ferrari understeers more, try harder still and the tail will slide in direct response to the throttle. In this sense particularly, it is more honest, and you can balance the car with the right foot. Cutting the power will have a similar although lesser effect. That said, such a manoeuvre requires alert reactions to carry through, because the torque will push the 328's tail to an alarming angle even at very high speed, especially on wet roads. The Ferrari, though, is definitely a driver's car.

It had good ride, damping and body control. Its composure flat out at over 160 mph was exemplary. The brakes, although extremely powerful, were a shade overservoed, and there was a tendency to lock a front wheel, especially on wet surfaces.

It is undeniable that the 348 is a better car dynamically than the 328, but the old car became one of the great Ferraris, and remains one of Pininfarina's finest achievements.

FERRARI 328 GTB/GTS

ENGINE

Cylinders: V8 (90-degree), transverse, mid-mounted.

Capacity: 3,186 cc (191 cu in).

Bore/stroke: 83/73.6 mm (3.27/2.90 in).

Valve gear: dohc per bank (driven by toothed belt), four valves per cylinder.

Compression ratio: 9.8:1.

Fuel system: Bosch K/KE-jetronic fuel injection.

Maximum power: 270 bhp/7,000 rpm.

Maximum torque: 224 lb ft (304 Nm) 5,500 rpm.

TRANSMISSION

Type: 5 speed manual, rear-wheel drive, limited-slip differential.

Mph/kph per 1,000 rpm in top gear: 21.2/34.1.

SUSPENSION, WHEELS

Front: independent, by double wishbones, coil springs, anti-roll bar.

Rear: independent, by double wishbones, coil springs, anti-roll bar.

Steering: unassisted rack and pinion.

Brakes: (Front) ventilated discs/(Rear) ventilated discs, servo assisted.

Tyres/wheels: front 205/55 VR 16 -7J, rear 225/50 VR 16 - 8J.

DIMENSIONS

Length: 167.5 in (425.5 cm).

Width: 68.1 in (173 cm).

Height: 44.5 in (113 cm).

Wheelbase: 92.5 in (235 cm).

Front/rear track: 58.5/57.7 in (148.5 146.5cm).

Weight: GTB 2,789 lbs (1,265 kg), GTS 2,811 lbs (1,275 kg).

Fuel tank: 16.3 gallons (74 litres).

PERFORMANCE

Maximum speed: 163 mph (262 kph).

Acceleration: 0-60 mph (96.5 kph) 5.5 sec.

Standing km: 25.7 sec.

Fuel consumption (average): 22.5 mpg (12.6 litres/100 km).

FERRARI 348

How do you replace a classic? It's tough, but it needs to be done eventually. Ferrari's transformation of the 348 is much more interesting from a technical and engineering viewpoint (because serious dynamic issues have been addressed by a good team of development engineers), but the shape will be the aspect that people talk about first.

Quite simply, the 308/328 was probably the prettiest production car that Ferrari ever built. You can look at the 348 and decide it looks quite nice when approached carefully from the right direction, but it certainly couldn't be called pretty.

Least flattering is the full frontal view, and that dummy grille is a cop-out: if a grille is not needed, why have one? Someone from either Pininfarina or Ferrari should have his knuckles rapped for that. An innovative and aerodynamic approach would have made more sense. In the press hand-out (referring to the Testerossa-style side strakes) is the following remark '. . . on a Ferrari a technical requirement becomes a stylistic theme and nothing is simply there for decoration.' That hardly seems true.

Also, Ferrari's use of a slot in only one side of the front air dam seems like affectation, as it did when it first appeared on the other side of the Testarossa. What's wrong with symmetry?

The chief engineering we have here is that instead of a transverse engine and in-line gearbox, everything has been turned through 90 degrees. The main reason for this, however, was not a search for better cornering behaviour. Like the Testarossa, the 328 had a centre of gravity that was too high for ideal handling, and the rearrangement has permitted the engine to be lowered by more than 5in.

The dimensional changes are in line with the current move towards extra width and height: almost 2in shorter than the 328 (but with 4in extra in the wheelbase), the 348 is 6.5in wider, and 1.7in taller. It weighs 3,227 lbs, an increase of more than 225 lbs, due mainly to extra equipment, but also due to the more rigid tubular chassis.

It used to be said that the heart of a Ferrari is its engine. Certainly that was true in far-off days,

when the rest of the car left a lot to be desired in many ways. Though beautiful, many of the old Ferraris which today command extortionate sums under the gavel of auctioneers didn't actually handle or stop or ride very well even by the standards of their day, and it didn't pay to examine the quality of the finish too closely. But they usually had superb engines, which makes up for a lot. Some say that a Ferrari with fewer than 12 cylinders is not a true Ferrari, which is of course total nonsense.

It looks good, and it goes superbly, but it doesn't *sound* like a V8, in fact the noise it makes is more like a high-pitched turbine than anything else, the characteristic whine of the flat-plane crank. It hasn't got the hard edge of the Lamborghini's V8 (similar to the old Cosworth DVF) or the deep, throaty rumble of the high performance American engines. It isn't an unpleasant noise, but neither does it make the hairs on the back of the neck stand on end. This engine is simply an efficient device to be used to the full.

Now with 3,405cc (the bore and stroke both mildly enlarged, respectively 85 and 75mm), peak power of this *quattrovalvole* unit has risen from 270bhp at 7,000 rpm to 300 at 7,200 and peak torque is up from 224lb ft to 238, but more significantly at 4,200 rpm rather than 5,500. The red line is now at 7,500 rpm, 200 rpm lower than before. Now with a catalytic converter, the engine is fully managed (for both its injection and ignition) by a Bosch Motronic M2.5 system.

The extra urge lower down really is noticeable, and the smoothness of delivery is matched by very few engines from anywhere in the world: since this is conjoined with exquisite driveline smoothness, you can stand brutally on the throttle at low revs, and it will just light up and take off without any hesitation. It certainly does take off too, with 0–60 mph in 5.5sec and a top speed of 275 kph (171 mph). Anybody sensible who wants a useable high-performance car should choose the 348 instead of the Testarossa, but nobody sensible buys cars like this anyway.

The 348 has an entirely new gearbox which feels very similar to the 328 gearbox. There is the same need to concentrate on the 'dog-leg' first into second, the same precision otherwise – as long as you treat it with sympathetic aggression (slow lazy changes are out of the question), and the same 'clack' as you snap from one ratio to

the next through the traditional gate.

The clutch also feels unchanged, quite heavy, but very pleasant once the car is moving. The ratios permit 47, 71, 104, and 137mph in the intermediates, with 23.2 mph/1,000 rpm in fifth.

Fuel consumption is reckoned to be between five and fifteen percent better than in the 328. Of similar importance to Ferrari owners is the larger fuel tank – now up to 21 gallons.

Bridgestone G71s never seem to perform badly on any car. At the front of the 348, these ZR-rated tyres are 215/50, and at the rear 255/50, on 17in rims.

Though all components have been changed, the suspension is essentially similar to that of the 328, with double wishbones at each corner, springing by coils, and no use yet of 'active' damping. The frequencies of the front and rear suspensions have been carefully tuned to reduce dive under braking.

It was fun testing the 348 at Ferrari's Fiorini test track, which has a useful mixture of corners of varying severity. In the hairpins, the 348 would want to understeer gently, but this could be altered with the throttle – ease off a little and then back on hard. Up to a point this could be described as easy adjustability, but once the tail had been pushed beyond a certain angle, it was uncatchable. This is often so with mid-engined cars, but the 348 is definitely better than its predecessor in this respect, even though its polar moment has been reduced by resiting the water and oil radiators in the centre.

On the road the 348 simply felt neutral, safe and adjustable, so you may wonder what is the point of provoking extremes on a test track. It's fun, and it makes for more exciting photographs, but the more serious reason is simply to explore what happens when the limits of adhesion are exceeded: somebody, somewhere, will do so at some time, and possibly not on purpose.

The greatest assets of the 328 (apart from its stunning looks) were its steering and chassis feel which have been carried over and, if anything, improved. Half a turn of the wheel is enough to get through a hairpin, thanks to much higher gearing than in many modern sports cars. Even at parking speeds, however, the steering is not especially heavy, and on the move it is superb, communicating small variations in grip with changes in perceived weight, the minutest adjustments to line being delivered in perfect proportion.

Though the discs have been slightly enlarged (made possible by the use of larger diameter wheels), the most significant change to the braking is the adoption of ABS. Undoubtedly, anti-lock braking has been the major safety innovation of recent years, but there is a drawback on a dry test-track: you cannot hold the car just below lock-up point with precision. Some of the satisfaction goes with the efficiency. On the road though, this was not noticeable, and the brakes simply felt nicely weighted, discreetly servoed and powerful.

All-round visibility in the 348 is much better than in most mid-engined cars, and the large door-mounted mirrors are ideal, both when travelling forwards and when reversing. Generally, they don't create their own blind spot. We had no opportunity to check out the efficiency of the big twin headlights, since by the time the sun had dropped towards the industrial smog of the Emilian plain, we already had to be back at the factory.

At first it is hard to spot the changes to the interior, and the character of the 308/328 has been carried forward into the 348. But there have been significant improvements, not least of them being an important increase in legroom and headroom, and a better driver's seat.

The leather upholstered seats not only look nicer than before, but they give better lateral location (especially noticeable around the circuit), improved lumbar support and – perhaps best of all – better padding in the cushion.

The driving position is excellent, with left foot braced aginst a footrest where the wheel arch intrudes, and right sliding down the central tunnel on to the throttle. So-called 'heel and toe' changes are facilitated by the well-devised pedal arrangement.

Of course, this promise of perfection will end in disappointment for British 348 buyers: a disadvantage of mid-engined cars is that the offset pedals are much more noticeable in a right-hand drive car, where it is the right leg that operates at a strange angle.

Also much neater is the design of the door trim, and the internal opening mechanism is among the best anyone has yet devised.

The instruments are much the same as before, the main four (speedo, rev counter, oil pressure, and water temperature gauges) housed under a

leather trimmed cowl, with the oil temperature and fuel gauges in the centre console. There is no longer a battery condition indicator.

Improved stalks are used, and the switches are pretty good, but Ferrari, like many other manufacturers, still has not found a sensible place for the hazard warning flasher button. Also the fog lights lack 'braille' identification.

Heating and ventilation systems in Italian cars have moved in recent years from effectively non-existent to a point where they are now almost as good as anything from anywhere else. The controls of the 348's air conditioning are not bad when you get used to them, and the ventilation on ram effect is especially good (with A/C switched off) – you don't have to wind the windows down any more! Swivelling cheese-cutter grilles are used these days, more effective but less aesthetically pleasing than the old swivelling split-disc vents.

This car has clearly been recognized at Maranello, and the level of interior noise at that kind of cruising speed of 70-100 mph has been greatly improved. The engine is quieter and there is much reduced whine from the transmission and fewer road/tyre noises. There was some wind rustle around the frameless windows, but it did not become severe.

Granted that a car like this is not designed with practicality as a priority, people still like to take some luggage with them and the 348 does provide adequate space at the front.

The chief reason for this relatively good carrying capacity is the decision not to supply a spare wheel, not even one of those 'space saver' devices.

There is no doubt that the 348, from a dynamic point of view, is a serious and important step forward from the 328. Besides being much faster, it handles better.

FERRARI 348

ENGINE

Cylinders: V8 (90-degrees) in-line, mid-mounted.
Capacity: 3,405 cc (204 cu in).
Bore/stroke: 85/75 mm (3.35/2.95 in).
Valve gear: dohc per bank, driven by toothed belt, 32 valves.
Compression ratio: 10.4:1.
Fuel system: Electronic injection integrated with Bosch Motronic ignition.
Maximum power: 300 bhp/7,200 rpm.
Maximum torque: 238 lb ft (323 Nm)/4,200 rpm.

TRANSMISSION

Type: 5-speed manual, rear-wheel drive, limited-slip differential.
Mph/kph per 1,000 rpm in top gear: 23.2/37.3.

SUSPENSION, WHEELS

Front: independent, by double wishbones, coil springs, anti-roll bar.
Rear: independent, by double wishbones, coil springs, anti-roll bar.
Steering: unassisted rack and pinion.
Brakes: (Front) ventilated discs/(Rear) ventilated discs, servo assisted, ABS.
Tyres/wheels: front 215/50 ZR 17 -7.5J, rear 255/50 ZR 17 - 9J.

DIMENSIONS

Length: 166.5 in (423 cm).
Width: 74.6 in (189 cm).
Height: 46.0 in (117 cm).
Wheelbase: 96.5 in (245 cm).
Front/rear track: 59.1/62.1 in (150/158 cm).
Weight: 3,227 lbs (1,452 kg).
Fuel tank: 20.9 gallons (95 litres).

PERFORMANCE

Maximum speed: 171 mph (275 kph).
Acceleration: 0-60 mph (96.5 kph) 5.5 sec, 0-100 mph (161 kph) 13.3 sec.
Standing km: 25.2 sec.
Fourth gear: 40-60 mph (64-96.5 kph) 5.0 sec.
Fifth gear: 50-70mph (80.5-113 kph) 7.3 sec.
Fuel consumption (average): 20.0 mpg (14.2 litres/100 km).

FERRARI 412

Ferrari's last front-engined car, the 412, ceased production in 1989. It was an enigma. Few journalists drove it, but rather too many who had not were prepared to express an opinion, based either on memories of the 400 (the 412's predecessor) or even on blinder prejudice.

If leading motoring journalists were asked to compile a list of the 10 most exciting cars in the world, it is unlikely that the 412 would rate a mention.

Why is this? After all, the 412 is elegantly designed, and also the most traditional of all recent Ferraris, a two-plus-two coupé powered by a front-mounted V12 driving the rear wheels: just like the Daytona.

Perhaps the reason for the dismissive remarks is that the majority of 412 buyers, like those who bought 400s, chose the automatic gearbox. Perhaps it is because, to some eyes, the absence of flamboyant styling tricks like those employed on the Testarossa (another Pininfarina design) makes the 412 'bland'. Maybe it looks too much like a road car rather than a Group C racer that has been tweaked just enough to get through Type Approval regulations. But mainly we come back to blind prejudice.

The vast majority of 412s sold in North American and North European markets were automatics. The five-speed manual gearbox was only supplied 'on request'. So, the car tested here, the manual 412, is one which makes the Aston Martin Vantage seem a commonplace sight.

There was certainly nothing bland about the 412 specification. In this age of stupendously fast 'supercars', 0–60 mph in just over 6 sec and a top speed of 155 mph may seem a bit 'weedy', but such performance will be sufficient for most occasions. There are not many places where 200 mph can be achieved even if it is permitted.

Its engine had a great deal in common with that of the Testarossa, including its bore and stroke dimensions (82/78 mm) and hence its capacity 4,943 cc. Both received fuel via Bosch K-Jetronic fuel injection (that is the mechanical type) and both had Marelli Microplex digital ignition. The blocks and heads were constructed in light alloy, with cast alloy pistons running in cast iron wet liners with a 'cermental' coating.

Where the 412 mainly differed from the Testarossa, apart from the fact that its cylinders were set in a 60-degree Vee rather than horizontally opposed, was in its cylinder heads.

Twin overhead camshafts driven by chains were used, but alone among recent Ferraris the V12 has only two valves per cylinder. These were operated via thimble type tappets. The 412 has a higher compression ratio than the Testarossa, 9.6:1 instead of 9.2, but not surprisingly both power and torque outputs are substantially down.

If you want enough power to melt the road surface, let alone the tyres, the 412 does not provide it. Even so, 340 bhp at 6,000 rpm is substantial and the torque peak of 333 lb ft is at 4,200 rpm with 300-plus available from only 2,000 rpm onwards.

Even with its lower outputs, the 412 is a very impressive performer, easily capable of storming up to 140 mph on many straights, despite the weight of almost 4,000 lb.

Its acceleration is strong: after reaching 60 mph in 6.4 sec, it passes the quarter-mile in 14.6 sec and covers a kilometre in 26.6. Not blindingly fast, perhaps, but undeniably quick. The way it does it is superb, as the V12 is silkily smooth throughout its wide torque range, and the sound it makes is musical: not a Daytona-style howl, but on the other hand it does not have that car's mechanical clatter. This refinement is in some contrast to the old 400, which slurped its fuel through Webers, throbbed noisily at idle, had chattering cam chains and valve gear, and sometimes hesitated when full throttle was applied. In several ways, the 412 is vastly superior.

Overall the car is fairly quiet, with negligible wind roar even at 140 mph, though there is a lot of road-generated noise (suspension clonking and surface roar) and a small background whine from the transmission in the intermediates.

In this class of car, fuel economy is not paramount, which is just as well as the 412 is unlikely to return more than 15 mpg. However, the 25.5 gallon tanks permit a range of well over 350 miles.

By absolute standards, the 412 sits on big, fat Michelins, but by comparison with the wilder fringes of the supercar market (Countach, F40 and – to a lesser extent – the Testarossa), the coupé's Michelin TRXs are quite narrow: 240-/55 VR415 on 180TR rims.

What is expected of a traditional type of high-performance car is that it should understeer mildly at moderate cornering forces, have enough power to neutralize itself, and be capable

of being steered on the throttle at whatever angle the driver chooses. The 412 does exactly that.

Some drivers prefer this type of behaviour to the astounding grip exhibited by many of those roadgoing racers with centrally-mounted engines. To drive a Testarossa hard, for example, you really have to wind yourself up, and persuade yourself that yes, it really can go into this bend at this speed. The 412's limits are substantially lower, but in many ways it is more fun to drive quickly, surprising as this may seem.

If you go into a bend a bit too fast, you simply allow the car to wind on the requisite amount of corrective lock, and proceed. That is what motoring used to be, before the clever necromancers in the tyre industry stopped making compounds out of banana skins.

When, as in the case of the 412, there is a classic suspension design (double wishbones on each corner) to go with the traditional engine location and when the chassis is well designed, you have a formula for highly enjoyable driving.

The steering seems lighter than was its predecessor's, and it is now considerably more direct, though the turning circle is still about twice that of a London taxi. Kickback is much reduced, and only occurs at all over bad potholes.

There is more roll than in the mid-engined monsters, but it is very well controlled, and the poise of the car on reasonably smooth roads is outstanding. The 412 turns in well, its angle can be altered more or less at will and has no nasty surprises in store, the 40 per cent limited-slip differential operating without any unpleasant

snatch. Though the adhesion of the tyres is good, even in the wet, it does not dominate the handling.

This all sounds close to perfection, but while it may be *close*, it is not quite there. The only serious criticism concerns the damping. At low speeds this, with well-matched spring rates, gives a remarkably smooth ride, if not a particularly quiet one. Over many surfaces at speed, damping control seems also to be good, but on a bumpy minor road, a few deficiencies appear, as the body floats rather more than is desirable.

It is difficult to understand why anyone, other than a partially disabled driver, should wish to buy a Ferrari with an automatic gearbox. In any case, although once among the world's best, the

GM400 used in the 412 (the same gearbox that is found in the V12 Jaguars) now seems dated.

Ferrari's own five-speed manual may not be the fastest changing gearbox in the world, with rather a long movement, but it is certainly positive, and well sprung towards the third/fourth plane (fifth is on the 'dog-leg'). The clutch, though heavier than that of the average saloon car, is fairly light by the standards of high-performance cars. Shifting ratios smoothly is as easy in the 412 as in any of the ZF or Getrag-gearboxed opposition.

Overall gearing is not outstandingly high. The 4.3:1 final drive produces 23.4 mph/1,000 rpm in the overdrive fifth (fourth is direct). Maximum speeds in the intermediates are 40, 68, 92 and 115 mph, while if 158 mph is attainable it would involve venturing 250 rpm into the red sector.

With big, ventilated discs on all four wheels (11.8 in at the front and 11.7 at the rear), the 412 has the sort of stopping power that is required in such a powerful and heavy car. The pedal is not as heavy in operation as those of some rivals, and its feel and the progression of the system are just right. It is reassuring to have ABS in such a car, and in the Ferrari the Bosch system works so discreetly, that you would not know it was there until those heart-stopping moments when it is required.

Once theoretical advantages of a centrally-mounted engine (superior handling and aerodynamics) are set aside we must return to the question of what we want our high-performance road car to be. If a vestige of practicality is

FERRARI 412

ENGINE

Cylinders: V12 (60-degree), in-line, front-mounted.

Capacity: 4,943 cc (297 cu in).

Bore/stroke: 82/78 mm (3.23/3.07 in).

Valve gear: dohc per bank, chain-driven, two valves per cylinder.

Compression ratio: 9.6:1.

Fuel system: Bosch K/KE-Jetronic fuel injection.

Maximum power: 340 bhp/6,000 rpm.

Maximum torque: 333 lb ft (451 Nm)/4,200 rpm.

TRANSMISSION

Type: 5-speed manual (unpleasant three-speed also available), rear-wheel drive, limited-slip differential.

Mph/kph per 1,000 rpm in top gear: 23.4 37.6.

SUSPENSION, WHEELS

Front: independent, by double wishbones, coil springs, anti-roll bar.

Rear: independent, by double wishbones, coil springs, anti-roll bar.

Steering: power-assisted worm and roller.

Brakes: (Front) ventilated discs/(Rear) ventilated discs, servo assisted, ABS.

Tyres/wheels: front and rear 240/55 VR 16 -7.5J.

DIMENSIONS

Length: 189.3 in (481 cm).

Width: 70.9 in (180 cm).

Height: 51.8 in (131.5 cm).

Wheelbase: 106.3 in (270 cm).

Front/rear track: 58.1/59.4 in (147.5/151 cm).

Weight: 3,976 lbs (1,805 kg).

Fuel tank: 25.5 gallons (116 litres).

PERFORMANCE

Maximum speed: 155.4 mph (250.0 kph).

Acceleration: 0-60 mph (96.5 kph) 6.4 sec, 0-100 mph (161 kph) 16.1 sec.

Standing km: 26.6 sec.

Fourth gear: 30-50 mph (48-80.5 kph) 5.9 sec.

Fifth gear: 50-70mph (80.5-113 kph) 7.2 sec.

Fuel consumption (average): 14.7 mpg (19.2 litres/100 km).

required, then the old formula is preferable by far: a front-mounted engine with either four-wheel drive or rear-wheel drive. This is the only way in which reasonable accommodation of people and luggage may be achieved.

This is not to suggest that the 412, which is a long car, is the world's most efficient people carrier. But it is a very comfortable two-seater, with occasional accommodation for two more and a well-proportioned luggage space. The driving position will suit drivers of most sizes. There is plenty of legroom, just enough head-room, and the major controls are generally well disposed.

The pedals are especially good, with a massive rest for the left foot and perfect spacing for 'heel-and-toe' changes. The seats are electrically adjustable, and shaped to give very good lumbar and lateral support.

The interior of the 400, even 10 years ago, was ugly, outdated and an ergonomic mess, capturing neither the old-world charm of an Aston, nor the high-tech, precision-fit efficiency of the Porsche 928. The 412 is closer to the latter, with expensive materials immaculately assembled in a highly-attractive and well-conceived design. Wisely, the token piece of wood veneer was abandoned, and there was more extensive use of leather than in almost any other car.

The instruments were also greatly improved, with orange markings on black dials, both simple and easily read. Between the large speedometer and rev counter are gauges of water temperature and oil pressure, and a bank of three dials in the centre console, angled towards the driver, display oil temperature, battery condition and the time of day. The stalks and switchgear are similarly neat and modern.

It is, or was, unusual to discover a successful heating and (more especially) ventilation system in an Italian car but, even if the controls are rather more scattered than seems necessary, the 412's climate controls work rather well, much better than the air conditioning in 7-series BMWs, if not quite as well as that of Rolls-Royce and big Mercedes-Benz models. It is possible to obtain a reasonably successful bi-level setting, and extremes of temperature are dealt with well.

Perhaps if Ferrari disconnected the power assistance of the steering, people would say, 'Wow! This is a real muscle car, just like the Daytona – you can't drive it under 100 mph unless you have the biceps of a superhero'.

The 412 is really too subtle to be described as a supercar. In fact, it may be that it is altogether too subtle ever to be properly appreciated in an age of raucous vulgarity.

FERRARI F40

Driving the fastest road car in the world around a motor racing circuit does not, *per se*, make us nervous. We've done it twice, at a patchily damp Donington Park, and in the pouring, belting rain at Castle Combe (Britain's bumpiest race track).

But it is impossible to banish from the mind the sheer cost of this beast. Initial quotes from insurance companies were designed to dampen our spirits: the first quote we had for cover offered a mere £25,000 excess on a value of several hundred thousand pounds, with the suggestion that we should pay £2,500 for 'no more than an hour on the track, and as long as Mr Mason drives to the circuit . . . ' They had preceded that with, 'Well, just how fast are you going to drive it?' Insurance companies don't like to be told: 'As fast as it will go . . . '

Mr Mason (Nick Mason, the Pink Floyd drummer, and owner of many valuable cars which he enjoys using in the manner for which they were intended) did indeed drive the car to Donington, but we managed to arrange to drive the car on the road as well as the track for our second experience in it, which involved Gordon Murray, the designer of the McLaren supercar.

Nick is urbane and soft-spoken, and not at all like a rock star who still plays to packed houses all over the world. To questions about rev limits, he is direct: 'Look, it's here to be used, and if you think you can get on top of it, then you must be very serious indeed. Just take it when you're ready . . . ' And with that he went off in search of a cup of coffee.

But despite Nick's soothing words, apprehension remained about the numbers involved. Not only that, but we didn't want to be the idiots who hooked the wrong gear in a moment of stress and laid 10,200 rpm on the engine, something which we gather is an accepted fact in the life of a Formula One team manager. Not in motoring journalism, it isn't. News travels fast.

No, we weren't nervous about actually driving the thing because we knew it would have been properly prepared by the men of Maranello. It wouldn't have any hideous vices, like terminal lift-off oversteer, or brakes that lock up and spin you around. And then there was that gloriously firm bucket seat reaching up under the armpits to clamp the torso, full harness belts to pull you in deep. It all adds to a feeling of having been made for the purpose.

The whirring starter sounds distant in the recesses of the tail, followed by a Fiat-like hum. The engine is very, very smooth, sending not a buzz or tremor through the body. The clutch is heavy and gears are guided accurately by a clacking aluminium gate, but they need a firm

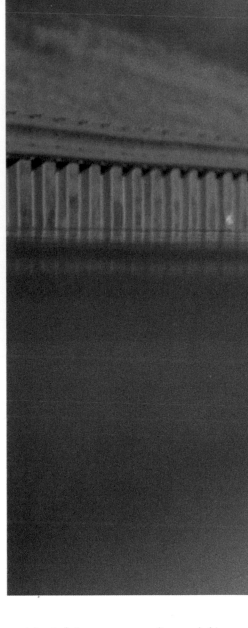

push. You can't expect the lever to fall into the slit as it does in the Porsche. We had read somewhere that the steering was heavy but it isn't heavy at all. We slip out on to the track, which is wetter than we want it to be but there's a promise of more rain, so we'd best get on.

There's no hint at all of what is about to follow. The engine still feels smooth, but flat and woolly, and pushing the throttle at low revs has no effect at all. But already, the steering has the sense of a delicious instrument. Alive without kicking, it just tugs a little at the fingers as the ripples disturb the fat tyres. Let the revs rise. Suddenly there's a whoosh of air from behind, and we are swept effortlessly forward. Let the oil warm a little more, listen to the clatter of stones flicking up under the wings.

Find second for the chicane, don't be brutal, just firm, make sure the clutch is fully down. Hit it. The revs erupt, and instantly the wheels spin and shudder, the tail slews up the greasy kerb, more wheelspin, lift a little then plant it again, hold the wheel with left hand only, quarter of a turn of reverse lock, straighten, revs shudder as the wheels find grip. Punch third gear. Hold all the way to 7,750 rpm and Redgate. Push really hard on the drilled brake pedal, push even harder. The car grumbles and grinds as the calipers clamp the huge Brembo discs. Find second and turn in. Understeer. The nose runs wide and the tyres chirrup with a quarter-turn of steering, but not for long. The boost arrives in an instant, and the tail slides wide, tramp on and off the throttle to keep the boost, and yet stop the wheelspin going out of control. The slide goes on all the way to Holly Wood. Take third, and head over to the right ready for the Craners. It's wet here. Gentle understeer though, even with foot hard in it, then a twitch. We're too far over to the right, have to brake before the car's straight. No matter, it grumbles the speed away as we fish for second.

Don't be brutal . . . relax, just push. More boost, and through the Old Hairpin with no understeer, just a long, long slide. The rear wheel slithers up the concrete run-off area, lurches the car back straight. It feels so taut, no rattling or shaking, just tight and true. Now there's the twitch at Coppice, tug the car over to the left to brake, they feel grindy, but we're still stopping. Flick the steering wheel to the right. This is just like a little sports racer with lots of power. Commitment into the corner kills the understeer – or so they say. Watch the wheelspin on the way out though. More revs equal more boost equals more power and if one wheel bites it'll turn you whichever way into the wall . . . A little helps you change direction until you learn the limits. Is this really a road car ..?

Enter McLeans for the last time, and go in a bit faster. Power on early, boost, and . . . wheelspin. This isn't a slide. The revs have climbed too quick, this is a moment . . . right hand full circle to the left . . . lift off and get ready to grab the wheel for another bit. It's come back. Time to reflect a little, wait for the track to dry perhaps . . .

That was overdriving. Later, the track nearly dry, we found the car to be a gear up in most places, which meant the arrival of power was not so savage, and progress not so sideways. This of course is quicker, and so much easier. Then, the Craner Curves were easy at 120 mph in fourth, but stopping became a big problem at the bottom. The exit from Coppice was quicker

FERRARI F40

ENGINE

Cylinders: V8 (90-degree), in-line, mid-mounted.

Capacity: 2,936 cc (176 cu in).

Bore/stroke: 82/69.5 mm (3.23/2.74 in).

Valve gear: dohc per bank, driven by toothed belt, four valves per cylinder.

Compression ratio: 7.8:1.

Fuel system: Weber-Marelli electronic injection integrated with ignition, twin turbochargers and air/air intercoolers.

Maximum power: 478bhp/7,000 rpm.

Maximum torque: 425 lb ft (576 Nm)/4,000 rpm.

TRANSMISSION

Type: 5-speed manual, rear-wheel drive, limited-slip differential.

Mph/kph per 1,000 rpm in top gear: 28.6/46.

SUSPENSION, WHEELS

Front: independent, by double wishbones, coil springs, anti-roll bar.

Rear: independent, by double wishbones, coil springs, anti-roll bar.

Steering: unassisted rack and pinion.

Brakes: (Front) ventilated discs/(Rear) ventilated discs, unassisted.

Tyres/wheels: front 245/40 ZR 17 -8J, rear 335/35 ZR 17 - 13J.

DIMENSIONS

Length: 174.4 in (443 cm).

Width: 78.0 in (198 cm).

Height: 44.5 in (113 cm).

Wheelbase: 96.5 in (245 cm).

Front/rear track: 62.8/63.4 in (159.5/161 cm).

Weight: 2,430 lbs (1,100 kg).

Fuel tank: 26.4 gallons (120 litres).

PERFORMANCE

Maximum speed: 201.3 mph (324 kph).

Acceleration: 0-60 mph (96.5 kph) 3.9 sec, 0-100 mph (161 kph) 7.8 sec.

Fuel consumption (average): 13.5 mpg (21 litres/100 km).

---

too, and the F40 would reach 225 kph (140 mph).

We were also allowed to drive the F40 on the road: straight out into London's rush hour, at 6 pm one December evening, wearing a Brembo full seat harness in amongst the black cabs and the big red buses. The F40 may be temperamental, but it is also very wide, with poor visibility, and its clutch action is painful and difficult in stop-start traffic.

It is ludicrous as a road car and most uncomfortable. The seat, unlike those of real racing cars, is not tailored to fit a specific pair of buttocks, so it is simply very hard, and the ride is also rock solid. The windscreen mists up miserably in damp weather, and the heater is inefficient. The engine, and more especially the gearbox, take several miles to warm up.

The finish (especially inside, when the doors have clanked shut) is quite poor, compared with, for example, a Countach. Everything has been done to eliminate weight, down to pull strings like those in early Minis to open the doors. It might look as if it has a high-tech composite chassis, but all that carbon fibre conceals old-fashioned steel girders.

And then there is the matter of actually driving it: out in the countryside, the F40 reveals its true self. It is a wild animal, and full travel of the throttle pedal – in any gear – makes the horizon tear open ahead of the screen like a zip. It is all achieved by the power-to-weight ratio, and no subtlety is involved.

So it's not really a road car, and it's not quite a racing car. But if there are more diverting ways of having some very expensive fun, we have yet to find them.

FERRARI TESTAROSSA

The Testarossa is not pretty like the GTO and 308/328, or pretty and butch like the Daytona, but it bristles with latent aggression. From whichever angle you look at it, it is a complex blend of dramatic curves.

In Pininfarina's original design, there were to be no horizontal slats along the sides, just large holes for the air intakes. If you can imagine the car without those distinctive features (or if you have seen the Koenig Testarossa, the only conversion in which the German has created something more discreet than the original) it is apparent that the inspiration for the styling was the ground-effects Grand Prix cars of the early 1980s. The only really odd effect is the single air scoop cut out of one side of the front air dam, a styling trick carried on to the 348.

Some may consider the 512 BB to have been more elegant, but there is no denying that the Testarossa is better proportioned than its predecessor. It is also substantially bigger overall, an extra 3 in long at 176.6 in (two extra inches are built into the wheelbase), and a fraction taller. But most of the increased size is in the width: at 77.8 in, though a thumb-joint narrower than the substantially shorter Countach, the Testarossa is 5.8 in wider than the Boxer, and while there is only 0.4 in difference in the front track, an extra 3.8 in has been added to the back axle.

This enhances the Testarossa's formula car look, and visually disguises the fact that at only 280/45, the rear tyres are far narrower than is usual in cars of this type. However, the reasons that led Ferrari to widen the car to this extent were not mainly aesthetic, as we shall see.

Lifting the counter-balanced engine cover –

hinged at the trailing edge of the roofline – reveals not the traditional mass of Webers fighting each other for air, but a cast aluminium bunch of bananas that looks like it might be – and is – of Stuttgart origin. Absorbed into a large corporation long before the same fate befell either Aston Martin or Lamborghini, Ferrari had the investment backing to be able to make fuel injection work. The massive flat-12 is a work of art as well as of science. Yet for all the adjacent high technology, a Ferrari chassis remains a fine example of the blacksmith's art, built for function rather than display. The entire rear section is bolted to the main tubular frame for relatively easy removal of the engine and transmission, as was the case with the Boxer.

As before, the engine is mounted above the gearbox, which gives a centre of gravity relatively high for a supercar, and it was mainly for this reason that widening the track was

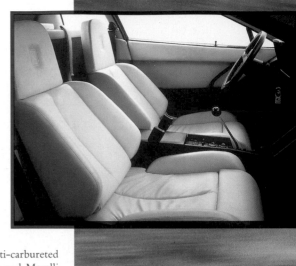

considered an advantage.

With identical internal dimensions – the bore is 82 mm and the stroke is 78 mm – to those of the Boxer, the Testarossa's capacity is 4,942 cc. But its eponymous red-painted cylinder heads contain four valves per cylinder, making a total of 48, driven by twin belt-driven camshafts on each bank, and the power output is substantially higher at 390 bhp, peaking at 6,300 rpm. Peak torque is 333 lb ft at 4,600 rpm, but more significant is that it delivers 260 from only 1,000 rpm.

When the engine is fired up, hot or cold, all 12 cylinders go to work immediately, with no sign of the gasping and spluttering of multi-carbureted engines. Bosch K-jetronic injection and Marelli

Digiplex ignition have replaced that old romance (which must have woken many of the more respectable citizens of select neighbourhoods in the early hours of mornings gone by as wealthy playboys attempted unsuccessfully to sneak home stealthily) with pure efficiency. It is a marvellous engine, with no flat spots and no signs of temperament, and one of the smoothest in the world, though certainly not among the quietest. Trickle along at 1,000 rpm and bury the throttle pedal into the floor: no hesitation, just a solid surge all the way to a top speed which is a click or so above 180 mph.

Despite its substantial weight the acceleration from rest is blistering. Especially high revs are not needed to make it smoke away from the line and the 0-60 mph time is not far above 5 sec. Beyond 100 mph it is really remarkable, still leaping forward stongly when the throttle is opened wide at 120.

The gear lever makes the typical Ferrari *clack* as it is moved about the open gate, but it is possible to make smooth, *slow* changes, whereas

FERRARI TESTAROSSA

ENGINE

Cylinders: flat-12, in-line, mid-mounted.
Capacity: 4,942 cc (296.5 cu in).
Bore/stroke: 82/78 mm (3.23/3.07 in).
Valve gear: dohc per bank, driven by toothed belt, 48 valves.
Compression ratio: 9.2:1.
Fuel system: Bosch K/KE-jetronic fuel injection.
Maximum power: 390 bhp/6,300 rpm.
Maximum torque: 333 lb ft (451 Nm)/4,600 rpm.

TRANSMISSION

Type: 5-speed manual, rear-wheel drive, limited-slip differential.
Mph/kph per 1,000 rpm in top gear: 26.5/42.6.

SUSPENSION, WHEELS

Front: independent, by double wishbones, coil springs, anti-roll bar.
Rear: independent, by double wishbones, twin coil springs, anti-roll bar.
Steering: unassisted rack and pinion.
Brakes: (Front) ventilated discs/(Rear) ventilated discs, servo-assisted.
Tyres/wheels: front 225/50 VR 16 -8J, rear 280/45 VR415

DIMENSIONS

Length: 176.6 in (448.5 cm).
Width: 77.8 in (197.5 cm).
Height: 44.5 in (113 cm).
Wheelbase: 100.4 in (255 cm).
Front/rear track: 59.8/65.4 in (152/166cm).
Weight: 3,315 lbs (1,505 kg).
Fuel tank: 25.3 gallons (115 litres).

PERFORMANCE*

Maximum speed: 180 mph (290 kph).
Acceleration: 0-62 mph (100 kph) 5.8 sec.
Standing km: 24.1 sec.
Fuel consumption (average): 16.0 mpg (17.7 litres/100 km).

*Factory figures

in the V8 models applied brutality is required.

At 140 mph, the Ferrari runs straight and true, and the steering does not become excessively light, so it seems there is adequate downforce. Like all today's supercars (except the F40!), the Testarossa has such high limits of adhesion on a dry surface that it is rarely possible to exceed them. Despite the relatively small rubber contact patch, grip is phenomenal. In most bends, it remains fairly neutral, with mild understeer which can easily be adjusted on the throttle. But there is a lot of roll, and the car feels a lot softer than a Countach, an experienced driver expecting a taut, semi-racer will be disappointed. To the extent that such a car can be practical at all, the Testarossa is ahead of most mid-engined rivals, with a comfortable cockpit for two people, neat interior design, a fair sized luggage space and an efficient air conditioning system.

The Testarossa's replacement will probably have a 348-style transverse gearbox, and that should be an extremely desirable car.

FORD SAPPHIRE RS COSWORTH

Nobody could accuse Ford of short-changing on performance with the Sapphire Cosworth, there simply is nothing as fast as this car for the money.

This Ford Cosworth is a fine example of development engineering. Early versions, in the three-door bodyshell with that wildly indiscreet rear wing, demanded intense concentration of the driver. It is fair to remark that this is true of any car with this level of performance, but they are not all so uncompromising.

It was not that the handling was poor, or even that grip was in short supply. It was purely a question of engine characteristics. If the gears were used to ensure that the 16-valve 1,993 cc four-cylinder engine was constantly high up in the boost zone of its Garrett turbocharger, no serious problems arose. But letting the revs drop, and using too much of the throttle pedal travel, off and then on when approaching a bend, could lead to very serious trouble.

What may have seemed like a relatively minor increase in pressure on the pedal (because nothing much happened for the first couple of seconds) could whizz the turbo into warp drive, and suddenly something like 100 per cent more torque came whistling along the propshaft than was intended.

The resulting wheelspin would lead with grim inevitability, especially at the apex of a greasy bend, to a massive oversteering slide that really needed to be caught before it had begun. Some people failed to do so.

The solution to the problem is interesting. A study of the bare figures of the Sapphire Cosworth (201 bhp at 6,000 rpm and 204 lb ft at 4,500 rpm) will not reveal the difference between this and the 'old' RS. Subtle programming changes to the Weber/Marelli system (governing the injection, ignition and turbo boost strategy) result in 80 per cent of that peak torque figure being delivered at 2,300 rpm.

Turbo 'lag' is still noticeable but far less alarming, small adjustments to throttle position do not bring such coarse results, and the rear tyres no longer light up at the first opportunity.

It still is not a car for the inexperienced, but the thinly concealed streak of malevolence has disappeared in the wash.

Despite our test track results of 'only' 142 mph, to all intents and purposes this is a genuine 150 mph car, and sprints from rest to 60 mph in a mere 5.9 sec. Its in-gear acceleration analysis, produces fair figures, too. It has outstandingly good handling, brakes and gear-change. It is true that the steering, in a straight line on a bumpy road, feels less precise than that of some other cars (in particular the M3). Once lock is applied, it gives plenty of feel in most circumstances, though in very tight curves it is less than perfect in this respect.

But that is a mild criticism, and the chassis is simultaneously forgiving and satisfying in its behaviour. The mild understeer that is the car's

FORD SAPPHIRE RS COSWORTH

ENGINE

Cylinders: straight four, in-line, front-mounted.

Capacity: 1,993 cc (120 cu in).

Bore/stroke: 91/77 mm (3.58/3.03 in).

Valve gear: dohc, driven by toothed belt, four valves per cylinder.

Compression ratio: 8.0:1.

Fuel system: Weber-Marelli injection, Garrett AiResearch TO3 turbocharger.

Maximum power: 201 bhp/6,000 rpm.

Maximum torque: 204 lb ft (276 Nm)/4,500 rpm.

TRANSMISSION

Type: 5-speed manual, rear-wheel drive, limited-slip differential (viscous coupling).

Mph/kph per 1,000 rpm in top gear: 22.8/36.7.

SUSPENSION, WHEELS

Front: independent, by MacPherson struts, lower track control arms, coil springs, anti-roll bar.

Rear: independent, by semi-trailing arms, coil springs, anti-roll bar.

Steering: power-assisted rack and pinion.

Brakes: (Front) ventilated discs/(Rear) plain discs, servo assisted, ABS.

Tyres/wheels: front and rear, 205/50 VR 15 - 7J.

DIMENSIONS

Length: 176.9 in (449 cm).

Width: 66.9 in (169.9 cm).

Height: 54.2 in (137.7 cm).

Wheelbase: 102.7 in (261 cm).

Front/rear track: 56.8/57.5 in (144/146 cm).

Weight: 2,755 lbs (1,250 kg).

Fuel tank: 13.2 gallons (60 litres).

PERFORMANCE

Maximum speed: 141.9 mph (228 kph).

Acceleration: 0-60 mph (96.5 kph) 5.9 sec, 0-100 mph (161 kph) 15.7 sec.

Fourth gear: 30-50 mph (48-80.5 kph) 6.9 sec.

Fifth gear: 50-70mph (80.5-113 kph) 6.5 sec.

Fuel consumption (average): 26.8 mpg (10.5 litres/100 km).

---

natural habit can easily be adjusted if a tighter radius is required, or even just for the hell of it, and it will change its attitude gently and gradually. Traction from the 205/50 VR15 Dunlops is remarkable, even on wet roads. Ride quality also is more than acceptable, not only for this type of car, but even by absolute standards.

Another factor in the car's improved behaviour is the use of stiffer front springs and a lower front roll centre. The result is better body control and improved lift-off characteristics.

The brakes are superbly powerful, and the anti-lock works discreetly and reassuringly. The gear ratios are ideally suited to the engine, and the lever can be moved around the five-speed gate as rapidly as required, matched by a perfectly-behaved clutch.

As well as being a dynamically excellent driving machine, the Sapphire Cosworth is exceptionally practical, with plenty of space in the front seats, enough in the back, and masses of space for luggage. After all, it started off as a company car . . . and that is its problem.

There are few specific criticisms that can be levelled at it. It is very noisy and unrefined, but

not to the point that it will induce ringing in the ears, while the heating and ventilation system is no better than adequate.

In its dynamics, the Sapphire Cosworth is more than a match for the opposition here. Its race-car performance and handling are skilfully

blended with just enough compliance to make ride quality at town speeds acceptable, and it is among the fastest cars from point to point currently available at any price. It represents extraordinary value for money.

The only problem is its image: it looks from

the inside like a salesman's car, from the outside like a salesman's car with a cheap add-on wing and ugly wheels, and above all it has a Ford badge. Its purchasers will come from two relatively slim bands of the market: intelligent enthusiasts who want it for what it can do, and plasterers with a fat wad.

It should be added that there is now a 4x4 version of the Sapphire Cosworth. Its extra power compensates for increased weight, and the performance figures are nearly identical. This car has impressive dynamic abilities, although it is not as enjoyable as the rear-drive-only model.

FORD TAURUS SHO

I t has been a widely held view in Europe that some of the worst cars on four wheels are made in the United States. True, some of America's 1970s offerings made a serious bid for the accolade, but then, the same is true of the Japanese. Ironically it was Japan that forced the States to move their automotive industry into the 1980s.

Ford in particular realized that if it did not invest heavily in new technology pretty soon, then it could leave too much catching up to be done. It is also interesting to note that American manufacturers in general do not worry too much about Europe's establishment 'quality' cars. The likes of Porsche and BMW are far too expensive by the time they get to the USA to be any kind of volume threat. So, with little whizzers like the Honda CRX having become a part of the US motoring scene, the promise of luxury performance cars like Nissan's rear-drive 32-valve V8 powered Infiniti, and Toyota's V8-engined 250 bhp Lexus began to loom as a realistically priced threat to mainstream middle-sized Americana.

Ford's line of defence has been much strengthened by the performance version of the Taurus, the SHO (Super High Output) although it has to be said that the best bit of the car – the 24-valve V6 engine – is made entirely by the Japanese Yamaha concern. The Taurus is a Granada-sized saloon with modern concession to the aerodynamic look (the drag coefficient is 0.33 thanks to flush glass, wrap over doors, high tail) and surprisingly, drives through the front wheels in a transverse mounted engine with end-on gearbox. Basic Taurus models apparently handle well, even if they are rather underpowered, and are well packaged and well equipped. (Ford apparently imports Scorpio Granadas for those

Americans who want European, but must have a Ford. The Taurus, however, is probably a better car.)

The SHO offers performance per pound to America in the same manner as the Sierra Cosworth did in Europe. This Taurus is not a limited edition special, however. It is a series production car and, as far as we can tell, there is no other full production car anywhere with front wheel drive and five seats that goes as fast for the money or, incidentally, does it while driving the front wheels.

A tie-up with Yamaha was Ford's quickest solution to the technology drought, although the SHO's V6 will not be used in any other Ford car. (Yamaha's total production capacity for the engine is already fully committed.) With an eye to the future, and frightened of falling behind in the technology race, Ford has since turned down Yamaha's proposal for a 48-valve V8 version of the Taurus engine (a probable cost of one million dollars) preferring to spend a billion dollars on their own multivalve V8.

Yamaha's handiwork is sublime. The iron block, twin aluminium head V6 puts out 220 bhp at 6,000 rpm and 200 lb ft torque at 4,800 rpm. Lift the lid, and the technology is visible, like taking the engine cover from a Formula One car. Twin plenums sit above each bank of the transversely mounted power unit, and a snakepit of cast aluminium inlet pipes nestles in between, rather like the Alfa's 164 V6. The SHO's 12 pipes feed an elaborate intake system, originally developed by Yamaha for the Toyota twin-cam range. Each inlet valve has its own port on the head and each cylinder has one long inlet pipe for low speed torque and one short, which is better at high speeds. Beyond 4,000 rpm, a butterfly valve allows both tracts to feed together, making the

best use of multivalve breathing ability, but the point at which the long and short pipes chime in together is exactly where each develops its maximum torque, thereby neatly avoiding any steps or surges. A single belt at the front of the engine drives one inlet cam per bank; the exhaust cams are each driven by a chain running across from the back of the inlet cams.

It works. Sounding rather like a Porsche but slightly gruffer, the engine pulls easily from 2,000 rpm, taking on a yet harder edged note as the tachometer needle soars round the dial. Steel crank and rods will indulge 8,500 rpm apparently with ease, but the ancillaries tended to self-destruct, and so the rev limiter gently makes its presence felt at 'only' 7,300 rpm. Response to the throttle is instant; the flywheel is racer-light which allows instant pick up, but needs a little care when starting from rest – it is quite easy either to surge the revs against the clutch, or to stall the engine. The top speed, of 143 mph is identical to the BMW 535i's, and although standing starts are predictably traction-limited, the Taurus never-

theless sneaks ahead of the German car, taking 16.9 sec to reach 100 mph while the 535 needs 18.7 sec.

Yamaha's automotive masterpiece unfortunately drives through a modified Mazda truck gearbox, the only transmission in the corporate parts bin which would cope with the torque. The gear change threatens to spoil the package. Long of throw, notchy and vague, it is the only real let down to be found. It would have been easier perhaps to spoil the engine with an indifferent chassis, but such is not the case. This is a powerful front drive car, therefore there is some wandering when you plant it in second gear on patchy-wet or uneven surfaces, but Ford engineers have all but eliminated the tugging at the wheel which usually goes with it. Smooth roads allow this Taurus to demonstrate simply formidable grip from 215/65-15 Goodyear Eagles on 6 in rims, and a remarkable honesty of chassis. That's not to say it is twitchy. Tramp on and off the throttle round 80 mph motorway exit sweepers and the car just adjusts its attitude accordingly

without needing great sudden armfuls of opposite lock to catch lift-off waywardness.

The suspension is certainly firm (no less than 30 per cent stiffer than basic, which always helps stability under power) and simple (MacPherson strut/lower links at both ends), which helps. Lacking extensive front drive experience, Ford was anxious not to be caught out by torque steer criticism and, accordingly, the engineers claim a breakthrough with the SHO's geometry. Wheel offset is a relevant factor, and much use is made of rubber bushes which move in one direction and stay stiff in another. These appear on both engine and suspension mounts, and of course, there are equal length driveshafts.

The technical stuff, and what amounts to a fairly predictable handling appraisal cannot convey just how alive and exciting the SHO feels. The steering is much meatier than expected, and the feedback through a thick wheelrim is always informative without being tiringly restless. The turn-in too is *so* crisp without being nervous, amazing for a comparatively big car, and yet the

chassis copes very well on the limit. There is no trace of debilitating understeer, even under full power with lock applied. The car just squirms a touch and goes. Possibly the ride is a little on the firm side but it does not jiggle and controls the body with masterly precision.

Apart from the gear change, frankly it is difficult to find fault with this car. Perhaps the glass area looks a little on the small side, as if it had been fitted with aftermarket double glazing, which accentuates a heavy waistline, and the heavy underbumper treatment is ugly. Mercedes does it much more subtly. Ford's idea was that they wished to hide the twin exhaust pipes and

the fuel tank from public gaze.

Inside, the leather covered front seats are fully electric, the analogue dials clear and European in style, as is the switchgear, and there's air conditioning and an excellent multispeaker stereo radio/cassette without which no American car seems complete. The price is substantially less than that of a VW Jetta GTi. In America, the BMW M5 costs three times as much. Whatever the rate of exchange, or wherever you think of importing it, the Taurus is something of a bargain, and it suggests that some of the European manufacturers are fooling their customers.

FORD TAURUS SHO

ENGINE

Cylinders: V6 (60-degree), transverse, front-mounted.

Capacity: 2,986 cc (179 cu in).

Bore/stroke: 89/80 mm (3.50/3.15 in).

Valve gear: dohc per bank, chain and belt driven, four valves per cylinder.

Compression ratio: 9.8:1.

Fuel system: integrated electronic injection and engine management.

Maximum power: 220 bhp/6,000rpm.

Maximum torque: 200 lb ft (147.5 Nm)/4,800 rpm.

TRANSMISSION

Type: 5-speed manual, front-wheel drive.

Mph/kph per 1,000 rpm in top gear: 25.6/41.5.

SUSPENSION, WHEELS

Front: independent, by MacPherson struts, tranverse links, coil springs, anti-roll bar.

Rear: independent, by MacPherson struts, trailing arms, transverse links, coil springs, anti-roll bar.

Steering: assisted rack and pinion.

Brakes: (Front) ventilated discs/(Rear) plain discs, servo assisted.

Tyres/wheels: front and rear 215/65 VR 15 -6J.

DIMENSIONS

Length: 188.4 in (478.5 cm).

Width: 70.9 in (180 cm).

Height: 53.9 in (137 cm).

Wheelbase: 106.1 in (269.5 cm).

Front/rear track: 61.6/60.4 in (156.5/153.5 cm).

Weight: 3,539 lbs (1,605 kg).

Fuel tank: 15.4 gallons (70 litres).

PERFORMANCE

Maximum speed: 143 mph (230 kph).

Acceleration: 0-60 mph (96.5 kph) 6.7 sec, 0-100 mph 16.9 sec.

Fifth gear: 30-50 mph (48-80.5 kph) 12.1 sec, 50-70 mph (80.5-113 kph) 12.2 sec.

Fuel consumption (average): 21.7 mpg (13 litres/100 km).

FORD THUNDERBIRD SUPER COUPÉ

Compared with the hi-tech, front-drive, multivalve Taurus, the latest Thunderbird 'super coop' is rather more traditional in its appeal. A good ol' rear-drive muscle car, with limited accommodation, and wearing one of America's most evocative car names, the styling is very reminiscent of the BMW 6-series with a slightly heavier waist treatment. Japan may have been the catalyst, but BMW was certainly the role model. Undeniably it is very striking and handsome in a rather heavy-handed sort of way, almost as if a whole dose of aftermarket body kitting had been added by the manufacturer.

The power unit is a 3.8-litre, iron block V6 with aluminium heads and pushrod operated valves. Cramming the space between the vee, though, is a belt driven Eaton Roots-type supercharger which blows at a maximum of 12 psi. This liberates 210 bhp at a mere 4,000 rpm, but a massive supergrunt's worth of torque, 315lb ft at 2,600 rpm. The combination of this and a five-speed manual gearbox is one of the easiest ways to fill a road with smoke yet discovered. Even the auto version has the sort of torque converter that engages straight away (this is preferred in the USA, where the roads are based on a grid system with millions of traffic lights, unlike Europe which prefers roundabouts). Just tread the throttle and the rear wheels light up instantly. In fact it is difficult not to pull out from the kerb with the tail smoking at an angle to the direction of travel.

The engine could not be described as refined. Certainly not in the BMW class, but then few things are. The supercharger belt adds a little whine and the blower's rotors clatter on tickover, but you hardly need to use the kind of revs which make the engine thrum. It is not quite as fast as it looks, however; 143 mph is respectable without being shattering, and even 315 lb ft cannot overcome a weight penalty which amounts to around 3,800 lb. Rest to 60 mph takes 7.1 sec, 100 mph occupies 20.4 sec. From behind the wheel, there is an immediacy of response that starts at about 1,000 rpm which makes the Thunderbird feel quicker than its figures suggest.

The extra weight can partly be explained by the no compromise suspension, upper and lower wishbones at both front and rear, with extra toe controlling links connected to massive H-shaped lower wishbones at the driving end, anti-roll bars front and rear, electronically-controlled shock absorbers and enormous chassis rails to

support the lot. Mindful of this, the first mile or so is faintly disappointing. The low speed ride is jiggly, like the worst aftermarket shocker conversion, but as you press on, it does smooth out quicker than expected; thereafter the big car belies its weight feeling taut and responsive. At higher speeds, the integrity of the suspension design shows up, coarse throttle or brake inputs having little or no effect on grip at speeds below 100 mph. Low speed understeer is unsurprising given the stiff shockers, though easily neutralized with the brake pedal but steering weighting is lighter than the Taurus's – somewhere similar to a BMW 535's. On the open road, the car's basic

good balance and lack of roll makes the grip from 225/60 VR 16 Goodyears seem greater than it really is, but it may require more lock than intended to get round the corner. Basic understeer is greater than that found in the front-drive Taurus. The Thunderbird has a slightly more Transatlantic feel to its cockpit than the Taurus. There are more colours on the instrument dials where SHO has white on black. Velour starts, Japanese-style, on the door trims and spreads to the seats which boast full electric adjustment including side wings which come in to restrain the torso against those g-forces (leather is optional). It is comfortable, and the range of

adjustments should accommodate even the pickiest of driver. Not as cheap as the Taurus, the Thunderbird is still outstanding value compared with equivalent Europeans.

The Taurus and Thunderbird are not directly comparable. One is a five seater, the other a 2 plus 2. One has a space age engine and carefully developed simple suspension, the other race car suspension and a 1950s engine with a blower. It would be fair to say that the Thunderbird is cruder, more muscular, slightly old fashioned despite its ideal suspension.

FORD THUNDERBIRD SUPER COUPÉ

ENGINE

Cylinders: V6, in-line, front-mounted.

Capacity: 3,791 cc (227.5 cu in).

Bore/stroke: 96.5/86.4 mm (3.80/3.40 in).

Valve gear: single central camshaft, pushrod ohv, two valves per cylinder.

Compression ratio: 8.2:1

Fuel system: electronic injection, Eaton Roots-type supercharger (belt-driven), air/air intercooler.

Maximum power: 210 bhp/4,000 rpm.

Maximum torque: 315 lb ft /2,600rpm.

TRANSMISSION

Type: 5-speed manual, rear-wheel drive, limited-slip differential.

Mph/kph per 1,000 rpm in top gear: 37.4/60.1.

SUSPENSION, WHEELS

Front: independent, by double wishbones, coil springs, anti-roll bar.

Rear: independent, by double wishbones, coil springs, anti-roll bar.

Steering: assisted rack and pinion.

Brakes: (Front) ventilated discs/(Rear) plain discs, servo assisted, ABS.

Tyres/wheels: front and rear 225/60 VR 16 -7J.

DIMENSIONS

Length: 198.8 in (505 cm).

Width: 72.8 in (185 cm).

Height: 52.8 in (134 cm).

Wheelbase: 113.0 in (287 cm).

Front/rear track: 61.6/60.2 in (156.5/153 cm).

Weight: 3,819 lbs (1,730 kg).

Fuel tank: 15.8 gallons (72 litres).

PERFORMANCE

Maximum speed: 143 mph (230 kph).

Acceleration: 0-60 mph (96.5 kph) 7.1 sec, 0-100 mph (161 kph) 20.4 sec.

Fifth gear: 30-50 mph (48-80.5 kph) 13.1 sec, 50-70 mph (80.5-113 kph) 12.0 sec.

Fuel consumption (average): 20.2 mpg (14 litres/100km).

HONDA NS-X

The steering writhes as with right foot to the floorboards we accelerate up the slip road onto Honda's banked, high-speed loop. The engine sings with a well-tuned harmonic induction roar that is, superficially at least, as arousing as the scream of any Ferrari V8, demonstrating the value of Honda's years of motorcycle engine experience.

The power flows smoothly and authoritatively, though at exactly 5,000 rpm a butterfly in the induction tract opens with an almost perceptible click and the engine gains an added burst of zeal that amplifies the action as the single overhead camshaft drives four valves per cylinder, via rocker arms, to their ultimate frenzy at 7,500 rpm. The entire experience is closer to ecstatic than any Japanese car before. Far closer than Nissan's disappointing and ill-prepared

Mid-4, and infinitely nearer than even the most scintillating of the clinically correct mainstream of Japan's automotive pride. But it has not crossed the line between 'very good' and 'magic'.

Reactions to the Honda NS-X when it was first unveiled to a sycophantic, perilously pro-Honda American audience at the Chicago Auto Show were excitement and awe. At first sight, to a crowd predisposed to admiration, the car was the quintessential Japanese supercar. Honda's Formula One experience, not to mention success, had laid the groundwork for instant credibility, and the NS-X was immediately accepted as a Ferrari-clone. It even looks like a Ferrari. Though Honda takes all the credit for the design, Pininfarina was a design consultant, and this shows. From the front, one might confuse the

NS-X with a Ferrari BB512, while in profile, with its jet-fighter glass canopy, the car is a virtual mimeograph of Ferrari's experiment with four-wheel drive, the 408.

A more exciting design might have been preferable, but perhaps Honda felt it wise not to attack consumer preconceptions. If Honda had persevered with the Pininfarina-styled HP-X, a somewhat impractical though intriguingly futuristic design that, at its unveiling at the 1984 Turin show, gave the world its first positive indication that Honda had embarked on the supercar trail, it would have tested consumers' tastes as well as their willingness to accept the very notion of a Honda supercar.

Ferrari can get away with building a car as weird as the Testarossa looked when it was new, but Honda probably could not. Rather than

stretching the design envelope, Honda simply rounds off the rough edges of established clichés. Honda asserts, of course, that it designed the NS-X with careful attention to practical considerations such as all-round visibility and stowage space, and in these respects they may have made some progress over what we consider normal in the ranks of the exotics. The car's aerodynamics have also been honed to the point where it drags through the air with a drag coefficient of 0.31, probably the lowest of any supercar. But there is nothing conceptually new. It is a safe, conservative design, and that was probably wise: a controversially-styled Honda might have alienated buyers even before the first cheque book had been tempted.

If the exterior does nothing to widen our metaphorical horizons, then the interior at least deserves credit for extending the literal ones, with easily the best all-round visibility of any exotic car. Only a Porsche 911 comes close, but not very. Apart from a minor 'dead angle' created by the B-pillars, the NS-X has the all-round view its canopy style would suggest.

Yet with the interior trappings, though, it is clear that the Honda is not in the business of radical innovation. The layout of all the controls is fine, excellent in fact. The instrument panel, too, is a paragon of ergonomics with huge, clearly marked dials for speed (up to 180 mph on the dial) and rpm (with a 7,500 red line), and smaller but equally clear and informatively marked dials for temperature, fuel, oil pressure and battery voltage. It is the most complete instrument package on any Honda, and it is functionally impeccable, but stylistically it is a marriage of BMW and Porsche 928, without the charisma.

Arguments about aesthetic charisma ultimately degenerate into debates of taste. Most people seem to find it attractive enough, which suggests that its looks are at least palatable. Honda cannot be rebuked for achieving that, but inside and out a bit more spirit of adventure would have been welcome. Neither a Porsche 911 or a Ferrari 328 (both of which were conveniently on hand for comparison at Honda's Tochigi proving ground) can match the Honda's ergonomics, but in fathoming their controls and peering at their ill-positioned, obscurely marked dials there is a challenge that helps make them interesting. In contrast, the NS-X is just boringly efficient.

Returning to the cockpit, the NS-X shifts smoothly up through a gate as well defined and super-slick as in any Civic or Prelude. The lever is short enough to create a flick-switch feel, yet long enough to take away the weight, and the cogs slip unobtrusively and with reassuring precision. Speed builds rapidly, and the dial is soon registering more than 150 mph, though even in fifth this is close to the red line, so there is obviously little more to come. Honda claims 250 bhp and 155 mph for this prototype. A four-speed automatic is also available.

Since the car's first public unveiling (and only since then) the decision has been taken to fit the three-litre, 90 degree V6 with twin-cam variable valve timing and lift (V-TEC) heads, that will lift the peak of the power curve to around 270 bhp, and will allow a higher red line – probably around 8,000 rpm. The power gain, compared with the sohc 24-valve engine in the test cars, is not as great as the 33 per cent hike achieved in the Integra's production V-TEC engine over its normally-valved counterpart, but that is a reflection of the high-state of tune of the NS-X's single-cam engine. For instance, while the Integra's engine gets around 4 mm extra valve lift when V-TEC switches to 'high power' mode, the NS-X's V6 already has nearly as much lift as tolerances would allow, and the V-TEC

addition is a mere 0.3 mm. However, Honda has added another twist because the standard 'low power' cam lobes have staggered timing characteristics that open one inlet valve per cylinder out of phase with the other to unbalance in the inlet flow for swirl, better mixing, and superior low speed combustion. Any detrimental effect this might have had on high speed breathing is avoided by switching to a single high speed cam lobe that operates both of the inlet valves simultaneously at high rpm. It is a typically clever Honda touch, though unfortunately we were not able to sample the results as the prototypes all have the sohc engine.

Within the confines of the test track, and in less than ideal conditions, the Honda is comfortably the fastest of the assembled group, but so it should be with its power and its aerodynamics, not to mention its light weight, courtesy of a body, engine and suspension constructed entirely of aluminium. It is an expensive construction technique for which Honda decided to build a new manufacturing facility at Tochigi, but the lightweight alloy produces a total weight saving of 440 lb, and helps Honda achieve its chosen compromise of weight and performance.

When Honda started its supercar quest it began, logically, with a mid-engined CRX. There was also a mid-engined, rear-wheel drive, underfloor (MRU) conversion based on the original City (Jazz), but that was an experiment in alternative packaging rather than sporting car

balance, and led to the latest TN Acty Microvan. The mid-engined CRX was the first prototype sports car, and its light weight made it attractive.

Honda has the technology to do whatever it chooses, but the company decided carefully to analyse the philosophy of what would inevitably be its corporate flagship. The research looked at all of the world's sports cars, and placed them on a two-dimensional chart with axes for power-to-weight (which equates to performance) and power-to-wheelbase (which Honda sees as a measure of handling nimbleness). Virtually at the intersection of these axes you will find Formula One cars, so from the assumption that an F1 car is the ultimate, any car that lies on the line bisecting the angle between the two axes will be the ultimate sports car at its performance or power level. The NS-X is on that line. So, is the CRX, but there is a difference. Honda admits that a CRX is fun, but its performance is inadequate to maintain the driver's interest. The NS-X rectifies that, and sits on the chart right next to a Porsche 911 Turbo.

There is no doubt that the NS-X performs well, and it handles well too, with admirable turn-in response and good control of subsequent yaw reactions. The suspension is basically a double wishbone system all round, though the rear features an additional toe-control lateral link to ensure toe-in reaction to side forces. The front is even more sophisticated, with a 'compliance control link' between the upper and lower wishbones to ensure that any compliance steering of either wishbone will be transferred equally to both, thereby preserving the predetermined camber and castor settings, and giving greater steering and handling precision.

Around the handling track the NS-X is, as Honda has said, well balanced, and it is certainly easy to drive at a cracking pace. An average driver in average conditions might prefer the NS-X to either the Ferrari or a Porsche 911 but for the driver who has mastered the intricacies of the 911's handling, driving the NS-X an inoffensive but uninspiring experience. A lot of drivers criticize the 911's quirks – lots of initial understeer and tricky final oversteer – but in so doing they are unwittingly admitting their own deficiencies. The Porsche does not tolerate fools, although it has been engineered over the years to help them avoid killing themselves. It is a sullen hulk until the driver begins to feed in the right inputs, when it transforms itself into a highly responsive tool. Driven in the right manner the Porsche 911 does exactly as it is told, and the rewards for the driver are commensurate. The NS-X makes few demands, but when a driver with the skill to master a 911 starts imposing his will, the NS-X is unable to respond in kind.

The handling section of Honda's test course has a series of switchbacks from left to right in a variety of radii, and in the Porsche 911 it is possible to track through them at speed in a virtually continuous opposite lock slide. The driver *thinks* the car into changes of direction by delicately altering the front to rear weight distribution with the throttle and, only when necessary, the brakes, while the steering is used as a source of information first and an implement of directional control second. Get it right and the 911 flows elegantly through even the tightest of bends. The NS-X just cannnot do it.

With a 57 per cent rear weight bias the NS-X is not as tail-heavy as a 911, but its behaviour suggests it is more so. In transient situations it is always the rear end that takes over; the mass behind the driver rolls into corners slightly, but perceptibly, out of phase with the front. The driver's job is reduced from manipulating that car to catching it. As such things go the NS-X is unlikely to go out of control and few drivers will get into trouble, but drivers seeking extra satisfaction will not find it here.

The NS-X is a fine product that irons out many of the irritating inconveniences that have come to be accepted in high performance cars. Americans will love it: it is easy to drive and will no doubt be easy to live with. But it is bland.

The sad thing is that we have seen it all before. In the 1950s and 1960s Britain and other countries produced some great superbikes, motorcycles of great performance and handling. They leaked oil and were generally unreliable, and they demanded a lot of skill from their riders. But when they were ridden as intended they were thrilling. Then in 1969 Honda launched its CB750 Four. On paper it was a remarkable machine, a high performance, four-cylinder motorcycle with better performance than most European rivals, and a super-slick engine that was reliable (and never leaked oil). It was easy to ride and own, and it

paved the way for a generation of Japanese superbikes. But the experience of motorcycle riding has not advanced one iota, and may even have receded. Today's Japanese superbikes are superb machines in every respect, but they do not involve the rider in the way the old bikes did. That's sad.

Maybe the time has come for Honda to build

a supercar like the NS-X, and maybe it is a good thing, but I am not able to say so. A car that does not challenge its driver is a car without charisma. There is a place for cars like the NS-X in society, but let us hope that the NS-X does not mark the beginning of the end for charismatic sports cars.

HONDA NS-X

ENGINE

Cylinders: V6, transverse, mid-mounted.
Capacity: 2,977 cc (179 cu in)
Bore/stroke: 90/78 mm (3.54/3.07 in).
Valve gear: dohc per bank, driven by toothed belts, four valves per cylinder.
Compression ratio:
Fuel system: programmed digital injection.
Maximum power: 270 bhp/7,300 rpm.
Maximum torque: 210 lb ft (285 Nm)/5,500 rpm.

TRANSMISSION

Type: 5-speed manual (4-speed automatic also available), rear-wheel drive, limited-slip differential.

SUSPENSION, WHEELS

Front: double wishbones, coil springs, anti-roll bar.

Rear: double wishbones, coil springs, anti-roll bar.
Steering: unassisted rack and pinion.
Brakes: (Front) discs/(Rear) discs, servo assisted, ABS.
Tyres/wheels: front 205/50 ZR 15 - 6.5J, rear 225/50 ZR 16 - 8J.

DIMENSIONS

Length: 169.9 in (431.5 cm).
Width: 70.9 in (180 cm).
Height: 46.1 in (117 cm).
Wheelbase: 98.4 in (250 cm).
Front/rear track: 59.4/60.0 in (151/152.5 cm).
Weight: 2,974 lb (1,350 kg).
Fuel tank: 13.2 gallons (60 litres).

PERFORMANCE

Maximum speed: 162 mph (260 kph).
Acceleration: 0-62 mph (100 kph) 6 sec.

ISDERA IMPERATOR 108i

Ever tried to buy a Lamborghini Countach? If you have the money to spare, then you will know that exchanging it for a Countach is not easy. The factory made only 180 per year, and those were already sold at least two years in advance. The waiting lists are long for a hugely expensive car. So imagine the consternation amongst the ostentates if they made only one Countach every four or five months. The point is, though, that provided the car is outrageous, fast and stylish, exclusivity goes a long way to guaranteeing sales. The price, it would appear, has little bearing on the demand.

The Countach market provides the small Isdera factory near Stuttgart with its three customers every year. If he could build more, says Isdera Principal Eberhard Schulz, he could sell them, with no problem at all. And, he might have added, they have to be paid for in advance, such is the demand for the cars.

There is no doubting the Isdera Imperator's striking appearance. Less angular than a Countach, less fussy than a Ferrari Testarossa or F40, it has no wings, skirts or spoilers, not even a deep chin under the grille. Although there are plenty of air-seeking ducts to soothe engine, brakes and occupants, none disturbs the car's profile. It is undeniably futuristic, a Star Wars impression reinforced by the gullwing doors, but at the same time it is smooth, compact and

uncluttered; there are no stuck-on flares to cover the wheels, for instance. Even with its near-flat screen and smooth lines, it does not look like a Group C racer, which ironically nowadays sets it apart from most of the rest.

Beneath the startling gullwing profile, the car is built to a fairly conventional mid-engine specification. A multi-tubular spaceframe chassis is jig welded, then galvanized for rust proofing, and the fibreglass body is glued and riveted to the chassis. Motive power comes from Mercedes's 5.6-litre V8, driving through a ZF transaxle. The latter is the brutal, indestructible five-speed synchromesh item that has seen service over the years in the GT40, BMW M1, De Tomaso Pantera and so on. It is expensive but well proven, and has been in production for so long that there are ratios available to suit almost any application. Rear suspension of the

Imperator – it is the Latin for conqueror or emperor – is based on Porsche's 928 Weissach axle.

The 928's rear end was designed well before the four-wheel steering fashion, and was intended to provide a measure of passive geometry change to help keep the car safe. Anyone who drove an early 928 and experienced the Skoda-like lift off oversteer will know that the system left much to be desired. Schulz is particularly rude about the set-up, arguing that its greatest attribute is availability, although he claims that for use in his creation, stiffening the bushes and adding an extra link has made it quite acceptable. A large cast aluminium semi-trailing arm and blade-type transverse link form the lower location and another cast transverse link does service as the upper. Koni spent some time developing the coil-over shock absorbers, and much care

went into rate of springs and stiffness of roll bars. Wheels are 9.5x15 front, 12.5x15 rear BBS spoked aluminium, with Porsche Group C style air-extracting wheel trims. Rubberware is respectively Pirelli's 285/40 and 345/35 section P7s front to rear, sizes originally developed for the Countach.

At the front, the Porsche 928 again provides the suspending medium, although it is a more geometrically cast aluminium upper and lower twin wishbone arrangement, together with coil spring shock absorber units.

Nothing revolutionary so far: use of proven components is arguably a strength rather than a weakness while the quality of those parts helps further; the Porsche suspension castings, hubs and brakes are beautifully made, as you might expect. Use of Porsche hardware also brings access to brakes of adequate ability (928S4 brakes are bigger still and will be standard on all Imperators), with ABS if so desired. The same is true of the Mercedes engine. The aluminium V8 is universally accepted as a beautiful piece of workmanship, probably more so since the Sauber Mercedes World Sports Prototype cars have used a turbo version of the same V8 to mount a successful challenge to the might of Tom Walkinshaw's Jaguars.

Now a perennial burning question: is this car a practical proposition? The performance figures are shattering, the styling is striking, but would

it stand the test as an everyday conveyance? Little things like non-existent rear and three-quarter visibility, ease of parking, noise, poke-and-hope gear changes, hopeless ventilation . . . They are all important considerations. Well, the Imperator is certainly exciting to look at and ride in. It's not perfect, but it is *Teutonic.* That is the ever-so-slightly arrogant assertion made by Schulz about his car, and his nation. It is intended to beg the question about usability.

Driver and passenger sit well forward in the car – look how close the door is to the wheel arch – consequently the pedals have to clear the inner wheel wells. If you have big feet you must remove your shoes in order not to depress both brake and accelerator together, and to be able to depress the clutch at all. Stockinged feet experience no discomfort thereafter, which must say something about the integrity of the pedalwork. That apart, there is plenty of legroom for a tall driver and the cockpit is spacious and airy, despite the fact that none of the windows can be opened. Fortunately, Mercedes provides the appropriate air conditioning unit to go with the big V8 and it dispenses copious draughts of freezing air to face, hands and stockinged feet.

Sitting so far forward has its advantages. The car's nose slopes steeply away straight from the windscreen, the wheels tucking neatly into the triangle without need for haunches to clear the tyres, and this means that the road is visible. Few

things are more intimidating than a performance car that denies its driver adequate vision in order to place it through the lanes.

Rear vision would be hopeless were it not for a periscope immediately above the head, and a curved mirror gives a panoramic view of the road behind with the added advantage that it does not clutter the windscreen either.

Taking the expected niggles in turn, the gullwings are another surprising advantage. They will open in a space a few inches wider than the car. They swing up completely out of the way and release such a large opening that elegant ingress or egress is simple whatever your age or attire. It is also a simple matter to open the door just before a parking manoeuvre so you can stick your head out and avoid kerbing those vastly expensive wheels and tyres.

The Mercedes engine is noisier than expected. Apparently adequately-sized silencers exacerbated an already tricky underbonnet heat problem (hence the plethora of ducts), and there is a fair degree of mechanical rustling and drumming. The test car was fitted with an AMG four-valve-per-cylinder conversion, which increases the power output to a very strident 390 bhp, delivered at 5,500 rpm. This is a lot of power in 2,750 lb, and will propel the Imperator 108i from a standstill to 100 mph in 11.5 seconds, quick enough to dispose of the Porsche 911 turbo (12.3 sec), Lotus Espirit turbo (11.9 sec) or su-

ISDERA IMPERATOR 108i

ENGINE

Cylinders: AMG Mercedes-Benz V8, in line, mid-mounted.

Capacity: 5,547 cc (338.6 cu in).

Bore/stroke: 96.5/94.8 mm (3.80/3.73 in).

Valve gear: dohc per bank, chain-driven, 32 valves.

Compression ratio: 10.0:1.

Fuel system: Bosch KE-jetronic fuel injection.

Maximum power: 390 bhp/5,500 rpm.

Maximum torque: 317 lb ft (430 Nm) / 3,750 rpm.

TRANSMISSION

Type: 5-speed manual, rear-wheel drive, limited-slip differential.

Mph/kph per 1,000 rpm in top gear: 31.3/50.4.

SUSPENSION, WHEELS

Front: independent, by double wishbones, coil springs, anti-roll bar.

Rear: independent, by semi-trailing arms, upper transverse links, coil springs, anti-roll bar, Porsche-Weissach geometry.

Steering: assisted rack and pinion.

Brakes: (Front) ventilated discs/(Rear) ventilated discs, servo-assisted, ABS.

Tyres/wheels: front 285/40 VR 15 -9.5J, rear 345/35 VR 15 - 12.5J.

DIMENSIONS

Length: 166.1 in (422 cm).

Width:72.3 in (183.5 cm).

Height: 44.7 in (113.5 cm).

Wheelbase: 98 in (249 cm).
Front/rear track: 58.3/55.5 in (148/141cm).

Weight: 2,750 lb (1,238 kg).

Fuel tank: 20.9 gallons (95 litres).

PERFORMANCE

Maximum speed: 178 mph (286 kph).

Acceleration: 0-62 mph (100kph) 5.5 sec, 0-100 mph (161 kph) 11.5 sec.

Fuel consumption (average)★: 24.6 mpg (11.5 litres/100 km).

★Factory figures

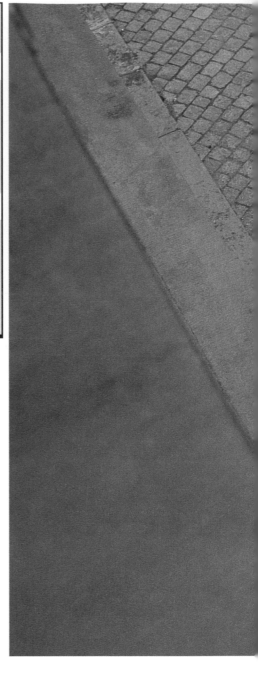

premely grunty De Tomaso Pantera (13.5 sec) with its similar 5.8-litre American C8/ZF trans-axle power-train.

The Imperator's gear change is acceptable with familiarity, but it needs to be shown who is boss. The flat lever in its slotted aluminium gate grates and clacks in use and can hang up the change, especially from first – situated in the racer's preferred across and back dog-leg position – to second. A cable gear change should cure the problem.

There is no need to use the gearbox much. The engine's sheer flexibility and pure urge allows the driver to clunk solely between fourth and fifth, which is enough to see off most things. Top speed is claimed just short of 180 mph, although we didn't quite manage that, and as the speed rose to an indicated 250 kph (155 mph), the car began to feel more and more like the racer it doesn't resemble. Downforce seemed to grow

with speed, the steering firmed up as the air pressed down, and the car felt ever more pushed to the ground, with steering true and accurate.

The suspension is actually quite supple which gives a superb ride without the peculiar nodding head sensation that some mid-engined cars occasionally display over indifferent surfaces, and yet roll is restrained – a carefully achieved optimum. Traction through tight corners is predictably excellent, although a sufficient tweak of throttle in first will eventually send the tail scurrying wide. In second, a good bootful brings understeer on a dry road, not much though, and nothing like as much as you find in a Countach or De Tomaso. More power still keeps the car almost neutral although oversteer is then difficult if not impossible to provoke on a dry road once out of bottom gear. Lifting off in the corner will do it, and the origins of the rear suspension make themselves known with just a touch of oversteer –

again only gentle. It is very hard to provoke the car. If you want to be a proper hooligan, then now is the time to tread the throttle, and you can hold the tail wide and smokey, balancing with steering which is as sharp as only a mid-engined car's can be. It is a little too much assisted perhaps, and every movement of the rather large wheel provokes a reaction, so you need to be tidy and accurate with your inputs, but the car is never nervous. It is about as good in this department as Ferrari's yardstick 328 or the original 911 Carrera Rs, only without the rear-engined diagonal rock.

Because the driver sits so far forward, the Imperator creates a delightfully different cornering sensation – the seat seems to sweep round *with* the nose rather than the mass of the car appearing to pivot round the driver. All mid-engined cars feel a little like this, which is part of the joy of driving them, but the Isdera actually felt more

responsive than most, without needing constant revision of line which becomes extremely tiring. It's a good balance.

In fact, the Imperator is a pretty good package, combining comfort, speed, distinctive styling, driver vision and so on. The suspension setting is well defined, and it is quick in a subtle, lazy way – the best way.

The test car had covered 49,000 (hard) miles, which promptly made the occasional creak from the doors entirely forgivable. More impressive still was that the trim had survived intact, a trick which has eluded some Italian supercar manufacturers. The electric seats still worked and the doors shut with a satisfying clunk and did not rattle. A lot of thought has gone into the car's design and development. And it has one supreme advantage over the F40 and 959. You can buy one, if at an extremely high price.

LAMBORGHINI COUNTACH

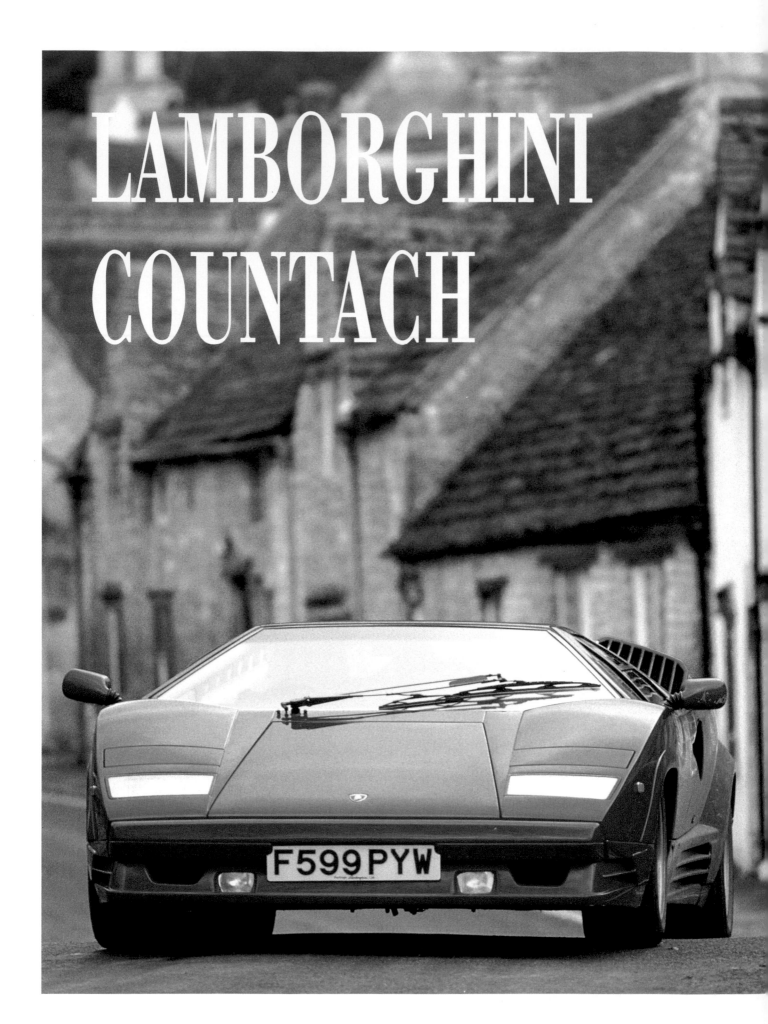

orget the suggestion that it is 'unstable' at high speed without that monstrous rear wing. Ignore those who claim that the Testarossa's 180 mph makes it the world's quickest production car. The Countach is the King of Supercars, and nothing else even comes close.

We arrived at the factory at Sant'Agata Bolognese early one morning. It was explained that although we would be allowed to drive the car later in the day, for insurance reasons it was necessary for a 'test driver' to be behind the wheel for the maximum speed runs, to be carried out on the *autostrada*. This turned out to be Grand Prix driver Pierluigi Martini, in his own Countach, minus unnecessary rear wing.

Italian motorways have marker posts every kilometre, with no half-kilometre signs. This is fine for the ordinary motorist, but it means that if a timed high speed run is being undertaken, realistically maximum revs need to be reached about 5 sec before the first post, and held all the way through to the second one. This is an elapsed time of something like 20 sec at maximum speed, and at the sort of speed being considered here, it is a problem, especially with a very definite need to leave a bit of space for braking.

The *Quattrovalvole* 5000S runs arrow-straight at its maximum speed. There *was* a tendency for the front end to become light, but a small but significant change in both the overall ride height and in the attitude of the car (it is now pitched ever so slightly forwards) has altered that.

We turned off on to a different *autostrada*. At last we got a time – 12.3 sec – but the car was still accelerating for at least two-thirds of the distance. A check with the calculator reveals that that represents 292.7 kph, or 181.9 mph.

Finally, we turned on to yet another *autostrada*. It was clear, and the rev needle flicked wildly just inside the red sector, and the speedometer read 320 kph. This was it. We passed the first kilometre post. Those tiny specks in the far distance were beginning to be identifiable shapes. Though they would not be aware of it even if they used their rear-view mirrors, soon they could become a braking area. Click! We passed the second kilometre post and Martini was safely, *very* firmly on the brakes to haul us down to traffic speed. We had covered a flying kilometre in 11.46 sec, which is 314.1 kph, or 195.2 mph.

This is not the end of this section of the job, however: it is necessary to time the car in the opposite direction, too, in order to eliminate factors such as wind speed and direction, and gradient.

On the way back we covered the kilometre in 12.1 sec, which means 297 kph, 194.9 mph. The car may have had a tiny bit left to come, but even so it works out a mean speed of 305.8 kph and 190.1 mph.

Unlike most high-speed rivals the Countach is a production car, even if it is hardly in the volume business. More than 1,000 Countaches have been built since the first LP400 appeared in 1973. The last of the anniversary models was produced in March 1990.

It was in 1985 that the King of the Countaches, the *Quattrovalvole* 5000S, took its bow. Until this point, the Countach had always had two camshafts above each bank of six cylinders, but now for the first time it was supplied with four valves per cylinder, a total of 48. At the same time the stroke was stretched to 75 mm, and the six downdraught twin-choke Webers changed from 45 DCOE to 44 DCNF. Power went up to a massive yet nominal 455 bhp at 7,000 rpm and torque to 369 lb ft at 5,200 rpm. Many engines produced more than 470 bhp in some instances.

What of the acceleration? These days a 0-60 mph time of 5.0 sec is about even par in the supercar league. Only the F40 can beat the Countach's 4.2 sec. Simply give it lots of revs to break the tenacious grip of the enormous rear tyres, dump the clutch and go. It goes all the way in first gear if you ignore the red-line change-up at 58 mph, and you're into third at 80 mph, reaching 100 mph in an almost incredible 10.0 sec. Carry on and 120 mph comes up in 14.1 sec, 130 mph in 17.2 and 140 in 20.5.

Respecters of red lines on rev counters, will never see more than 183 mph if the Countach's needle works properly, for that is the road speed (ignoring tyre growth, which may be a factor) at 7,500 rpm – there is a precautionary yellow sector before that, starting at 7,000 rpm.

The engine has an unburstable feel to it, all the way up its range. Shortly before maximum speed is reached the note deepens perceptibly.

Starting the Countach from cold calls for a sequence of actions which almost form a ritual. Switch on the ignition and wait for the ticking of the fuel pumps to fade away. Turn the key further and listen to the ferocious, hungry growl, emanating only from multiple carbureters on a multi-cylinder engine, which then settles into a deep rumble. It is necessary to wait a little longer for the various fluids to warm.

Even if the movements through the slotted gate (with first offset to the left and reverse protected from accidental selection by a sprung locking tab) are rather long, it is really a question of quickness of hand movement. The Fitchel and Sachs clutch is *very* heavy.

This is something that simply must be put up with, but we did wonder about the unusual with, but we did wonder about the unusual amount of force required of one's right foot in initially depressing the throttle. After that, throttle response is miraculously smooth.

Although maximum torque seems high up the range at 5,200 rpm, our acceleration figures in top and fourth show that the curve must be a very flat one. Indeed, the response to flooring the throttle at only 1,500 rpm in top (about 36 mph) is simply instant, smooth, turbine-like acceleration, and the figures from 40 mph onwards are outstanding.

The driver able to afford a Countach will not be worried by anything as trivial as fuel consumption, but will want to be able to travel quite a few miles on a full tank, or rather tanks since there are two which are inter-connected. The total capacity of 26.4 gallons gives a range of over 250 miles even asuming lead-footed driving, which may result in something like 9 mpg.

The servo-assisted discs are all ventilated, and all mounted outboard, and they are the size of dinner plates: 11.2 in at the rear and 11.8 in at the front.

When burbling around waiting for a gap into which to propel this projectile, one becomes aware of a few noises that are normally drowned out by the howl of the engine (even so, since much of that marvellous bellow is left behind, it is still just possible to have a conversation at over 180 mph, if you can think of a good reason to do so). There is quite a lot of transmission whine in the intermediates, and the tyres and suspension make plenty of noise over surface irregularities (though no more so than is the case in a Porsche 911). However, wind noise is virtually absent, as are any creaks or rattles, confirming the belief that the chassis is impressively rigid.

The first surprise is that the unassisted rack and pinion steering, is light in the straight ahead position even at very low speeds; then you glance at the speedometer and realize you are travelling at about 80 mph. It is only when manoeuvring in a tight space that the poor lock (common to all fat-tyred supercars) and a fair degree of weight make their presence felt. With an overall rubber contact patch unequalled by any other road car (the rear tyres are 345/35 VR 15 on 12 in rims, and the fronts are 225/50 VR 15 on 8.5 in rims), it is hardly surprising that dry road grip is outstanding. But roadholding is one thing and overall handling another, and the more impressive aspects of the Countach are how well balanced it feels, how much true feel of the surface is fed to the driver via the wheel and through the chassis, and how progressively and predictably it responds to suggestions that it should change direction. Again, it is working with the driver.

The point is that the Countach does not have that combination of apparently limitless grip and then abrupt breakaway which can be so fraying to the nerves, not to mention potentially damaging to the rest of the system. Instead, there is a steady feedback to the driver so that if an adjustment to the line becomes necessary, the driver can make it before a crisis is reached. Although very neutral in general terms, it does eventually push its nose wider under power in most circumstances. Ease pressure on the throttle, and it will come back on line.

In a tight bend, even in the dry, it is possible to punch the tail out with a brutal and sustained stamp on the throttle pedal.

Another surprising aspect of the car, is the comfort of the ride. Everything is relative, but in comparison with almost any high-performance car, the Lamborghini shines. At low speeds over rough surfaces it jiggles, but without sending violent shocks vertically through the spines of the occupants. Travel just a little faster and it smooths everything out, and at very high speed there is no tendency to float.

Underneath that extraordinary shape, with its single curve sweeping from nose to tail, underneath the beautifully hammered aluminium panels, is a 'birdcage' space-frame chassis of such complexity that it defies the imagination. For a number of different considerations, it is ideal for the engine in a mid-engined car to be located longitudinally, and that is the case in the Countach. Normally, the gearbox is then mounted behind it, in unit with the final drive.

However, in the Countach, the gearbox is ahead of the engine, and the drive passes back via a shaft through the crankcase.

Attached to this frame at either end is suspension of classic racing pedigree: unequal-length double wishbones, with angled coil spring/damper units and an anti-roll bar.

Getting in and out of the Countach requires some agility, but inside it is considerably less cramped than an Esprit, for example, and it does not give the same claustrophobic feeling. Even for tall drivers, there is just about sufficient headroom, and, though it is necessary to drive with knees bent, the in/out adjustability of the steering wheel avoids dangerous contact between hands and thighs when lock is applied. The pedals are offset to the centre because of wheel arch intrusion, but they are well spaced. The handbrake lever pokes out of a recess next to the wide central console. The switches, stalks and instruments are all simple; they function well, but there is nothing in particular to mention about them. Likewise the trimming is competently executed, though it does not give that air of plush luxury that you find in an Aston Martin or the crisp, modern and efficient environment of the latest Ferrari.

The seats are of a true 'bucket' design, the frames forming a single curve from headrest to tip of cushion, and they can be adjusted for tilt as well as to slide fore and aft. They offer good lateral location and are acceptably comfortable for journeys of moderate length. The engine cover and luggage space release levers are concealed in the door jamb, and the carpeted luggage space, though by no means large, is not too bad for this type of car. The front lid conceals a temporary spare wheel, the battery, and the brake servo.

The Countach's interior may not be claustrophobic, but the all-round view from it is not a strong point. Its forward vision is acceptable when you get used to looking through that huge pane of glass set in a shallow incline: ahead of you, it is just possible to see the highest peaks of the front wheel arches, but the nose is out of sight.

Reversing a Countach in a confined space is a minor nightmare, and the preferred technique

LAMBORGHINI COUNTACH 5000 Quattrovalvole / Anniversary

ENGINE

Cylinders: V12 (60-degree), in-line, mid-mounted.

Capacity: 5,167 cc (311 cu in).

Bore/stroke: 85.5/75 mm (3.37/2.95 in).

Valve gear: dohc per bank, chain driven, four valves per cylinder.

Compression ratio: 9.5:1.

Fuel system: six Weber 44 DCNF downdraught twin-choke carbureters.

Maximum power: 455 bhp/7,000 rpm.

Maximum torque: 369 lb ft (500 Nm)/5,200 rpm.

TRANSMISSION

Type: 5-speed manual, rear-wheel drive, limited-slip differential.

Mph/kph per 1,000 rpm in top gear: 24.4/39.3.

SUSPENSION, WHEELS

Front: independent, by double wishbones, coil springs, anti-roll bar.

Rear: independent, by double wishbones, coil springs, anti-roll bar.

Steering: unassisted rack and pinion.

Brakes: (Front) ventilated discs/(Rear) ventilated discs, servo assisted.

Tyres/wheels: front 225/50 VR 15 -8.5J, rear 345/35 VR 15 - 12J.

DIMENSIONS

Length: 163.0 in (414 cm).

Width: 78.7 in (200 cm).

Height: 42.1 in (107 cm).

Wheelbase: 98.4 in (250 cm).

Front/rear track: 60.4/63.2 in (153.5 160.5cm).

Weight: 3,293 lbs (1,494 kg).

Fuel tank: 26.4 gallons (120 litres).

PERFORMANCE

Maximum speed: 190.1 mph (305.9 kph).

Acceleration: 0-60 mph (96.5 kph) 4.2 sec, 0-100 mph (161 kph) 10.0 sec.

Fourth gear: 40-60 mph (64-96.5 kph) 6.0 sec.

Fifth gear: 50-70mph (80.5-113 kph) 6.2 sec.

Fuel consumption (average): 12.6 mpg (22.4 litres/100 km)

seems to be to open the door and sit on the sill. This really is a car designed for the open road, and once there, visibility is fair.

Until recently, Italian cars have not been known for the efficiency of their ventilation systems, which is odd for such a hot country. The Countach has air conditioning, but its performance is only adequate.

At times in the past, Lamborghini's standards of finish were perhaps not as high as might be wished, but now, the Countach is as beautiful close up as it is from the other side of the street, and the panel fits are particularly impressive.

It is a crazy vision made into reality. It costs a fortune. It is totally impractical. There is no way that buying it could be justified by any rational argument, but if you are a true car enthusiast and immensely wealthy, who needs arguments?

The Countach is dead. The last of the Anniversary models was produced at Sant'Agata at the end of March 1990, bringing to a close a remarkable 17 years of production. Lamborghini's replacement, the Diablo, was officially launched in Monte Carlo on 20 January 1990.

On paper, the Diablo looks like an updated Countach, but it is very much more in tune with the times, in so far as that does not sound somewhat ridiculous in discussing a two-seater with a V12 engine putting the best part of 500 bhp through 335-section rear tyres.

Those who thought that the Gandini-designed Cizeta Moroda V16-T gave a sneak preview of the Diablo were right. The front end of the Diablo – and indeed the sides of it, as far back as the rear of the doors – is very similar to the Cizeta, and it will be hard to tell the two apart on the rare occasions that they appear in a rear view mirror. The front wing line of the Diablo is more striking, but the side window shape (better for vision) is rather awkward, especially at its low forward extremity, where door and windscreen pillar meet front wing.

But from the 'B-posts' back, the Diablo is very much more attractive, with excellent detailing. It is particularly pleasing from low down in the rear, its rear wings recalling the shape of the original LP500 show car, and another echo of the early Countach may be seen in the scalloped rear arches.

There are a few too many apertures in the car from an aesthetic point of view, but there is a great deal of heat to be dissipated from this machine, and the Diablo looks less like a mobile food processor than some modern mid-engined cars. Not everyone will like the engine cover, but it allows much better rearward vision than the tall carbureter box of the Anniversary.

Incidentally, if you really insist on impairing the rearward view, the factory has designed a new rear spoiler. Nobody at Lamborghini likes it, since (as with the Countach) it cuts down the top speed while conferring no benefit in stability.

The Diablo retains the Countach's singular engine/transmission arrangement, in which the five-speed gearbox is mounted ahead of the longitudinally-aligned 48-valve engine, and drives the rear wheels via an enclosed shaft running back through the sump. Engineering

Director Luigi Marmiroli says that alternative configurations were assessed, but none was considered superior.

But the Diablo is much more than simply a reskinned Countach. The entire car has been re-engineered from nose to tail and Marmiroli (an ex-Grand Prix engineer) jokes that the only common component is the bull badge on the nose.

The engine has been enlarged from 5,169 cc to 5,709 cc (and is, as a consequence, slightly less 'over-square'). It produces 492 bhp at 7,000 rpm, and peak torque of 428 lb ft is delivered at 5,200 rpm: and all that is with twin catalytic converters, whereas the Countach's Bosch K-jetronic injection system (for US-specification models) could not get anywhere near the carbureted version's 455 bhp. The improvement, says Marmiroli, is largely due to the efficiency of Lamborghini's new sequential multi-point injection system which is integrated with its electronic ignition. So now, for the first time, Lamborghini's flagship will have the same engine throughout the world.

It has the same gearbox worldwide too, but it is also all-new. It had to be redesigned to be attached to a transfer box for the four-wheel-drive version of the car, the Diablo VT (which is due in 1991 when an electronically activated clutch will become available as an option).

The chassis is still a multi-tubed spaceframe, but the tubes are now square in section. Though the round-section tubes are theoretically superior, Marmiroli says that the Diablo is 30 per cent stiffer than the Countach in torsion. Square tubes make production considerably easier, simplifying welds and saving weight.

Materials in the body and chassis have been carefully selected so that the most appropriate is chosen in each area. Thus high-strength alloy is

LAMBORGHINI DIABLO/DIABLO VT

ENGINE

Cylinders: V12 (60-degree), in-line, mid-mounted.

Capacity: 5,709 cc (342.5 cu in).

Bore/stroke: 87/80 mm (3.43/3.15 in).

Valve gear: dohc per bank, chain driven, four valves per cylinder.

Compression ratio: 9.5:1.

Fuel system: L.I.E. electronic sequential multi-point injection, integrated with ignition.

Maximum power: 492 bhp/7,000 rpm.

Maximum torque: 428 lb ft (580 Nm)/5,200 rpm.

TRANSMISSION

Type: 5-speed manual, rear-wheel drive (VT: four-wheel drive), limited-slip differential.

Mph/kph per 1,000 rpm in top gear: 20.8/33.5.

SUSPENSION, WHEELS

Front: independent, by double wishbones, coil springs, anti-roll bar.

Rear: independent, by double wishbones, coil springs, anti-roll bar.

Steering: unassisted rack and pinion.

Brakes: (Front) ventilated discs/(Rear) ventilated discs, servo assisted.

Tyres/wheels: front 245/40 VR 17 -8.5J, rear 335/35 VR 17 - 13J.

DIMENSIONS

Length: 175.5in (446 cm).

Width: 80.3in (204 cm).

Wheelbase: 104.3 in (265 cm).

Front/rear track: 60.6/64.6in (154/164 cm).

Fuel tank: 22 gallons (100 litres).

Weight: 3,640 lbs (1,651 kg), VT: 3,741 lbs (1,697 kg).

PERFORMANCE*

Maximum speed: 202 mph (325 kph).

Acceleration: 0-62 mph (100 kph) 4.1 sec.

Standing km: 20.7 sec.

Fuel consumption (average): 17.7 mpg (16.0 litres/100 km).

*Factory figures

used for the central passenger 'safety cell', while a lesser alloy is used for the front and rear 'crumple zones'. Much of the body continues to be panelled in aluminium (or rather aluminium alloy, which apparently improves the quality of the surface) but the front and rear sections are in composites, as are the engine cover and front lid.

Lamborghini learned a great deal about the advantages and disadvantages of composites with the Evoluzione Countach in the late 1980s. That was a fully composite car; it was too rigid for the barrier tests!

One of the drawbacks of the Countach was that its wheel arches did not permit the use of the 17 in rims which have been introduced in recent years and which not only give good results with the massive Pirelli P Zero tyres (F40 sizes: 245/40 at the front and 335/35 at the back), but also allow larger brake discs to be used. Actually the rears on the Diablo are the same size as before, but the fronts are now 13 in in diameter (also identical to the F40).

Anti-lock brakes are not part of the existing or projected specification. Marmiroli says this was a purely engineering decision, not based on the difficulties of making ABS work with four-wheel drive. The intention is to leave as much feel in the hands of the driver as possible.

It will be interesting to see the effects of this philosophy, which also rules out power-assisted steering in the Diablo VT, which will have a limited-slip front differential. Its central viscous coupling will never permit more than 20 per cent of the torque to arrive at the front wheels.

'This is not a rally car,' says Marmiroli. 'Of course, with big tyres like that, you are still going to have difficulties in bad weather. Our aim with the VT, though, is to take away the traction problems which can be suffered in first gear when the driver is trying to put a lot of power on to a damp road.' The VT will also have electronically-controlled damping, but it will not have fully 'active' suspension or four-wheel steering. Coil springs are preferred in Sant'Agata.

Marmiroli says he is pleased that there will be no shortage of competition for the Diablo. Two rivals are being produced by ex-Lamborghini men, Claudio Zampolli's Cizeta and the Bugatti (the latter, engineered by the great Paolo Stanzini – who created the Countach – is considered by most of those in the know to be the greater threat).

The aim is to build 500 Diablos per year. That is two per day and a 20 per cent increase on the Countach's final, record-breaking year. Marmiroli believes that because the difference in cost will not be large, all Diablos will be VTs.

At under 176 in, the Diablo is the same length as a Montego, and not much longer than the Countach, the gearbox location aiding compactness. But the width has increased to more than 80 in (2 in wider than the F40), and that is still barge-like even if 8 in narrower than the Cizeta.

As well as a wider track, the Diablo has a longer wheelbase than the Countach, which not only aids handling but improves internal space. The increased height of the car also gives better headroom, though it is still too easy to bang your head when getting in or out. The interior is considerably tidier, but remains largely conventional.

Electric operation of the windows is retained, more useful now that the windows are deeper than letter boxes, but the inappropriate provision of electric adjustment of the seats has been abandoned. The only unusual aspect of the instruments is that the two major dials are outside the wheel rim.

The Countach weighed in at 3,293 lb in its final form. The enlarged Diablo tips the scales at 3,640 lb (the VT is almost 1,020 lb above that). This means that the power/weight ratio is marginally worsened, so the quoted acceleration figures are quite remarkable: 0-100 kph in 4.1 sec, and the standing kilometre in 20.7 sec, both of which are *just* better than Ferrari's staggering 2,250 lb F40 can manage. Aided by a drag coefficient of 0.31, which is not bad for a supercar – though the frontal area is massive – is

said to be 325 kph (202 mph), and again, no doubt, coincidentally – that is 1 kph better than Ferrari's claim for the F40.

Nobody (including the factory) is exactly sure how many Countaches have been made since the first production LP400 of 1974, by which time Ferruccio Lamborghini had severed all connection with the car company he had created. It is certainly less than 1,500. Volkswagen makes four times as many Golfs in a day. Will the Diablo last through to the year 2006, and if so, who will then own Lamborghini?

LAMBORGHINI

JALPA

Some cars get tantalizingly close to fulfilling their makers' hopes and ambitions, only to fail. The reasons are sometimes mysterious. The Jalpa is a case in point. Intended to be Lamborghini's answer to the Ferrari 308, it was well engineered and well built. One day soon it will probably be a highly valued 'classic'. But in its own time it failed.

Perhaps the appearance had something to do with it. It was not ugly, but it was no match for the little Ferrari in looks; something was lost at Sant'Agata in converting the Silhouette as the Jalpa production car. Something was also gained – a lot of weight, and at 3,300 lb, it was substantially heavier than its rivals.

The Jalpa we tested was disappointing in several respects, and did not match up to the memories two of our testers had of a previous test car. We remembered a rather wild and temperamental machine, but undeniably a thoroughbred in character, perhaps the sort of car that Ferrari made a couple of decades ago. Flawed, certainly, but with a raw *machismo* appropriate to the marque which carries a fighting bull as its emblem.

The pressure required to operate the throttle in our test Jalpa was almost equivalent to the pressure required to operate the brakes in a Daytona. The Lamborghini's brakes, in contrast, were soggy in feel and combined long pedal travel with a tendency to lock the front wheels without warning on slippery surfaces. Coupled with a flat spot and some hesitation on part throttle, this made driving with precision virtually impossible, despite the inherent flexibility of the 3,485 cc four-cam V8.

Use full throttle, however, and the engine note is fabulous, the closest you can get to the sound of the venerable three-litre Cosworth Grand Prix engine in a road car. We remembered the previous car we had driven, with that wonderful roar, but without the fluffiness from the four twin-choke Webers, and without the pumping iron action of the throttle pedal.

On paper at least, the Jalpa had the power to do the job: 250 bhp at 7,000 rpm and a useful 232 lb ft of torque at 3,500 rpm. However, apart from the weight penalty, it was no standard-setter aerodynamically. Even so, with a maximum speed a whisker short of 150 mph and 0-60 mph in less than 6 sec, it was still a very quick car.

Another aspect of the earlier Jalpa that we recalled was a remarkably fine compromise between ride and handling. The fine ride quality of the chassis, with its ability to soak up most surface irregularities, despite a fair amount of noise generated by the big P7s (205/55 VR front, 225/50 VR rear on 7.5J x 16 in rims), was as evident in our test car, but something seemed awry in the handling.

Understeer under power was stronger than expected, and steering feel was less acute, but the most disquieting aspect of the car's behaviour was its tendency to lurch into untidy oversteer when closing the throttle halfway through a bend. There was none of the delicate precision of the Ferrari here: this one wanted to bite back, and hard. Perhaps a damper or two had seen better days, or perhaps someone had scuffed a kerb too hard.

Getting a gearbox gate with the planes parallel to the wheelbase seems to have been beyond the Jalpa's engineers, and the angle is awkward. Springing within the gate is also poor, but once you get the knack of the rather ponderous movement, changes can be positive enough.

Without the benefit of programmed ignition and injection (and in our test car, without the pleasure normally associated with carbureters), you cannot expect to obtain more than 17 mpg in a Jalpa if you drive fairly hard.

If you give the Jalpa the benefit of the doubt in the above-mentioned areas, then what are you left with?

The answer, when the Jalpa was being produced, was not a 3U8 GTS at a slightly lower price; the lower price concealed running costs which were likely to be higher. An optimist is a man who thinks he might *just* be able to afford to run a Lamborghini.

Instead it was a character car in the old tradition, one that required pampering and love and attention; one that was designed for fast, long journeys on a sunny summer day rather than for the day-to-day slog that can be soaked up by a Porsche 911, or these days perhaps a Ferrari 348.

The Jalpa had a remarkably practical interior. The trim was not as neat as it might have been, and the ventilation pathetic (though the heater was powerful), but there was plenty of legroom, headroom was just about adequate for tall drivers, and there was a feeling of spaciousness that is rare in mid-engined cars.

The Jalpa's roof panel was designed to be stowed behind the seats, and attaching it was simple enough, but the panel was far too heavy. Even at high speed, a topless Jalpa generated surprisingly little wind roar or buffeting. Mind you, at 120 mph or more, there are enough Lotus 49-style sounds from the rear for it to be difficult to tell.

LAMBORGHINI JALPA

ENGINE

Cylinders: V8 (90-degree), transverse, mid-mounted.
Capacity: 3,485 cc (209.1 cu in).
Bore/stroke: 86/75 mm (3.39/2.95 in).
Valve gear: sohc per bank, driven by toothed belt, two valves per cylinder.
Compression ratio: 9.2:1.
Fuel system: four downdraught twin-choke Weber 42 DCNF carbureters.
Maximum power: 250 bhp/7,500 rpm.
Maximum torque: 232 lb ft (314 Nm)/3,500 rpm.

TRANSMISSION

Type: 5-speed manual, rear-wheel drive.
Mph/kph per 1,000 rpm in top gear: 20.4/32.8.

SUSPENSION, WHEELS

Front: independent, by MacPherson struts, lower wishbones, coil springs, anti-roll bar.
Rear: independent, by Chapman struts, reversed lower wishbones, trailing links, coil springs, anti-roll bar.
Steering: unassisted rack and pinion.
Brakes: (Front) ventilated discs/(Rear) ventilated discs, servo assisted.
Tyres/wheels: front 205/55 VR 16 -7.5J, rear 225/50 VR 16 - 7.5J.

*Factory figures

DIMENSIONS

Length: 170.5 in (433 cm).
Width: 74.0 in (188 cm).
Height: 44.9 in (114 cm).
Wheelbase: 96.5 in (245 cm).
Front/rear track: 59.1/61.2 in (150 155.5cm).
Weight: 3,304 lbs (1,500 kg).
Fuel tank: 17.6 gallons (80 litres).

PERFORMANCE*

Maximum speed: 147.6 mph (237.5 kph).
Acceleration: 0-60 mph (96.5 kph) 5.8 sec, 0-100 mph (161 kph) 16.0 sec.
Standing km: 26.8 sec.
Fourth gear: 30-50 mph (48-80.5 kph) 4.3 sec.
Fifth gear: 50-70mph (80.5-113 kph) 6.1 sec.
Fuel consumption (average): 16.7 mpg (16.9 litres/100 km).

LAMBORGHINI LM002

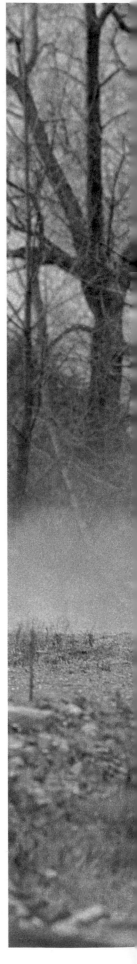

The trouble with ultimates is usually finding some ways of employing them usefully. It's all very well having the fastest, the loudest, most powerful, most waterproof, heaviest, lightest and so on, but mere superlatives do not make for a practical experience on the road: it is not much fun boasting about a concept.

Take the Lamborghini LM002. A three-ton amalgam of steel, fibreglass and aluminium wearing the famous prancing bull badge and powered by a Countach engine; 100 mph over rough ground is absolutely no problem. Well, that's amazing, but how often do you need to travel at 100 mph over rough ground? There would have to be something else we could do with a Lamborghini LM.

It is certainly a talking point at gas-stations. Talking of which, sticking the nozzle in the tank involves climbing up on the back like a perching monkey, and then climbing down to reset the pump at least once. 'Are you paying by cash or credit card . . ?' comes the anxious question over the PA system before the counters all clear to zero. This car is definitely the ultimate as far as thirst goes. But just in case that is not quite ultimate enough, there is a version of the LM available with the 7.2-litre powerboat motor. This apparently produces 420 bhp, slightly less than the smaller engine's 450 bhp, but delivered exactly 1,000 rpm lower down the scale, at 5,800 rpm and with more torque.

Torque output from the 5,167 cc, all aluminium, 48-valve four cam V12 – borrowed in unaltered, six-carbureter form from the 'old' Countach – is just under 400 lb ft. Substantial, but delivered at a comparatively high 4,500 rpm. Swift progress therefore demands energetic use of the gearbox, because the engine does not really start to go until the tacho shows at least 4,500 rpm; but then it can be argued that a high torque peak makes for less wheelspin when the going is slippery, and a high rpm capability allows the use of low gear ratios which hides the lack of torque. In the LM, the engine was suitably powerful, and handy. Still, you cannot argue with the performance, on or off road.

So, understatement is not a gift-wrapped LM, and it costs a fortune, whatever it is used for. Apparently nearly 100 are being used by armies, predominantly in the Arab world, and to date the other 250 or so have been sold to private customers, mainly in Italy. But unless you are an upmarket mercenary it seems that the LM is something of the ultimate in toys.

Ultimates need to be verified, so we took the Lamborghini to the Millbrook test track and strapped the fifth wheel on it. Now it might have been imagined that such a heavy vehicle round the banked Bedfordshire concrete would have been a wobbling handful. No racing truck was ever *that* good. But contrary to all expectations, well before the 12-cylinder wail reached 5,500 rpm in fifth, the steering had stopped wandering, and the whole thing took on a surfeit of stability. Flat out at a genuine 122 mph seemed positively anticlimatic. It gives the feeling that it would do that all day, or at least until the 50-gallon tank, which was emptying at just under a gallon per lap, ran dry. The Lamborghini man sitting alongside, however, was disappointed. He reckoned that 7,000 rpm in fifth was perfectly feasible, whenever you felt like it. However, the drag from 325/65 VR 17 Pirelli rubberware must amount to a few mph round the two mile curve.

Then it was time to see whether the factory's claim of 7.8 sec from rest to 60 mph was true or not. Thinking about it, it should be. Making the Lamborghini fly through the gears was rather dependent on mechanical sympathy, or lack of it, but thankfully the process was less painful than with some, because the two-wheel-drive-only facility allowed a drop of wheelspin which looked after the clutch. Not that there was ever any feeling that you might break the specially developed five-speed ZF transmission. Hurrying the shift only left the right palm tenderized against chunky synchromesh, and the clanking and shrilling from the transfer gears suggested teeth of substantial proportions beneath the enormous central tunnel.

Unusually perhaps, the all-drive system on the LM is only part time; drive to the front wheels

locking hubs to 'drive', then grasp the lever on the transmission tunnel with both hands, and you *will* need both. Wrestle the lever into four-wheel drive – everything about this machine with the possible exception of the steering demands muscle – and proceed. Now this is amazing and addictive. It jolts a fair bit – the driver's backside lifts from the seat on occasions, and there's a bonk from the rear suspension every so often as a wheel drops to the limit of its travel. But only afterwards do you realize just how rough was the terrain, and that you had been travelling at some 70 or 80 mph.

Since the old Austin Gypsy of the 1960s, there has been no production off-roader with all-round independent suspension, but the advantages are plainly obvious, if expensive. Not least, it allows all the differentials and propeller shafts to be tucked away up inside the chassis, and on the LM these and other fragile items like the exhaust system are protected by steel tubes. There are simply massive twin wishbones for front and rear suspension, with coil springs and telescopic hydraulic dampers. Brakes are full-powered like a Citroën's, and are just about up to the performance.

is engaged by a large lever alongside the transmission tunnel, and there are freewheeling front hubs to reduce the transmission drag still further and improve the fuel consumption.

The fastest possible getaway involved winding the engine beyond the start of the 6,500 rpm red line (maximum power is at 6,800) and dropping a foot off the clutch pedal. There is a prompt howl from the rear Pirellis, the engine bogs down, then gathers momentum once more as the

4,000 rpm mark is passed, and away you go. The result? 100 mph came up in 24.6 sec, and 60 in 7.8, the latter of which is as quick as a 16-valve VW. Now remember that the LM weighs three tons, and will go almost anywhere, and that is certainly impressive. It is, as far as we know, the fastest *production* off-roader in the world.

That left only the rough-terrain driving to test, which of course is the whole point of this vehicle. Having found a suitable venue, stop, twist the

The LM's ride isn't as supple as a Range Rover's, it has firmer damping and is actually more comfortable for that, but it does not nod its front like the British all-wheel drive car, and has a better ability to float over the rough. It also rolls much less, has vastly better ground clearances and much longer wheel travel. It does,

LAMBORGHINI LM002

ENGINE

Cylinders: V12, in-line, front mounted
Capacity: 5,167 cc (310 cu in.)
Bore/stroke: 85.5/75 mm (3.37/2.95 in)
Valve gear: dohc per bank, chain driven, two valves per cylinder.
Compression ratio: 9.5 : 1.
Fuel system: six side-draught Weber 44 DCNF twin-choke carbureters.
Maximum power: 450 bhp/6,800 rpm.
Maximum torque: 369 lb ft (500 Nm)/ 4,500 rpm

TRANSMISSION

Type: 5-speed manual, four wheel drive, limited-slip front and rear differentials
Mph/kph per 1,000 rpm in top gear: 18.4/29.6

SUSPENSION, WHEELS

Front: independent by double wishbones, coil springs.
Rear: independent, by double wishbones, coil springs.
Steering: assisted recirculating ball.
Brakes: (Front) ventilated discs/(Rear) drums, servo assisted.
Tyres/wheels: front and rear 325/65 VR 17-11J

DIMENSIONS

Length: 192 in (480 cm)
Width: 78.7 in (197 cm)
Height: 72.8 in (182 cm)
Wheelbase: 118 in (295 cm)
Front/rear track: 63.6/63.6 in (159/159 cm)
Weight: 5,947 lbs (2,697 kg)
Fuel tank: 63.8 gallons (287 litres)

PERFORMANCE

Maximum speed: 122 mph (195 kph)
Acceleration: 0-60 mph (96.5 kph) 7.8 sec, 0-100 mph (161 kph) 24.6 sec.
Fourth gear: 30-50 mph (48-80.5 kph) 7.8 sec.
Fifth gear: 50-70 mph (80.5-113 kph) 12.0 sec.
Fuel consumption (average): 9.4 mpg (30 litres/100 km).

however, cost nearly four times as much as the Range Rover.

There are limited-slip differentials both front and rear, and – unusually for part-time 4WD – another in the centre which can be locked. The front and rear of the chassis are steeply angled too, which stops the ends hitting the ground when attacking a steep slope; Lamborghini claim approach and departure angles of 50 and 45 degrees respectively.

A lot of thought has gone into the design of the LM, and there are few compromises anywhere in this performance, which is not so surprising considering that it was originally designed for military use. In view of that, though, it is perhaps more surprising that it manages to be so comparatively civilized and nimble given its weight and size, and that it manages to combine the roles of fast road car and fastest off-roader with such apparent ease.

The LM will also climb. We could not find a slope steep enough to defeat it, and the makers say that it will manage a gradient of 160 per cent (1.6 in 1), as long as there is enough traction. Water, mud, sand, nothing seemed to defeat it. Combine this with its speed, and it makes a package which as far as we know is unique for a production vehicle.

There are some dynamic disadvantages however, apart from the economics. Narrow country roads show the LM's attraction for ridges, and its wanders quite alarmingly. This in turn shows up a large dead area in the steering, and straight line secondary road progress involves a fair

wheel-sawing impression of the average car driver in all those 1950s films. Although it is hardly fair to expect something of this size and weight to have super-sharp steering, once the play has been taken up, the expected understeer through the corner is only gentle, and grip on metalled roads surprisingly high.

On unmade surfaces, the power steering is sensitive enough to allow you to travel at enormous speed with the tail swaying gently from side to side. Twitch the wheel and the tail sways further in the desired direction, helping the turn. This is simple: the weight of the machine is soon forgotten, increased speed seems to make the car more nimble and responsive, and, provided it is given some commitment, the LM can be thrown about like an Escort rally car. It is as well to keep an eye on the rev counter, though. On rough terrain, when you are busy twirling the wheel, the V12 gives no mechanical hint of its approaching limits, and you could easily hang too many revs on it.

The interior is all cream leather in the best Italian luxury car traditions, the bovine aroma blending unhappily with a persistent smell of petrol, which is apparently a feature of the machine. There are electric windows and air conditioning as well as central locking, and a four speaker stereo radio cassette player that is barely audible above the gearbox whine.

It is a strange mixture. Latin luxury, with military styling. Hot hatch performance with off-road supremacy. It is ridiculously expensive, but there is no other car like it.

LANCIA 8.32

Perhaps the engineer in charge of this project began with a pure heart and was then over-ruled by the marketing department. In essence the body is modified from the standard Thema shell only in its extended front end, with a more vertical grille and a few other, very minor, alterations.

Clearly this was not considered sexy enough, so there is an absurd rear spoiler that pops up at the push of a button on the top of a steering column stalk. Raised or lowered, the perceptible effect on high-speed handling and stability is minimal. It has not been possible yet to carry out a back to back test of maximum speeds to check its effect objectively.

Lancia's identification badges on the car do not exaggerate the Maranello influence, and the only direct reference is to be found in the centre of the induction system cover: 'Lancia by Ferrari'. On the outside of the car there are '8.32' badges at front and rear, the first digit for the number of cylinders, the other two representing the number of valves.

Essentially this engine is the old 308 *quattrovalvole* in slightly detuned form: with a 90-degree crank throw (rather than 180), and alterations to the Bosch KE-jetronic fuel injection, Marelli/Weber digital ignition, and to the valve timing, it puts out 215 bhp at 6,750 rpm (compared with the 308's 240/7,000), but has more torque, 209 lb ft at 4,500 rpm. This indicates how much less 'peaky' the 8.32 is compared with the 308 (192/5,000). In the 8.32, more than 165 lb is available at only 2,500 rpm.

These outputs are well beyond what, only a few years ago, were considered prudent, or indeed even possible, in association with front-wheel drive.

Despite having to haul 3,080 lb off the line, the Lancia accelerates well up to 70 mph or so (the mystically significant 60 mph figure being achieved in 7.2 sec), and then pulls inexorably away up to a top speed of 149 mph, making it the world's most rapid front-wheel-drive car by a wide margin.

The in-gear figures are even better than those of the BMW M3, helped by the same combination of torque spread and lowish gearing: flat out in fifth, the V8 is less than 200 rpm short of its 7,000 rpm red line.

Despite its altered crank throw, the engine still makes a sound more like a high-pitched turbine whine than the characteristic pulsing of a traditional V8. It is a musical collection of sounds, with little whirrings and purrings at low speeds and a muffled scream with the pedal buried into the bulkhead. It might be called refined, but it is hardly quiet.

When trickling around in the lower gears, there is a disappointing degree of wind-up in the transmission, which does not do justice to the qualities of the power unit and makes smooth progress difficult. The rather rubbery, clonky gearchange does not contribute towards serene low-speed progress, either. Once you get moving, though, this is ironed out, throttle response is immaculate, and the inherent unloveliness of the strengthened turbo gearbox less obvious.

The way that the 8.32 delivers power on to the road is surprisingly clean. Floor the throttle from low speed and there is a small degree of torque steer, but it is noticeable only as a background characteristic even on a damp surface.

Squeezing the all-alloy V8 into this bodyshell must have given the engineers a few headaches, but its location just ahead of the front axle line and the use of equal-length driveshafts, combined with a good choice of tyres, have reduced to a minimum the unpleasant tendencies that could be expected. Interestingly, they are relatively skinny for this type of car: 205/55 VR 15 Goodyear Eagles. To this extent the chassis development of the 8.32 is a minor engineering miracle.

However, our test car was a difficult proposition on winding, bumpy roads. The power-assisted steering (a Servotronic system), which is effective in eliminating effort at low speeds, remained unnervingly light at speed and bereft of feel. On turn-in, the body rolled untidily, and the damping was poorly controlled on uneven, badly cambered surfaces, especially under braking. Understeer is persistent, to the degree that vigorous cornering is discouraged: closing the throttle in mid-bend has only a small effect on the car's desire to plough straight on.

If you were to conclude that these problems are the direct effect of lots of power combined with front-wheel drive, you would be mistaken. It is all a question of settings. The 8.32 is biased towards ride quality, and it is indeed very comfortable at moderate speeds.

All 8.32s sold in home markets are fitted with a complex electronic damping control system.

themselves are comfortable, combining well-judged padding with structural strength to ensure satisfactory location. There is no problem with the pedals, which are well spaced for heel-to-toe changes and allow room for the left foot to rest. The steering wheel adjusts for tilt but not reach, the only flaw in an otherwise highly adaptable driving position.

There is an element of over-design in the plague of fiddly markings on the speedometer and rev counter, but there are plenty of minor dials, and the warning displays are well conceived. The stalks are good, too, but the other switches are scattered at random. In particular, the rear window lifters are above the transmission tunnel, while the buttons for the front windows are in the armrests.

This works either manually (push a 'Sport' button and it firms up) or automatically, in response to cornering, acceleration or braking forces. But in that form too, the cornering behaviour remains deeply unsatisfactory.

Admirably comfortable and practical for a high-powered car, the Lancia provides plenty of interior space both in front and rear (to which access is easy), and the generous luggage space is not diminished by the gimmicky spoiler.

It is also very luxurious, almost ostentatiously so, with its wood veneer (which has a matt finish but which remains pleasing to the eye) and its Alcantara leather.

The seat controls are fiddly, and oddly the cushion lifts, but does not tilt. The seats

Powerful, though noisy, on its third and highest setting, the climate control system can warm up the interior rapidly, or keep it pleasantly cool on a hot day, but it is only moderately successful in bi-level mode.

All the potential is there for the 8.32 to be a great car. As tested, it fell well short of fulfilment.

LANCIA 8.32

ENGINE

Cylinders: V8 (90-degree), transverse, front-mounted.
Capacity: 2,927 cc (176 cu in).
Bore/stroke: 81/71 mm (3.19/2.80 in).
Valve gear: dohc per bank, driven by toothed belt, four valves per cylinder.
Compression ratio: 10.5:1.
Fuel system: Bosch KE3-Jetronic injection.
Maximum power: 215 bhp/6,750 rpm.
Maximum torque: 209 lb ft (283 Nm)/4,500 rpm.

TRANSMISSION

Type: 5-speed manual, front-wheel drive.
Mph/kph per 1,000 rpm in top gear: 21.8/351.

SUSPENSION, WHEELS

Front: independent, by MacPherson struts, lower wishbones, coil springs, anti-roll bar.
Rear: independent, by MacPherson struts, coil springs, transverse links, reaction rods, anti-roll bar.

Steering: power-assisted rack and pinion.
Brakes: (Front) ventilated discs/(Rear) ventilated discs, servo assisted, ABS.
Tyres/wheels: front and rear 205/55 VR 15 -6J.

DIMENSIONS

Length: 180.7 in (459 cm).
Width: 69.1 in (175.5 cm).
Height: 56.5 in (143.5 cm).
Wheelbase: 104.7 in (266 cm).
Front/rear track: 58.7/58.3 in (149/148 cm).
Weight: 3,080 lbs (1,397 kg).
Fuel tank: 19.4 gallons (88 litres).

PERFORMANCE

Maximum speed: 149 mph (240 kph).
Acceleration: 0-60 mph (96.5 kph) 7.2 sec, 0-100 mph (161 kph) 16.9 sec.
Fourth gear: 30-50 mph (48-80.5 kph) 5.6 sec.
Fifth gear: 50-70mph (80.5-113 kph) 7.0 sec.
Fuel consumption (average): 23.8 mpg (11.9 litres/100 km).

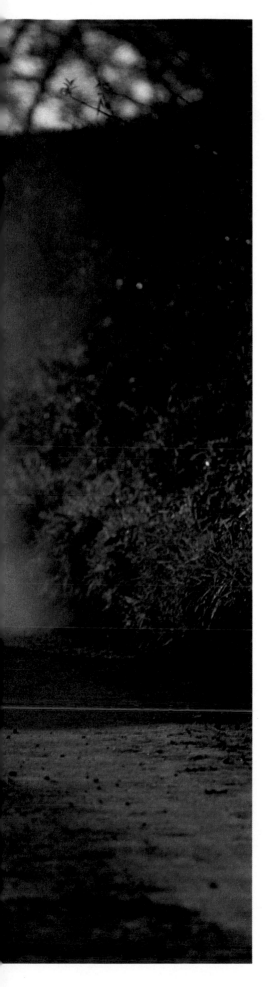

LANCIA DELTA INTEGRALE 16V

This appeared as a derivative of an existing four-wheel-drive performance saloon produced by Lancia, the primary difference being twice as many valves. Lancia have introduced new heads, and so now offer a 16-valve integrale.

This car was intended to boost Lancia's already formidable rally record; the idea was that as soon as the requisite 5,000 production units had rolled off the line, it would become Lancia's front line Group A machine with the maximum permitted 300 bhp output.

With its power output boosted from 185 to 200 bhp, the 16-valve integrale is considerably quicker than the earlier eight-valve version. The revised engine is also far, far smoother. But the downside is that, despite a new turbocharger and revised injection/ignition maps in the engine's electronic control unit, there is a much more noticeable 'step' in the power delivery, which makes this far more obviously a turbo unit than the eight-valve engine.

Unless the revs are kept up above 4,000 rpm, the 16-valve suffers from obvious turbo lag yet, ironically, because of the engine's greater smoothness, it is actually easier to drive at lower

speeds. Part of the reason is the improved torque that the 16-valve offers – 200 lb ft at 3,000 rpm. All in all, the 16-valve integrale is spectacularly fast on the road so long as the gear lever is kept on the move. Lancia's performance figures indicate a 138 mph top speed and 5.7 sec from 0-62 mph.

Among other significant changes and improvements are a redistributed torque split, which is now 47 per cent front/52 per cent rear compared with 56/44 on the eight-valve. More torque to the rear simply improves turn-in still further; the original was never too unwilling to change direction, but this move reduces understeer and increases driving pleasure. While the eight-valve car's tail can be provoked out of line, its basic characteristic lies somewhere between neutral and understeer. The 16-valve, on the other hand, positively relishes a handful of opposite lock when given a dose of throttle overload.

The brakes are upgraded and ABS is now offered as an option. Earlier, Lancia said it was physically impossible to fit ABS to the integrale without reducing the size of the oil cooler and

therefore increasing unreliability. But they seem to have managed it here, presumably without compromising the cooling system, perhaps because the large 7 in rims provide more space while allowing larger 205/50/15 low profile Pirellis to be adopted.

Gearbox ratios have been changed slightly and

a hydraulically controlled clutch has been fitted, so what Lancia offers now is a near perfect set combined with a gear shift that feels rather tricky at first but which, with increased familiarity, allows both fast and fluid changes.

The standard power steering is a model for small cars, and one that other manufacturers

LANCIA DELTA INTEGRALE 16V

ENGINE

Cylinders: harmonically balanced straight 4, transverse, front-mounted.

Capacity: 1,995 cc (120 cu in).

Bore/stroke: 84/90 mm (3.31/3.54 in).

Valve gear: dohc, driven by toothed belt, four valves per cylinder.

Compression ratio: 8.0:1.

Fuel system: IAW-Weber injection, Garrett T3 turbocharger.

Maximum power: 200 bhp/5,500 rpm.

Maximum torque: 224 lb ft (304 Nm)/3,000 rpm.

TRANSMISSION

Type: 5-speed manual, four-wheel drive, Torsen rear differential.

Mph/kph per 1,000 rpm in top gear: 23.4/37.7.

SUSPENSION, WHEELS

Front: independent, by MacPherson struts, lower transverse arms, coil springs, anti-roll bar.

Rear: independent, by MacPherson struts, lower transverse arms, coil springs, anti-roll bar.

Steering: power-assisted rack and pinion.

Brakes: (Front) ventilated discs/(Rear) plain discs,.

Tyres/wheels: front and rear 205/50 VR 15 -7J.

DIMENSIONS

Length: 153.5 in (390 cm).

Width: 66.9 in (170 cm).

Height: 54.3 in (138 cm).

Wheelbase: 97.4 in (247.5 cm).

Front/rear track: 56 1/55 3 in (142 5/140 5 cm).

Weight: 2,755 lbs (1,250 kg).

Fuel tank: 12.5 gallons (57 litres).

PERFORMANCE*

Maximum speed: 138 mph (222 kph).

Acceleration: 0-62 mph (100 kph) 5.7 sec.

Standing km: 26.1 sec.

Fuel consumption (average): 27.8 mpg (10.2 litres/100 km).

*Factory figures

could do worse than to attempt to emulate. It is admirably light at low and parking speeds, but provides plenty of feel at higher rates of progress. The combination of stunning performance, brilliant handling, excellent traction and first rate steering adds up to a near-epic package. But it's flawed.

The front Recaros offer plenty of lateral support, though, despite the myriad possible adjustments, they are still a little too short in the seat to be comfortable over longer journeys. And that is just about the nicest thing it is possible to say about the interior.

The fabric chosen for the seats and door panels is of very questionable taste; the instrumentation is lamentable (most of the tachometer and speedometer are obscure by the driver's hands at ten-to-two) and the secondary controls are weak to say the least. One item of trim on the test car (in the footwell) had fallen off, and there were more than enough squeaks and rattles to infer further problems in the future.

Outside the integrale, things improve considerably. Its lower ride height, low profile tyres and lid bulge which accommodates new air intake grilles add up to an unashamedly aggressive stance. And in case passers-by (or more likely drivers of passed cars) are left in any doubt, there are those little 16v badges to clear up any confusion.

When wallets are taken into account, there can be no better bargain among the current crop of performance cars than the 16-valve integrale. Even at twice the price, there are very few competitors that are quicker, at least up to 100 mph; above that speed its archaic aerodynamics start counting against it, and particularly against its top speed.

Largely academic maximum speed apart, the way in which the Lancia's performance potential can be used is virtually matchless. No other car at the price offers the same raunchy grunt, brilliantly precise steering, rally car balance and poise and almost rocket-like manner of transmitting power into motion. For an enthusiastic driver who wants supercar performance without paying supercar prices, the 16-valve integrale becomes an irresistible choice.

LISTER LE MANS

I f you believe everything you read in the motoring press, then the muscle car is dead. Nobody wants huge powerful motors driving the rear wheels anymore. We all want ceramic multivalve engines turning at hyper rpm and breathing ecologically perfect fumes, driving all four wheels as and when the computer decides that conditions warrant. Maybe somebody should tell the queues patiently waiting for Aston's Virage, or Mercedes's 500SL. Queues of would-be buyers, it should be added, who are willing to pay a considerable sum for what may well be an impractical mode of transport. Among these enthusiasts there are also those who would dearly love to buy British and exciting, but find themselves with a simple choice between Lotus-GM and Aston Ford. Now there is another choice: WPA's Lister Le Mans.

WP Automotive of Leatherhead, Surrey is well-versed in the art of toughening Jaguar's XJ-S boulevard cruiser. This they have been doing for some five years, the last three under the Lister banner. The six-litre and seven-litre versions are well engineered and beautifully finished. The Le Mans, however, is much more radical and represents the culmination of seven years' hard development on the various components, now installed in a shell which, although using Jaguar's sheet metal as a starting point, is so extensively restyled that it deserves to be regarded as a car in its own right, rather than a conversion.

Lister's original brief was to build a car which would seat four people and reach 200 mph, and although the latter has yet to be proved officially, it was the increased passenger space which caused the major problems. Some clever cutting and shutting within the original XJ-S wheelbase has liberated an extra three inches of legroom for the rear passengers, and production models will have deeper, individual bucket seats for each of the rear occupants, sitting them lower to give more headroom. This necessitated a new fuel tank, increased in capacity as well from 18 to 26 gallons, and made to fit behind the seats. This inevitably borrows from the luggage space which also has to accommodate one (10 in x 17 in) front wheel and tyre as a spare, so is rather limited, but the tail did swallow briefcases and overnight gear for four.

The original upright rear window has gone, replaced by one from another much loved British sports car, and the unsightly 'flying buttresses' have also gone the way of the cutting chisel. Larger rear windows are flush fitted which allows much more light into the cabin to add to the feeling of spaciousness. Trim is Connolly leather, which extends to the custom made Recaro front seats, and to the door panels. The suede finish to the dash is an option. Minor styling revisions have still to be made, some tidying round the rear which is rather busy at the moment, but there is no doubting the aggression that positively radiates from the car. From the rear three-quarters it looks like a blend of Ferrari F40 and Aston DB6, and yet the enormously fat 335/35/17 Pirelli P Zeros (designed for the F40) are mounted on 13 in rims with a good deal of inset which prevents them sticking out as much as you might expect. In fact the arches only add

3.5 in per side. Nevertheless, 77.5 in across the haunches is wide for a coupé – about the same as a Testarossa – but just for the record, at 78.9 in, the standard XJ6 saloon is wider than both.

To give some idea of the extent of the work that goes into the Le Mans, only the doors, windscreen glass, front suspension uprights and wishbones, power steering pump and alternator remain unaltered from the XJ-S, and the more you investigate the Lister's construction, the more areas you discover that have been changed, particularly the mechanical specification. In many ways this is more impressive than the overtly aggressive body treatment. The steering rack for instance is a special item which gives 2.3 turns between extremes and a pleasantly meaty weighting – the standard item's unbearable light-ness has been the subject of endless complaints in the press. But the method of mounting has also been revised: Jaguar's original mounts are rubber, designed to insulate from road noise at the expense of ultimate steering accuracy, and the previous solution has been to compress the rubber with washers, and put up with any clatter and kickback.

The Lister's front subframe has been firmly tied into the shell with extra mounting blocks because it was discovered to be flexing with steering inputs, even on standard sized tyres, and the geometry of the front suspension has been altered to remove some of the anti-dive. Dual rate springs do the job instead, appearing at both ends with matching Koni dampers, while the front brakes are four pot alloy calipers squeezing simply massive 13.2 in diameter x 15 in thick ventilated discs borrowed from a Group C World Championship sports racing car. Rear discs are 12.5 x 1 in with specially made AP alloy

calipers. The rear suspension is totally different, as is the gearbox, and a roll cage is built into the shell above the rear seats. It all gives the refreshing impression that much thought has gone into the car's construction and develop-ment.

Leaving aside the chassis and body for the moment, the heart of the car lies in the engine compartment. WPA's seven-litre engine im-presses both by smoothness and its sheer punch. This does not happen by chance. The standard

V12 Jaguar block receives specially made liners which feature Wills sealing rings between top face and cylinder head, while Cosworth supplies race-developed forged pistons. Main bearing caps are steel, as are the connecting rods – made for Lister in the style of the legendary American Carillo – and the crank is machined in-house from a solid steel billet. It takes at least two men to lift this, and the machine to cut it – a Dunbar and Cook no less – was a chance bargain spotted by WPA's Laurence Pearce. It had been used for

LISTER LE MANS

ENGINE

Cylinders: V12 (60-degree), in-line, front-mounted.

Capacity: 6,996 cc (420 cu in).

Bore/stroke: 94/84 mm (3.70/3.31 in).

Valve gear: sohc per bank, chain-driven, 24 valves.

Compression ratio: 11.2:1.

Fuel system: Marelli digital electronic injection.

Maximum power: 496 bhp/6,200 rpm.

Maximum torque: 500 lb ft (369 Nm)/3,850 rpm.

TRANSMISSION

Type: 5-speed manual, rear-wheel drive, limited-slip differential.

Mph/kph per 1,000 rpm in top gear: 33/53.

SUSPENSION, WHEELS

Front: independent, by double wishbones, coil springs, anti-roll bar.

Rear: independent, with driveshafts as upper links, lower wishbones, twin coil springs, anti-roll bar.

Steering: assisted rack and pinion.

Brakes: (Front) ventilated discs/(Rear) plain discs, servo-assisted.

Tyres/wheels: front 245/40 ZR 17 -10J, rear 335/35 ZR 17 - 13J.

DIMENSIONS

Length: 183.7 in (467 cm).

Width: 77.5 in (197 cm).

Height: 47.5 in (121 cm).

Wheelbase: 102 in (259 cm).

Front/rear track: 73.5/76 in (187/193 cm).

Weight: 3,965 lbs (1,798 kg).

Fuel tank: 28.2 gallons (128 litres).

PERFORMANCE

Maximum speed: approx 200 mph, (322 kph).

Acceleration: 0-60 mph (96.5 kph) 5.0 sec, 0-100 mph (161 kph) 11.6 sec.

Fuel consumption (average): 13.8 mpg (20.5 litres/100 km).

making marine engine cranks and drives from both ends of the bed which is apparently desirable in crank cutting. Bore and stroke of the seven-litre are stretched to an oversquare 94 x 84 mm, some way from the original 90 x 70.

The cylinder heads are interesting in that the 'fireball' high (12:1) compression, remote combustion chamber arrangement that appeared on the XJ-S HE, in an attempt to reduce the car's thirst, is not used on the Lister seven-litre. Instead WP Automotive manufactures its own

cylinder heads, using a combustion chamber similar in design to the pre-1980 cylinder head used on the Jaguar V12. Compression ratio is 11.2:1. Ports are flowed and polished, cams are specially made, as are the followers, which operate bigger valves and matching springs.

All this breathes through a specially cast throttle body, fuelled by Marelli digital electronic injection, and the engine develops 496 bhp at 6,200 rpm on Lister's in-house test bed, with no less than 500 lb ft of torque at 3,850 rpm. This latter figure is staggering for a road car: Aston's V8 Vantage can boast 400 bhp at 6,000 rpm with 390 lb ft at 5,000 rpm, the Ferrari F40 a mere 478 bhp at 7,000 rpm and 425 lb ft at 4,000 rpm. Only the Callaway Corvette's twin turbocharged Chevy iron could boast a victory of numbers over the Lister, and only in the stump pulling contest – 562 lb ft at 2,500 rpm.

The specification is mightily impressive, then. Does its performance match up? Unfortunately, the prototype had covered only 250 miles when it came to be tested, and we were unable to performance test the car. We did, however, test the engine in a Lister Mk3 fitted with similar suspension and tyres, and it is those figures which are reproduced here. Forget the zero to 60 mph, and look at 100 mph in 11.6 sec. There are few cars which can match that, and it lifts the seven-litre Listers into the genuine supercar bracket.

Although the power band is wide, and the V12 is happy to trickle smoothly from as little as 1,000 rpm in any gear, the rear axle ratio necessary to reach the coveted 200 mph without over revving the engine adds up to a 33 mph/1,000 rpm final drive, which inevitably blunts the car's ultimate accelerative capability, but does allow relaxed 2,100 rpm cruising at the legal limit. Customers who feel no need to travel at this speed can opt for a lower final drive. There is a manual five-speed Getrag gear box, complete with synchro on reverse, and features Lister modifications in the form of a larger mainshaft, Nitrided gears and an oil pump.

The noise the engine makes is unique. A strange combination of rumble and rasp exhausts from the specially made large bore system, an ursine growl that rips like fabric as the revs rise. There's no V8 rumble or four-cylinder howl, and no hint of individual cylinders working. It is more like a synthesized saxophone, and too loud for some tastes, but customers apparently refuse the additional silencers offered by WPA. There is no point in being shy and retiring when you drive something that looks like this. Inside, the exhaust intrudes but little, and road and wind noise are also commendably restrained despite the wide tyres.

Having 500 bhp at your disposal is all very well, but there is an awful tramping that

threatens to tear all the teeth off the transmission when substantially less than this kind of motivation is poured through the standard rubber-insulated XJ-S suspension. The solution is ingenious. Lister have retained the time-served Jaguar layout where the driveshaft acts as the top suspension transverse link, but added another diagonal rose-jointed link which turns the bottom location into a wishbone. The brakes have been moved outboard into the wheel rims to make room for all this, and the calipers now lie deep inside the inset of the massive rear wheels.

On the road, it works extremely well. Lifting savagely on and off the throttle or braking in a corner has no nasty effect on the car's tail, and there is a minimum of squat under power, combined with excellent traction. The amount of grip is astonishing, even on wet roads. Indeed, on dry tarmac making the Lister do anything but understeer gently is all but impossible. Ride is excellent, perhaps even a little too good – later models may feature slightly stiffer springing to cure a touch of float at higher speeds – but the car still changes direction well, turns in crisply and feels taut and responsive. You can feel drumming from the road a little more without all Jaguar's rubber in the suspension, but it is a small price to pay. The shell, too, was devoid of shakes even over really rough surfaces, although it would pay to be circumspect over speed bumps as ground clearance is fairly limited.

The Le Mans is a carefully conceived package, and the engineering is faultless, as is the quality of the finish and fittings. The styling is a matter of taste – you would have to be prepared to live with the attention that the car creates – but meanwhile orders pour in at an embarrassing rate.

LOTUS ESPRIT TURBO SE

You might have been forgiven for thinking that Lotus had already extracted all there was from its long-serving, four-cylinder engine. After all, 215 was a fair amount of horsepower, and the 153 mph to which it was able to motivate the Esprit was a fair amount of speed. Where is the V8?

Undoubtedly over 200 bhp *is* a lot from 2.2 litres but Lotus needed something more to complement the new smoothed-out, rounded-off Esprit body shape. It really needed to shut down Porsche and Ferrari in the performance stakes if it were to challenge them in the market place, not least because it needed a reason to trumpet the company's increased commitment to reliability and engineering integrity. Lotus could now announce 'the fastest ever unleaded British turbo . . .' and at the same time *quietly* to the press 'and by the way, we sorted out a few problems, while we were about it. . .'

The latest top of the range Esprit Turbo SE is massively quick. It is now faster than the Ferrari 328 (but not the 348), to which the model has always had to give best in the drag race, and faster on top speed and acceleration even than the mighty, musclebound 3.2-litre Porsche turbo with all its 300 bhp. We achieved a genuine 160 mph average in the Lotus, around the Millbrook track's two-mile bowl. From rest to 100 mph in less than 12 sec and to 60 in 4.6 is staggering for a series production road car.

Yet more impressive, and infinitely more useful, is the Esprit's in-gear performance. In fourth gear, the Esprit needs just 3.6 sec to nudge the speedo from 60 to 80 mph. This time would be about halved in third gear. It is the perfect answer to people who repeatedly ask what use there is in a car which can travel at 160 mph. If that kind of acceleration goes with it, there is plenty of use. Overtaking, within the sensible constraints of visibility and good manners, is simply never a problem.

The mind-numbing acceleration comes from a claimed 264 bhp, and the extra 50 is due to fuel injection and the charge cooler which now intrudes between the turbo and the engine's inlet manifold. The charge cooler needs a separate pump to circulate the hot liquid, and another radiator to surrender the accumulated heat back to the air, so it is more complex and expensive than an air-to-air system. It is, however, much more convenient in a mid-engined layout because the charge cooler itself is compact and needs no air ducts, so that the water radiator can be put up at the front with the others.

Cooling the inlet charge allows the engine to develop more power without harmful detonation and Lotus's power output claims may well be modest. Apparently the claimed 264 bhp is developed when the charge temperature entering the engine has stabilized from its post-turbo 140°C (284°F), down to 60°C (140°F), and when the car is travelling at 163 mph – conditions which are readily achievable at the Nardo test facility in Southern Italy, where much of the factory's testing was carried out. In colder climates, and with a charge temperature of about 20 °C (68°F), the power output can be as much as 280 bhp. Optimum boost pressure from the Garret TB03 watercooled turbo is 12.5 psi.

These statistics are yet more impressive still because the engine runs only on unleaded fuel, and has a proper catalyst with a lambda sensor which reports the state of emissions back to the engine management. It is one of the most refined large four cylinder engines anywhere. The rev limit has been increased to no less than 7,400 rpm; and it is easily possible to trip in the limiter without meaning to, so mechanically smoooth is the engine. Unfortunately for the enthusiast, the accompanying noise is hardly music, although nothing like as vocal as the Ferrari 328. The Lotus's four-potted soundtrack is all vintage Cortina piston slap when compared with the 328's Formula One V8 wail. But then listening to the radio's spoken word is at least possible at 100 mph in the Lotus, and in the Italian car it is not. At 100 mph in a 328, conversation is not possible.

General Motors supplied a lot of the electronic know-how that manages the engine's various functions, and there are now six injectors, one per cylinder and two extra in the intake tracts to supply extra fuel for high boost situations. There is a fail-safe ignition system incorporating one double ended coil per two cylinders, and an onboard diagnostic interrogation facility which can relay faults to a service centre. Meanwhile, the whole lot is electronically 'quiet', both on the car and on the radio waves.

The engine is not the only area to have received attention since we tested the first of the new shape Esprits. The suspension has been revised. That car was vastly effective in terms of grip and sheer cornering ability, but the ride was awful, the steering far too heavy and, on the limit, the car was intolerant of mistakes. (The latter is probably still true of Ferrari's 328, but in return that

ESPRIT TURBO SE

car offers such involvement with the driving process that you can forgive it.) The new shape Esprit had even lost most of the sharpness that had characterized the previous Giugiaro folded-paper design, and some of the nothing-shall-compromise-the-driving feel, which made that car a supreme pleasure. Any caprice had been surgically removed for the greater good of the customer. There was no doubting though that the Mk2 Esprit was a much better car overall, more modern and better made.

The SE now wears wider, specially developed Goodycar Eagles, 215/50/15 front and 245/50/16 rear. The suspension changes are designed purely

to cope with the extra grip available, which indeed is truly awesome. But the engineers did also admit that the previous car could have been a little easier to live with. Now the SE sits 10 millimetres higher, has one degree less castor to lighten the steering, has pro- rather than anti-dive suspension geometry at the front with stiffer springs – which has taken out some of the previous car's pitching and improved the ride – and there are now twin tube, low gas-pressure shock absorbers at the rear. All the chassis modifications will be passed on to the non-chargecooled Esprit.

The engineer's work has been supremely

effective. If the SE's forebear was a little difficult at times, it was never slow, yet the chargecooled SE is now so blindingly quick from A to B, and comfortable with it. The ride is taut and the body control superb without any low speed choppiness. The excellent grip tugs at the car through the fast corners, rocking the body on the springs – but it never moves off line. Accelerating harder through a corner needs more steering lock, which can be unwound after easing off. Cornering hard with noticeable understeer may not be the enthusiast's finely balanced ideal, but at least the foot can be kept down all the way through a roundabout; the inside rear lifts and smokes away a little of the excess rather than pushing out the tail. It is very easy, stable and safe, and all done at a surprisingly high speed. To make the car wag its tail is far from easy, requiring tricks like lifting off suddenly in the corner or turning in on the brakes and then hitting the throttle. Catching the result is reasonably easy – the car does a lot of the sorting out for you as long as you leave it alone – but it nevertheless requires a fair degree of physical effort. The Esprit's wheel can still not be twirled at arm's length, and it imparts a curious, springy sensation as the lock goes on, as if the steering only becomes sharp as the lock moves further away from straight-ahead – rather like the BMW

Saloon. The Esprit's helm could never be considered a subtle instrument, but at least it no longer fights back over the bumps . The brakes are unaltered mechanically but feature some specially developed pad material which is cooled by exhausted air from the oil cooler ducts. They are powerful and fade free but grumble when used hard.

There are no significant changes to the interior and it is a pleasant place for fast travel. There is plenty of room for head and legs, for people of average height, and the light and airy cabin is tastefully trimmed in crumpled leather. Air conditioning effectively reverses the effect of a large removable glass roof panel. Dials are small

and clear but the wheel's rim neatly hides half the rev counter, and the pedals are close to the floor and offset to the left. This means pointing the toe to operate the clutch, and operating the brake with a twisted foot, both of which can become tiring. At least there is a rest for the clutch foot, which is welcome.

Much has happened to the Esprit since 1972 and this latest evolution is a serious, up to date contender in Ferrari's corner, if not yet perhaps Porsche's.

But the magic of the original seems still further distant. It is as if the driver is being denied a relationship with something beautiful. The steering is lighter, but there is safe, front-drive style

LOTUS ESPRIT TURBO SE

ENGINE

Cylinders: four in line, in-line, mid-mounted.

Capacity: 2,174 cc (130 cu in).

Bore/stroke: 95.3/76.2 mm (3.75/3.00 in).

Valve gear: dohc, driven by toothed belt, four valves per cylinder.

Compression ratio: 8.0:1.

Fuel system: multi-point injection (integrated with ignition), Garrett TBO3 turbocharger.

Maximum power: 264 bhp/6,500 rpm.

Maximum torque: 261 lb ft (354 Nm)/3,900 rpm.

TRANSMISSION

Type: 5-speed manual, rear-wheel drive.

Mph/kph per 1,000 rpm in top gear: 23.1/37.2.

SUSPENSION, WHEELS

Front: independent, by double wishbones, coil springs, anti-roll bar.

Rear: independent, by upper and lower transverse links, trailing arms, coil springs.

Steering: unassisted rack and pinion.

Brakes: (Front) ventilated disc/(Rear) plain disc, servo assisted.

Tyres/wheels: front 215/50 VR 15 -7J, rear 245/50 VR 16 - 8.5J.

DIMENSIONS

Length: 170.5 in (433 cm).

Width: 73.0 in (185 cm).

Height: 44.8 in (114 cm).

Wheelbase: 96.0 in (244 cm).

Front/rear track: 59.5/60.0 in (151/152 cm).

Weight: 2,957 lbs (1,341 kg).

Fuel tank: 15.4 gallons (70 litres).

PERFORMANCE

Maximum speed: 160 mph (257 kph).

Acceleration: 0–60 mph (96.5 kph) 4.6 sec, 0–100 mph (161 kph) 11.9 sec.

Fourth gear: 30–50 mph (48–80.5 kph) 5.9 sec.

Fifth gear: 50–70mph (80.5–113 kph) 4.4 sec.

Fuel consumption (average): 25.5 mpg (11.1 litres/100 km).

understeer which increases as you push harder. The brakes are more powerful thanks to better friction material and better cooling, but the servo takes away any effort, and much of the feel. The gear change is light and easy, but the play that has crept in between lever and box means there is no satisfaction in a crisp gearchange.

We wanted the SE to have all the tactile pleasure of a Ferrari 328 without the temperament, and to wear a Lotus badge. In the great commercial scheme of things there is no earthly reason why it should. The Esprit SE is probably the best Lotus ever to come out of Norfolk, and it that is what the public wants, then so be it.

SEEING RED

LE IT

TRAILER REPAIRS

South Bramley-Moore
Dock

AMG MERCEDES

HAMMER

You know what to expect from it the moment you twist the key. The shoe-horned V8 thumps into life, shaking and rumbling as it idles. Touch the throttle and the whole car twists in brutal reaction, letting you know that it's not for show.

This is AMG's most potent Mercedes-derived model. The Hammer is a hot-rod based, in this instance, on the mid-range W124 coupé (you can also get it with the four-door saloon body, or even as an estate), but with the original four or six-cylinder engine exchanged for a vigorously tuned version of the big quad-cam V8. There's a choice of three capacities (5.0, 5.6 or 6 litres) to suit your particular fancy, all coupled to modified S-class automatic transmission, though a manual gearbox is available as an option.

Naturally the suspension, wheels, tyres, and brakes are all changed or substantially altered. Even the speedometer is replaced, presumably to avoid 'over-revving' the original. The new one reads to 320 kph! By the time AMG have finished, few Mercedes parts remain apart from the body.

The Germans prefer the Hammer to look completely standard. It is a wickedly fast 'Q-car' (or 'sleeper'), if ever there was one. A whole catalogue of body and interior parts is available if you want some visual enhancement. The version tested here is a wolf in wolf's clothing: a six-litre body-kitted coupé, with 385 bhp and enough torque to pull a house down.

AMG will sell you the parts to build a look-alike for a fraction of the cost, but without the 32-valve V8, it can't be called a Hammer.

Unfortunately, no test track in the UK is suitable to unleash this car's full maximum speed potential, but journalists at *Car and Driver* have timed a similarly equipped AMG at more than 180 mph.

From the outside, the AMG is probably as loud as German regulations allow. The deep-toned decibels hint at what is in store, and the note assumes a hard-edged yowl as the engine climbs on to its four cams. However, this Mercedes is not uncouth. There's a docile side to its make-up: slide the gearbox switch to E (which stands for 'Economy'. . .) and the torque oozes the car along with the rev needle barely above tickover. The throbbing exhaust note recedes to a quiet burble when cruising, aided by gearing set at around 30 mph/1,000 rpm in top. Don't think of this as a cruising gear, though.

The manual gearbox seems an unnecessary extravagance in the Hammer, not only because of the huge reserves of torque: the S-class

The usual huge Mercedes steering wheel has been replaced by a chunky four-spoke AMG wheel. It's a pity, though, that the rim obscures the instruments and you have to search for the horn buttons hidden in the spokes.

The steering could benefit from less assistance – it's too light a touch to guide such a serious missile. Thanks to that mass up front, the AMG runs straight and true. It also steers quickly and accurately. But don't be fooled. This car is a beast, which has to be mastered. You must grab it by the scruff of the neck and show it who's boss, but it needs to be done with a degree of caution.

Contrary to predictions, the Hammer doesn't feel nose-heavy in corners. Rather, it turns in strongly, displaying little stablizing understeer. As you'd expect, its behaviour is dominated by the driver's throttle foot – but even in steady state cornering, the back end feels 'loose' – squirming about over bumps, and tightening the line unexpectedly when you turn the power on or off. In truth it does feel over powered, as if the suspension and tyres are not up to taking the big-gun V8. Gone is the 'user-friendliness' and delicate balance of the standard W124 – replaced by something more ferocious and altogether more demanding. This is a car for the skilled enthusiast capable of taming nearly 400 horse power.

transmission does a masterful job in harnessing so much horsepower so smoothly. There's no jerking even when power-shifting on full throttle, while kickdown is quick and clean. Abort the flow of power, and the gearbox seems to disconnect the drive before softly engaging a higher ratio. Few drivers can shift a manual as capably.

It is possible to select first gear manually (in 'Drive' it is blocked), but be warned: an indiscriminate prod of the accelerator pedal will 'light up' the rear tyres.

At least the braking is up to the job – its purpose-designed system inspires confidence, giving enormous power in return for moderate pedal effort. The wide tyres thud like a machine gun when you drive over cat's eyes – this is the price you must pay for extra grip and steering accuracy, although there is no tendency to 'tram-line'.

The problem with the chassis is that the firm springing makes it feel lumpy at times. Yet oddly there are other occasions when control feels weak. In particular, the back end 'looseness' seems to be induced by insufficient damping. There is room for fine tuning.

The price of the AMG depends on what you started with and what you want to end up with. But since the engine alone costs as much as a BMW M5, it is not difficult to end up with a car costing far more than, for example, a Rolls-Royce Corniche Convertible, not that that car is aimed at the same type of buyer.

The result is a complete transformation of the original vehicle – a six-litre rocket that just happens to reside in a Mercedes bodyshell.

It's an aggressive animal whose handling is on the wild side – perhaps an inevitable consequence of trebling the power. Such a specialized motor cannot offer the value you get when buying an off-the-peg Mercedes, but value considerations have no place in a comparison of absolutes. Some must have the best, the most, the fastest, irrespective of the financial burden. And as long as that is the goal, there can be no substitute for the AMG. What can compare with such an adrenalin-pumping monster?

AMG MERCEDES HAMMER

ENGINE

Cylinders: V8 (90-degree), in-line, front-mounted.

Capacity: 5,953 cc (357 cu in)

Bore/stroke: 100/94.8 mm (3.94/3.73 in)

Valve gear: dohc per bank, chain-driven, four valves per cylinder.

Compression ratio: 9.8:1

Fuel system: Bosch KE-jetronic injection.

Maximum power: 385 bhp/5,500 rpm.

Maximum torque: 417 lb ft (565 Nm) 4,000 rpm.

TRANSMISSION

Type: 4-speed automatic, rear-wheel drive, limited-slip differential.

Mph/kph per 1,000 rpm in top gear: 29.5/47.2

SUSPENSION, WHEELS

Front: independent, by double wishbones, coil springs, anti-roll bar.

Rear: independent, by multi-link system, coil springs, anti-roll bar.

Steering: assisted rack and pinion.

Brakes: (Front) ventilated discs/ (Rear) ventilated discs, servo assisted, ABS.

Tyres/wheels: front and rear 235/45 ZR 17 -8.5J.

DIMENSIONS

Length: 186.5 in (474 cm).

Width: 68.5 in (174 cm).

Height: 56.8 in (144 cm).

Wheelbase: 110.3 in (280 cm).

Front/rear track: 60.6/60.2 in (154/153 cm).

Weight: 3,718 lbs (1,687 kg).

Fuel tank: 15.4 gallons (70 litres).

PERFORMANCE

Maximum speed: 185 mph (298 kph).

Acceleration: 0-60 mph (96.5 kph) 5.0 sec, 0-100 mph (161 kph) 12.6 sec.

Kickdown: 30-50 mph (48-80.5 kph) 2.2 sec, 50-70 mph (80.5-113 kph) 2.7 sec.

MERCEDES 500 SL

The first thing anyone should know about the new Mercedes SL is that it is not a sports car. It is a *sporting* car, large but with only two seats. It is vastly refined, taut and shake-free even in convertible form, but heavy as a consequence. It can be fast; of the three engines available, the new 32-valve V8 version develops 326 bhp, which is enough to propel it to 155 mph, to which speed it is electronically restricted (a common practice among German manufacturers, to demonstrate an environmental sensitivity).

The SL bristles with technology; there are 15 electric motors to operate a hydraulic hood which can be raised or lowered at the touch of a button. No clips or locks need be undone – even the windows are lowered and raised automatically during the operation – or there is an aluminium hardtop, included in the price. An electronically operated screen rises behind the seats which looks like a rollover bar with a hairnet infill but which is actually designed to counter buffeting at speed.

On the 500 SL there is a damping system which measures vertical acceleration of the body, wheel acceleration and angle, speed and overall body roll angle, and then adjusts the damping and the ride height to suit – all in a split-second. A rollover bar pops up automatically if the car begins to turn over, becoming fully erect in 0.3 sec – before the inversion is half complete.

More electronic guardians of the car's safe conduct include a differential lock which works when a driving wheel slips, at the same time backing off the throttle until grip returns.

The bottom of the new SL range is powered by the familiar Mercedes in-line six with its single chain-driven overhead camshaft, developing 190 bhp/192 lb ft of torque, but now with revised combustion chambers for cleaner emissions. The middle option is a 24-valve version of this engine, pushing out 231 bhp/200 lb ft, and featuring variable timing of the inlet camshaft. This appears on the range-topping 32-valve V8 as well, which yields 326 bhp, and 332 lb ft of torque.

We have seen variable timing before: Alfa's excellent Twin Spark two-litre twin-cam employs a similar system, and the idea is that at low speeds the inlet cam is retarded to give smooth running and low emissions, but advances at higher rpm to allow more power to be developed.

All is electronically controlled via the engine's Bosch KE-5 management system, which also monitors engine speed and load, and looks after emissions control, receiving information from a heated oxygen sensor in the exhaust system as well as the normal ignition and refuel functions.

The styling of the new car is clean, devoid of any Japanese gimmickry, and retains the long snout/short tail look of its predecessor, together with a Mercedes corporate appearance. This was a priority to the Germans, but the styling was not permitted to compromise the kinematics. This is apparently the potential for harming pedestrians with the exterior of the car, and the SL is designed to scoop up jaywalkers and roll them over the bonnet with a minimum of harm.

Those inside the car can rest easy too, because

the shell is massively strong – particularly against a three-quarter frontal impact – and much attention has been paid to overall body stiffness in order to eliminate the shakes which cheapen the ride of most open cars. There are even extra steel tubes within the shell, placed to stiffen up critical areas. The penalty of this and all those whirring little motors is that the SL tips the scales at almost 3,900 lbs – but, as with BMW and the Z1, the makers felt that the resultant air of quality was worth the weight.

And then there are the integrated seats. They move electrically every which way, carry the inertia reel for the belt so it is always in the correct restraining position no matter where it is adjusted, move the head restraint for similar reasons, heat up in cold weather, remember where you last adjusted it (along with the exterior mirrors, interior mirror, and steering

column rake and reach). See if you can fool it by shrinking a few inches overnight. All these adjustments may be made separately by touching buttons. In fact, buttons control most things in the SL, including the opening of lockers, glove compartments, all of which are locked centrally when you turn the key in the door. But the car is pleasantly understated despite the plethora of technology.

On the road it was surprising how the different engines affected the feel of the car. The big one is massively fast but there is just a hint of body float at high speeds, especially if rejoining the lane is a bit untidy after an overtaking manoeuvre. Mercedes engineers hinted that there might be a stiffer car for certain markets. The 24-valve six version felt rather more agile, possibly as a consequence of rather less mass in the engine compartment, and proved willing to

rev all day to its 7,000 rpm red line without protest. At the lower end, though, it felt rather leisurely, whereas the basic 12-valve type had these characteristics reversed.

The company has responded to the traditional complaint about the over-large steering wheel, and the diameter of the SL's tiller is reduced by a few millimetres. Unfortunately, its power assistance gives it luxury lightness, the gearing is low, and there is very little feedback.

There is no doubt that this car will be a massive success. It is beautifully finished, full of mostly useful features and it radiates elegant class. It is not a road burner and is not intended to be, but as the first engineering statement from a restructured and revitalized Mercedes-Benz, it is highly impressive.

MERCEDES 500 SL

ENGINE

Cylinders: V8 (90-degree), in-line, front-mounted.
Capacity: 4,973 cc (298 cu in).
Bore/stroke: 96.5/85 mm (3.80/3.35 in).
Valve gear: dohc per bank, chain driven, four valves per cylinder.
Compression ratio: 10.1:1.
Fuel system: Bosch KE5-Jetronic injection.
Maximum power: 326 bhp/5,500 rpm.
Maximum torque: 332 lb ft (460 Nm)/4,000 rpm.

TRANSMISSION

Type: 4-speed automatic, rear-wheel drive.
Mph/kph per 1,000 rpm in top gear: 28.1/45.2.

SUSPENSION, WHEELS

Front: independent, by strut and separate coil spring, lower wishbone, anti-roll bar.
Rear: independent, by multi-link system, coil springs, anti-roll bar, self-levelling.

Steering: power-assisted recirculating ball.
Brakes: (Front) ventilated discs/(Rear) ventilated discs, servo assisted, ABS.
Tyres/wheels: front and rear 225/55 ZR 16 -8J.

DIMENSIONS

Length: 175.8 in (446.5 cm).
Width: 71.3 in (181 cm).
Height: 50.6 in (128.5 cm).
Wheelbase: 99.0 in (251.5 cm).
Front/rear track: 60.2/59.8 in (153/152 cm).
Weight: 3.899 lbs (1,755 kg).
Fuel tank: 17.6 gallons (80 litres).

PERFORMANCE

Maximum speed: 155 mph (249 kph).
Acceleration: 0-60 mph (96.5 kph) 6.4 sec, 0-100 mph (161 kph) 15.0 sec.
Kickdown: 30-50 mph (48-80.5 kph) 2.2 sec.
Fifth gear: 50-70mph (80.5-113 kph) 3.0 sec.

MVS VENTURI

In the increasingly rare case of the small-scale car manufacturer, it is all too easy to be kind. He is usually a well-meaning enthusiast, fired with dedication to his brainchild, for which one is tempted to suspect critical objectivity. Cholet in central France is home of MVS. The preconception in this case is that here would be a car with performance and handling in abundance, a half-finished interior, rudimentary heating and ventilation, and a generous sprinkling of kit car Achilles heel that means the thing will be impossible to live with.

The basis of the Venturi is a sheet-steel tub chassis based around a Lotus/GTA-style central backbone, but with the outriggers and body mounting points extending much further, and with spaces panelled in steel. The plastic parts constitute much less of the basic structure than in some cars, which means that the end result is likely to be stronger but more laborious to produce. The chassis assembly is extensively rustproofed before the body is bonded on, which then forms a rigid monocoque, with a roll cage integral within the roof, as in the Esprit. Bodyshells are only available as a complete unit together with the chassis, which is the case in most modern saloons, although certain damaged parts can be replaced by the factory.

The Venturi uses the complete engine and transmission from Renault's 25 turbo. Because the 25 drives via the front wheels with engine in line ahead of the gearbox, the whole assembly can be slotted directly in the back of the MVS to place the engine in the middle and the gearbox behind.

The rear suspension of the Venturi is pure race car with MVS pattern cast uprights, transverse links – two lower and one upper – and four forward-facing radius rods. Attention to detail is already evident at this stage and where uniball joints have been used in place of rubber bushes they are properly protected by moulded rubber gaiters. At the front, there are twin wishbones supporting MVS aluminium uprights, and Konis are used all round to damp the coil springs.

So there is a stiff steel and fibre shell, with geometrically pure but costly multi-link suspension instead of the semi-trailing arms and struts which are almost universal. The engine is in the ideal low-polar moment position, and drives through a transaxle and double-jointed half shafts. There are large ventilated front discs and solid rear ones, all outboard, and all this sits on a set of MVS-designed Dial aluminium wheels with Michelin MXX tyres (205/55 ZR 16 front, 245/45 ZR 16 rear). But does it all work, or is it like so many attempts at racers for the road, for weekends and short journeys only?

The Renault package bolted into a subframe in the MVS is predictably untemperamental; unsurprisingly it sounds just like the GTA, and the gear change feels just like that of the old Lotus Esprit, with a weight of steel rods complicating the shift on its way to the box.

Shaped in the St Cyr wind tunnel by aerodynamicist Robert Choulet, the MVS has a drag coefficient of 0.31. The steering is pin sharp. The

MVS VENTURI

ENGINE

Cylinders: V6 (90-degree), in-line, mid-mounted.

Capacity: 2,458 cc (147.5 cu in).

Bore/stroke: 91/63 mm (3.58/2.48 in).

Valve gear: sohc per bank, chain-driven, two valves per cylinder.

Compression ratio: 8.0:1.

Fuel system: A.E.I. Renix electronic injection, Garrett T3 turbocharger.

Maximum power: 200 bhp/5,750 rpm.

Maximum torque: 214 lb ft (290 Nm)/2,500 rpm.

TRANSMISSION

Type: 5-speed manual, rear-wheel drive.

Mph/kph per 1,000 rpm in top gear: 24.9/40.1.

SUSPENSION, WHEELS

Front: independent, by double wishbones, coil springs, anti-roll bar.

Rear: independent, by two lower and one upper transverse links, trailing arms, coil springs, anti-roll bar.

Steering: power-assisted rack and pinion.

Brakes: (Front) ventilated discs/(Rear) ventilated discs, servo assisted.

Tyres/wheels: front 205/55 VR 16 -7J, rear 245/45 VR 16 - 8.5J.

DIMENSIONS

Length: 161.0 in (409 cm).

Width: 66.9 in (170 cm).

Height: 46.1 in (117 cm).

Wheelbase: 94.5 in (240 cm).

Front/rear track: 57.4/57.9 in (146/147 cm).

Weight: 2,756 lbs (1,255 kg).

Fuel tank: gallons (90 litres).

PERFORMANCE

Maximum speed: 152 mph (245 kph).

Acceleration: 0-62 mph (100 kph) 6.9 sec.

Standing km: 26.8 sec.

Fuel consumption (average): 24.0 mpg (11.8 litres/100 km).

turn-in to corners is as immediate as only a good mid-engined car's can be, sharper even than a Lotus or 328 Ferrari. There is no roll to speak of, no waiting for the suspension to soak up some of the body lean, and no aftermath of weight transfer as the rear of the car sways behind. Every move of the wheel is faithfully translated as a move of the nose. It really feels telepathic and because all the masses, including the passengers, are well within a 95 in wheelbase, there iss that superb feeling of the wheel as an extension of the arms. Such agility would be dangerous if there was any tail-happy oversteer lurking, but the MVS can ultimately only be provoked by entering a corner too fast on a trailing throttle and then booting it while the car is unbalanced. Even then this is not caused by rubber bushes squidging about and altering the suspension geometry, which is what occurs with trailing arms. Otherwise, the predominant characteristic is neutrality until you are going extemely fast, then understeer increases and the nose begins to run wide. Relax the throttle and it returns to line. The car's grip is simply enormous – easily in the Lotus class but with better balance; enough to pin you hard against the door when you start trying.

There is a catch, however. The steering is far too light for this kind of response. There is speed-sensitive electronic assistance, and although you can take your hands off the wheel at high speed on a bumpy road and the car will track perfectly straight, resting the hands on the rim at the recommended ten-to-two seems to make

the car wander. There *is* feel there, but not enough.

The Renault V6 is much smoother than it once was. Since the engine is completely unaltered from standard it unfortunately follows that the turbo lag which spoils the GTA and 25 comes with it. There's no such lag on the 5 and 11 turbos, so Renault is capable of extinguishing it. Performance of the Venturi is similar to the GTA's which means a claimed top speed of 152 mph and acceleration from rest to 62 mph in 6.9 sec, to 100 in 17.1 sec. That is quick without being startling; it is marginally more impressive in fifth gear, taking a claimed 9.1 sec to go from 80 to 120 kph. The chassis could easily handle more power, such as the factory-supplied, 280 bhp package for the Europa Cup, one-make, GTA circuit racing series.

The electrically adjustable seats easily accommodate two big people although they lacked a little sideways support. The instruments are easy to read, reasonably sized and attractively mounted in a wood dash which would not be out of place in an Aston or Jaguar. The car is quiet with little contribution from wind or road and, as the sun beams into a small cockpit, the (standard) air conditioning chills the interior with welcome speed.

Now for a closer look at the interior. Here is a French car with not the slightest suspicion of grey plastic anywhere inside. The all-leather coverings are made in-house, and beautifully stitched and stretched over nicely fashioned mouldings. The quality of the interior finish is more German than French, and the ambience was somewhere between Jaguar and Audi, traditional yet understated, and so very well finished.

We were able to try the car on a wet road, and it kept up its hitherto well mannered behaviour. Noteworthy, and welcome too, was the huge Mercedes-style Bosch wiper which lengthens while it sweeps in order to clear the extremities of the screen (borrowed, incidentally, as are the side windows, from the Renault Fuego). Heating, ventilation, wiping: all the sort of details that could let down a small-volume operation, but not in this case.

The styling we have left until last. The work of Gerard Godfroy, it may be a little thick in the midriff for some. Perhaps a two-tone paint job might lighten the car a little; a trick used by Tom Walkinshaw's men to tackle the same problem on the XJS. Otherwise, the MVS is remarkably uncluttered, smooth and simple of line. It also looks smaller than it really is. Most of the width of the wheels (7.5 in front and 9 in rear) is inset, which tidies the appearance yet further. As usual though, styling is a subjective matter.

The Venturi's standard equipment list is impressive indeed. It comes with electric windows, seats and mirrors, air conditioning, leather trim, central locking with remote 'plip' and alarm, tinted glass and stereo radio/cassette. It can be painted (by hand) in any one of 18 different colours (more by arrangement) and you can choose from no fewer than 25 shades of hide for the interior.

This is undoubtedly a serious car. We travelled far and fast enough in it to have uncovered any dynamic or practical flaws if there were any. It is extremely well finished, and never once did we hear a squeak or rattle from anywhere. It makes use of simple, readily available mechanical components, and dynamically it is the equal of the very best on the road. Somewhere between the response and balance of a 328 without the slight underlying nervousness, and with the outright grip of a Lotus and the comfortable ride of the GTA. The steering does need improvement though. The only disappointment was that it just didn't feel quick enough.

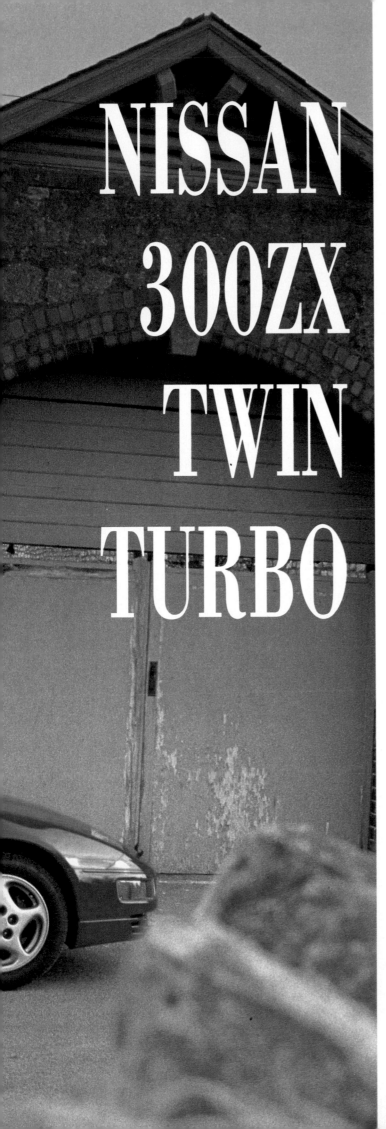

NISSAN 300ZX TWIN TURBO

Watch Nissan. After more than a decade of producing some of the world's duller cars, there is a new spirit at Japan's number two motor manufacturer. We saw the first signs of it at the Tokyo show in 1987, when Nissan produced a stunning array of concept models, including the Mid-4 supercar. President Yutaka Kume told us then that they represented Nissan's future: 'We have a new generation of young designers and we have given them their head. We need to attract younger customers, to change our image.'

That is beginning to happen. Look at the 200SX, widely considered to be among the best of the latest crop of middleweight coupés. In America, the 4.5-litre V8 Infiniti saloon promises to set a new standard for value in the Jaguar/Mercedes class. And this from a company that has never previously made a decent big car. Why, even the Maxima is getting good notices.

Where Nissan have been on top in the past is in the real sports car market. The Datsun 240Z entered the US market some 20 years ago, with its fusion of E-Type style and Porsche size and performance for just $3,500. It spelled the end of Britain's traditional two-seaters.

In terms of sales, Nissan's Z-car is the most successful sports car in history; nearly a million have been sold in the United States alone. But the car itself did not improve with age. The 260 and 280Zs had larger engines only to compensate for increasingly stringent US emissions regulations. The second generation ZX was fat and bloated compared to the original; a gadget-laden boulevard cruiser rather than a sports car. Fitting that with a strong, optionally turbocharged, three-litre V6 engine, to create the 300ZX, pushed the emphasis back to performance, but the car still felt clumsy.

We hoped for an all-new Z that would return to the principles of the original – a proper modern sports car. For a while the Mid-4 looked likely to show the way but now its future is uncertain. Enter in its place a new front-engined/rear-drive 300ZX – same name but a very different car from its predecessor. Shorter overall but longer in wheelbase, with a completely new body and chassis. And it is terrific. The only thing that stops this new model making the impact of the original 240Z is its price which puts it in a different sector of the market. To justify that it has to be as good as, or better than, a Porsche 944. No previous ZX could make that claim. The new one can. We gave a normally aspirated five-speed 300ZX a thorough work-out on the back roads of Michigan. Our conclusion was that this is a car which sits between the 944 and 928 in performance and ability, feels and looks more modern than both, and in most respects

Accelerating hard, there is a sporting growl in the engine's note, but otherwise only tyre roar disturbs the peace in the well-insulated cabin.

Given its readiness to go fast, it is just as well that the chassis is up to the task. It has multi-link suspension front and rear. At the back, the four-link set-up is much as the 200SX. The front suspension resembles the Honda Accord's distorted double wishbone layout, but with an extra link to control toe-in and camber changes during suspension movement.

The adjustable dampers of the earlier 300ZX have gone, but the compromise on the new one is better than that was in any phase. The ride is firm but generally comfortable, perhaps a little more so than a 944's.

On the basis of road, rather than test track, experience, we would say that it has handling balance that matches the Porsche's exemplary poise. Most of the time it feels taut and neutral, aided by nicely weighted, quick steering (which has a particularly sophisticated form of variable, speed-related, power assistance). There is plenty of grip from fat, low profile 225/50 VR16 Michelin Sport XGTV tyres – it has recorded 0.9 g on the skid pan. If you still find yourself approaching a corner too fast it understeers, though lifting off brings it

matches the driver-oriented design and fine build quality of the German cars.

Only the engine is related to what has gone before. The three-litre VG30 V6 now has four camshafts and 24 valves, variable valve timing and 'direct ignition' which, like the Saab Turbo system, provides a separate coil for each sparking plug and is controlled by the electronic engine management computer. It develops 222 bhp at 6,400 rpm and 274 lb ft of torque at 3,600 rpm; the variable valve timing is intended to improve low and medium-range torque. The power output, with three-way catalyst, is only a couple of bhp short of the previous two-valves-per-cylinder 300ZX Turbo. The normally aspirated car is good for 143 mph and 0–60 mph in 6.7 sec. The 300ZX Turbo will be speed limited to 155 mph.

From the driving seat the speed is deceptive. Because the engine is sweet and smooth, and this regular version has no 'step' into turbo boost, it is easy to find yourself going faster than intended.

NISSAN 300ZX TWIN TURBO

ENGINE

Cylinders: V6 (60-degree), in-line, front-mounted.

Capacity: 2,960 cc (178 cu in).

Bore/stroke: 87/83 mm (3.43/3.27 in).

Valve gear: dohc per bank, driven by toothed belt, four valves per cylinder.

Compression ratio: 10.5:1.

Fuel system: electronic sequential injection.

Maximum power: 222 bhp/6,400 rpm.

Maximum torque: 274 lb ft (372 Nm)/3,600 rpm.

TRANSMISSION

Type: 5-speed manual (4-speed automatic available), rear-wheel drive, limited-slip differential (viscous coupling).

Mph/kph per 1,000 rpm in top gear: 23.4/37.7.

SUSPENSION, WHEELS

Front: independent, multi-link, coil springs, anti-roll bar.

Rear: independent, multi-link, coil springs, anti-roll bar.

Steering: power-assisted rack and pinion.

Brakes: (Front) ventilated discs/(Rear) ventilated discs, servo assisted.

Tyres/wheels: front and rear, 225/50 VR 16 - 7.5J.

DIMENSIONS

Length: 169.5 in (431 cm).

Width: 70.5 in (179 cm).

Height: 49.2 in (125 cm).

Wheelbase: 96.5 in (245 cm).

Front/rear track: 58.9/60.4 in (150/153 cm).

Weight: 3,214 lbs (1,460 kg).

Fuel tank: 15.4 gallons (70 litres).

PERFORMANCE

Maximum speed: 143 mph (230 kph).

Acceleration: 0-60 mph (96.5 kph) 6.7 sec, 0-100 mph (161 kph) 18.6 sec.

Fuel consumption (average): 21.7 mpg (13 litres/100 km).

---

safely back into line. A viscous coupling limited slip differential is standard.

The brakes are ventilated discs all round with beefy four-piston calipers, visible, Porsche 959-style, through narrow-spoked alloy wheels. ABS is standard, and while we have no complaint about the braking performance, the pedal could be more communicative.

The new Nissan is a wider, more bulky and heavier car than the 944, and on narrower roads that will compromise its agility to some extent. It is only 1.5 in narrower than a six-foot 928 and feels it; strongly curved sides and an enormous, angled screen makes it difficult to place precisely. There is a lot of glass which makes for a light, spacious cabin but some aspects of driver visibility – rear quarters particularly – are not good.

However, the style and furnishings of the interior are superb. It takes the 'cockpit' ideal of the Porsche 928 a stage further, with driver and passenger seated in smoothly sculpted elliptical cut-outs, completely surrounded by heavy tweed trim. There is also something of the 928 about the instrument binnacle, though it isn't adjustable like the Porsche's. Generous seat adjustments will suit everyone (provided that the passenger does not want to recline into a sleeping position), the instruments are clear, conventional analogue, and all the controls are well placed. They operate sweetly too, with the kind of light effort one associates with small Japanese hatchbacks. The seat belts are housed in the trailing edges of the doors, Starion-style, and designed to be left buckled up to meet America's passive safety regulations; fortunately they can be released and used normally.

This wrap-round interior is very pleasing and made more so by the lack of wind noise. That is surprising given that the side windows are long and curved, have no exterior frame, and seal against the removable roof panels (the T-bar roof is the only version sold in the USA). The glass panels fit and remove easily but, despite black screen printing, are annoying when fixed on a bright sunny day and, if removed, the wind blows noisily and directly into the driver's ear. The side windows use the Audi system of concealed guide rails which with the windows and their black shadowing (more screen printing) wound down leaves a rather unsightly piece of track standing alone on the door, alongside the B-pillar.

The rear hatch is hinged from the B-pillar but does not extend very deeply so that there is neither much room nor easy access for heavy luggage. The space between the rear suspension turrets is arranged as a kind of raised tray, more easily reached from inside the car.

This version provided no possibility of sitting or even perching in the rear compartment but, as before, there is a 2 plus 2 version. It is 8.5 in longer, but, at a glance, almost indistinguishable from the two seater.

There is no chance of mistaking the new 300ZX for anything else, though. Judging by the reaction of other drivers in and around Detroit, the style is a hit. The opalescent yellow paint of the car we drove may have been the reason, but there is no doubt that this is a spectacular, almost futuristic-looking car. Everyone seems to approve of the profile, with the short engine lid taking maximum advantage of the compact V6 engine. The fish-like front, with its curious slit headlamps, is more controversial.

The boldly curved roof and side window line are straight from the ARC-X show car exhibited at Tokyo in 1987. Mr Kume's promise is being fulfilled: watch out, Nissan is fighting back. This new 300ZX is its front line weapon.

PANTHER SOLO

At the 1987 Frankfurt Motor Show, two specialist sports car manufacturers displayed prototypes which they tried to promote (as much to themselves as to the press and public) as saleable motor cars.

Sadly, Walter Treser's brave gamble ended in bankruptcy, but here in virtual production form is the Panther Solo – not the pretty and promising Solo shown in 1984 at the Birmingham Show. This one is based upon the very different Frankfurt Show prototype (then called Solo 2), which was predicted to go on sale by the middle of 1988. In engineering terms it is the same.

It has a composite 'survival cell' consisting of the roof, screen and door apertures bonded and fastened to a steel monocoque under-body. It is powered by the four-cylinder, 1,993 cc, 204 bhp Ford Cosworth Turbo engine, centrally mounted at an angle to the longitudinal axis. Transmission, via a Borg Warner T5 five-speed manual gearbox, is by a permanent four-wheel drive system devised by the small design and engineering company, Ramar. March Engineering also played a significant part in early development. The torque split gives 34 per cent to the front wheels, and 66 per cent to the rears; suspension is by MacPherson struts at the front, with wishbones at the rear.

Early on in our brief drive the car was reluctant to turn into corners, the unassisted rack and pinion steering felt too heavy on the initial movement into a curve, and then there was pronounced understeer. Easing throttle pressure would bring the car back into line, never actually into oversteer (though that could probably be induced on a test track).

The Solo sits on Goodyear Eagles, 195/50 VR15 at the front and 205/50 VR15 at the rear. The car was apparently supplied with 23 psi in the fronts and 27 in the rears. With the tyres warm, a forecourt pump suggested the fronts contained 26 psi so we raised them to 28. Who knows what the true figures might be.

This had the effect of lightening the steering on initial turn-in, and reducing the understeer, though this was still predominant

It seemed that there was a small penalty to be paid in low-speed ride quality but the chassis is basically very sound, with what seems to be an excellent combination of spring and damper rates.

All that is needed is fine tuning, and Panther would not be the first or the largest manufacturer to have erred on the side of understeer in order to avoid hassles from frivolous litigants. Solo buyers should adjust pressures in stages until the desired balance is achieved.

Without taking performance figures it is hard to judge exactly how fast the Solo is. Apparently it has pulled more than 150 mph at the Millbrook circuit, where tyre scrub removes a few digits, while 0-60 mph on the test track will take just under 6 sec. The Solo has the type of engine which needs the throttle buried in the floor to extract the best from it. But it does have a chassis which makes it feel as if it is going more slowly than is the case.

The difficulty in driving such a car is brought about by the combination of very high levels of grip with a relatively narrow usable rev band, and it is easy to drop into the 'turbo lag' zone, especially on unknown roads.

Gear change quality has been tuned towards a relatively stiff compromise which requires a bit of getting used to, but it is precise and quick, if almost notchy. The brakes (discs all round, ventilated at the front) seem powerful enough, though they whiff a bit if you give them some serious work to do. In testing on dry roads, the ABS system was not needed. The single most impressive quality of the Solo is that although it hardly rolls at all and pitch and squat have almost been eliminated, it nevertheless gives acceptable ride comfort: not in the Jaguar class, but not bad for a sports car.

Though the driving position is not perfect for a tall driver, there is room for adjustments to be made to suit individual customers – moving the seat runners further back, for example. This, together with relocating the clutch foot rest, would make long journeys easier. Incidentally, with a claimed torsional rigidity of 10,000 lb ft per degree (compared with 2,700 for the TR7,

though that was hardly a paragon), the Solo should be as safe a car as any in which to have a crash.

The driving position is generally well devised, with a sound arrangement of the major controls, the only minor drawback being one which afflicts all mid-engined cars: intrusion of the front wheel arches makes the pedals – which are well spaced – offset to the centre of the car. The seats are padded enough to hold the driver in place when cornering.

It is a refreshing change to find a car which does not have orange markings on a black background with red backlighting. The Solo's black-on-grey dials are conventional except that the rev counter is dominant and enormous. All switches and stalks and the door handles and locks are of Ford origin, and none the worse for that. On a warm day, the ventilation was no great help, but air conditioning is available at extra cost.

The main problem with the car is internal noise: there is almost a complete absence of wind roar, and the level of road noise is acceptable, but the engine is boomy, especially at high revs; and it needs to be revved hard for the performance to be fully exploited.

Visibility is not actually as bad as might be expected: there are some saloons which are harder to ease out of angled junctions, but reversing is very difficult because of the high rear deck. Luggage space is restricted; you can either have vestigial rear seats, or zip-up 'bins'. There is no room under the front lid.

In two years Panther has produced from a blank sheet of paper, an entirely new, modern sports car incorporating the latest technology and copying nothing which already exists. The company also moved factory (from Brooklands

to Harlow New Town) and most of the workforce changed, but all through this its other product, the very different Kallista, remained in production and will do for the forseeable future.

It is wrong to consider the original, short-wheelbase Solo as part of the present car's development. It was a pretty and interesting design exercise which was sadly killed off at birth by the appearance of the Toyota MR2.

The Solo as it is now bears virtually no relationship to that car, in its driveline, chassis or body. It is a good deal larger, but still, at 171 in, not a very long car, 8 in shorter than the Esprit, for example, but its 95.5 in wheelcase is only half an inch shorter and it is a cigarette pack narrower at 70.5 in.

The strongest single link between the two Solos is the designer Ken Greenley (whose partner John Heffernan designed the Virage for Aston Martin). Ken was hired by the Korean businessman Young C Kim, who then owned Panther, and he created both the Solos.

Mr Kim still owns 20 per cent of Panther (the other 80 per cent is owned by the Korean company Ssangyong, represented by Mr B U Kim, who is no relation), but no longer plays an active role in the running of Panther.

Unlike most designers, Greenley has not simply handed over the drawings, taken his fee, and moved on. 'It's become a bit of an obsession', he confesses. He is now a part of the Panther Car Company, with a finanical stake in the success of his project. He reports directly to managing director Mike Newman, who was also appointed by Y C Kim. Greenley and chief engineer Phil Gillott are the two men chiefly responsible for the development of the car.

There is no single factor which determines the success or failure of a sports car: a blend of

qualities is required. The Solo seems to have the performance, and holds the road and handles well, and does not ride too harshly. It has an unusual combination of leather, suede and composites in the attractively designed interior.

Beauty is subjective, but the important thing is that the car has as much 'presence' on the road as a Countach. Schoolgirls pout, and knowing schoolboys say, 'Oh look, it's the new Lotus Elan'. It is also one thing which a sports car needs to be these days: 'exclusive'. Panther hopes that does not mean the volume will be *too* low, but the decision to make a marketing point of the chassis numbers is clever: each car is individually numbered.

Mike Newman has taken a conscious decision to limit production to around 300 cars per year (100 of them in the UK); there are no plans to sell the car in the USA. This is half the original sales target. There will be no dealer network, and purchasing the Solo directly from the factory, it is hoped, will add a touch of personal service. Routine maintenance can be carried out by Ford RS dealers.

The Solo's major drawback is the interior noise level. The chief question is whether potential purchasers will consider the car to be in the same league as an Esprit Turbo (never mind Porsche 911 Club Sport), and worth the asking price. Cars as good as this have failed; worse ones have sold in reasonable numbers.

PANTHER SOLO

ENGINE

Cylinders: four in line, angled, mid-mounted.
Capacity: 1,993 cc (120 cu in).
Bore/stroke: 90.8/77 mm (3.57/3.03 in).
Valve gear: dohc, driven by toothed belt, four valves per cylinder.
Compression ratio: 8.0:1.
Fuel system: Weber-Marelli electronic injection, Garrett T31/TO4 turbocharger.
Maximum power: 204 bhp/6,000 rpm.
Maximum torque: 204 lb ft (276 Nm)/4,500 rpm.

TRANSMISSION

Type: 5-speed manual, 4-wheel drive.
Mph/kph per 1,000 rpm in top gear: 26.4/42.4.

SUSPENSION, WHEELS

Front: independent, by MacPherson struts, coil springs, anti-roll bar.
Rear: independent, by double wishbones, coil springs, anti-roll bar.
Steering: unassisted rack and pinion.
Brakes: (Front) ventilated discs/(Rear) plain discs, servo assisted, ABS.
Tyres/wheels: front 195/50 VR 15 -J, rear 205/50 - J.

DIMENSIONS

Length: 171 in (434.5 cm).
Width: 70.5 in (178 cm).
Height: 46.5 in (118 cm).
Wheelbase: 95.5 in (253 cm).
Front/rear track: 60.2/59.6 in (153/151.5 cm).
Weight: 2,430 lbs (1,100 kg).
Fuel tank: 12.5 gallons (57 litres).

PERFORMANCE

Maximum speed: 150 mph (241 kph).
Acceleration: 0-60 mph (96.5 kph) 5.7 sec.
Fuel consumption (average): 26.9 mpg (10.5 litres/100 km).

PLYMOUTH LASER

For many years Europeans were derisive about American cars, but the simple truth is that domestic US produced cars were ideally suited to American road conditions, and petrol is *still* only 95 cents per US gallon. No need for high-revving multivalvers here. Stick on the smog equipment and up the capacity to drive the air conditioning. The Japanese changed all that. They made the buyer feel cheated if he or she settled for a lesser amount of technology than was available – whether or not it was actually usable. It was there and available

for the same price. Not only that, they started building them on American soil . . .

Chrysler has a greater image problem than Ford, and after a financial crisis, reconstruction and painstaking return to profitibility, it found that greater collaboration with the Japanese was the only route to instant hi-tech. Thus Diamond

Star Motors was born, a Japanese American conglomerate which would between them produce a hi-tech range. The first products of this union are the Mitsubishi Eclipse and the Plymouth Laser, two cars identical in all but a few cosmetic respects, and yet, curiously enough sold in America under both badges.

The basis of this very attractive 2 plus 2 coupé

is a shortened Mitsubishi Galant floorplan and mechanicals, including a twin balancer shaft, two-litre, 16-valve turbocharged engine. Mitsubishi also designed the ever-so-slightly flashy interior, but Chrysler claims credit for the striking concept-car exterior shape. This space-age look, taking the current tail in the air fashion typified by Toyota's Celica one stage further, with just a hint of the Mitsubishi flying poached egg, record-breaking two-litre concept car. The Cd figure for the Laser is 0.33, while the only exterior body difference between Laser and Eclipse is the latter's tail spoiler, which drops its wearer's Cd figure to 0.29. Also something of a prerequisite on modern sport cars are big wheels; those on the Laser are 6 in inches wide, 16 in in diameter, wearing 205/55 Goodyear Eagles, all of which adds a distinct touch of racer to the futuristic look.

The balancer engine is a very good piece of engineering by Mitsubishi, and in the Laser it pokes out 190 bhp at 6,000 rpm, and 203 lb ft of torque at 3,000 rpm; this is 10 bhp or so short of the European Ford Sierra and Sapphire RS with similar torque but creamy, smooth and quiet all the way to a 7,000 rpm red line – beyond if necessary. By comparison the Ford feels positively vintage. The Laser's Mitsubishi built turbo is well matched to the engine, starting to blow in earnest from 2,000 rpm while the inevitable lag

is minimal. The Laser is quick too: top speed is 143 mph, and the 60 mph drag takes just 6.6 sec; 100 mph from zero occupies 18.5. Front-drive traction predictably takes a toll here. The gear shift is light, accurate and easy, with a typically Mitsubishi remote, clonky action.

The chassis has a distinct Mitsubishi flavour. It is highly competent, but not very alive, and gives minimal feedback to the driver. The car's turn-in is sharp enough, but the steering is far too light to have any real feel while over rough roads the front damping can find itself out of phase with the rear. Unleashing the considerable power produces a slight restlessness at the

wheel's rim – by no means disturbing – while cornering in the same state can suddenly find the inside wheel spinning and the revs soaring away. Torque steer, even on wet roads, is minimal – much better than say, an Escort turbo, because however heavy the foot, generally, the car stays on line. Only a severe dip under one wheel will have the car really diving about, but this should be a rare occurrence.

These characteristics having been duly noted, it must be said that the car is enormous fun. Its little foibles help to put back much of the sparkle that the Orientals love to exorcize. It has lots of grip, is enormously quick, has a neatly laid out,

if rather small Oriental grey velour cockpit, a stylish, easily read facia with big dials and it cuts a striking image in the car park. Perhaps it shows a legacy of its committee design procedure, a struggle between ideologies which, ironically, has avoided the sterilization of a great little car. Whatever, it knocks spots off such as the Escort RS turbo or Mazda 323 turbo 16. And best of all, it is amazingly cheap for a 143 mph car.

PLYMOUTH LASER

ENGINE

Cylinders: four in-line/front-mounted.

Capacity: 1,997 cc (120 cu in).

Bore/stroke: 85/88 mm (3.35/3.46 in).

Valve gear: dohc, driven by toothed belt, four valves per cylinder.

Compression ratio: 7.8:1.

Fuel system: electronic injection integrated with engine management, Mitsubishi TD05H turbocharger, air/air intercooler.

Maximum power: 190 bhp/6,000 rpm.

Maximum torque: 203 lb ft (407 Nm)/3,000 rpm.

TRANSMISSION

Type: 5-speed manual, front-wheel drive.

Mph/kph per 1,000 rpm in top gear: 23.4/37.6.

SUSPENSION, WHEELS

Front: independent, by MacPherson struts, lower wishbones, coil springs, anti-roll bar.

Rear: torsion beam axle, trailing arms, Panhard rod, coil springs, anti-roll bar.

Steering: assisted rack and pinion.

Brakes: (Front) ventilated discs/(Rear) plain discs, servo assisted.

Tyres/wheels: front and rear 205/55 VR 16 -6J.

DIMENSIONS

Length: 170.5 in (433 cm).

Width: 66.5 in (169 cm).

Height: 51.6 in (131 cm).

Wheelbase: 97.2 in (247 cm).

Front/rear track: 57.7/57.1 in (146.5/145 cm).

Weight: 2,677 lbs (1,215 kg).

Fuel tank: 13.2 gallons (60 litres).

PERFORMANCE*

Maximum speed: 143 mph (230 kph).

Acceleration: 0–60 mph (96.5 kph) 6.6 sec, 0–100 mph (161 kph) 18.5 sec.

Fifth gear: 30–50 mph (48–80.5 kph) 11.0 sec, 50–70 mph (80.5–113 kph) 8.5 sec.

Fuel consumption (average): 20.9 mpg (13.5 litres/100 km).

*Factory figures

PORSCHE 911 CARRERA 4

S hould a sports car be exciting or *involving to drive*? The question tends to imply some kind of additional compromise or short-coming – even if it is only lack of roof, or luggage space or something. Or, in addition, should a sports car be a shrine to supreme technology; electronic controls for engine, transmission, suspension, ventilation, seating? Should a disembodied voice inform you that a microchip has compensated for your ineptitude and revised the toe in and camber angles because you entered the corner too fast, retarded the ignition because you were in the wrong gear, and thrown away the keys because it is decided you are a moron? Might as well go by train, leave all the decision making to someone else.

Even if we are unable to settle on exactly what the sports car should be, the Porsche 911 is one of the all-time greats. It makes the right noises, achieves the right speeds, imparts the right amount of thrill to the driver. Fractious it can be, but only if it is used irresponsibly, and the reserves of performance before problems set in are still enough to see off just about anything else. Added to which, it has always been practical. The Bee-tle-like shape allows the driver better visibility, and with that the confidence to place the car on the road. The view of snub nose lines dropping sharply away, uncompromised by any lurking mechanicals beneath is as handy as it is unique. Its shape has always allowed a reasonable amount of luggage space and headroom, and you always know that the mechanical parts were unlikely to go wrong too often or fall to bits. Still more than that of course, it has always been an exciting car to drive – and this is the nub of the matter. The steering, hitherto unassisted, feels telepathically alive, the body taut, the engine's response electric

and the whole machine just waiting for inputs from throttle, steering or brakes. This of course is why it does not suit everybody, and why opinions of the machine have been, and probably always will be, sharply divided.

Over the years, improvements in tyre technology more than anything else have dealt with some of the 911's on-the-limit waywardness, and although it still persists, the threshold has been elevated to begin somewhere outside the sensible public road envelope. The everyday shortcomings of the 911, as ever, lie more with the heating and ventilating systems, facia layout and general ergonomics than in the dynamics.

So, having failed to lay the thing to rest in the late 1970s, and instead publicly committed to another 25 years of the rear-engined route, Porsche had the problem of what else to do in order to improve it, or rather make it different.

There is a limit to the increases in engine size and more and more aggressive body treatment accompanied by the ever bigger price tags to which we have grown accustomed over the preceding 25 years of the model's lifespan. Four-wheel drive was the only option left, and the Carrera 4 is the first of a family which already includes targa and cabrio variants, with a turbo to follow.

Four-wheel drive is primarily a tractive advantage. It distributes available power over twice as many wheels, which lessens the chance of wheelspin, and thus gives whichever tyre a better chance to steer or drive. But then, traction has never been the 911's problem, it is usually easier to make the clutch spin than the rear tyres. The 911's handling quirks have always stemmed from the engine's mass lurking aft of the rear wheels, giving excellent traction, but less good for making the front tyres stick when braking or accelerating because there is no weight on them. Then, decelerating in a corner, that weight in the tail tries to swing round a point somewhere in the middle of the car – known as polar moment. Four-wheel drive will not cure this. What it will do is allow the engineers to make the differences between power on and power off less marked. As any racing driver will testify, a better balance is more important than ultimate cornering ability. In the four-wheel-drive 911's case, the extra differentials and so on in the front of the Porsche handily add a little ballast where it is most needed (at the expense of most of the luggage space), while on the Carrera 4, the 911's

tendency to lock front wheels has at last been curbed by the fitment of ABS. The Carrera 4 is more than just a facelifted 911, however. It is largely a new car with, of course, new transmission, but with a new floorplan to accommodate it, a new engine stretched to 3.6 litres and with twin-plug ignition, new coil-sprung suspension, a new retractable rear spoiler and a new heating and ventilation system borrowed from the 959.

The main feature of the new Carrera is the four-wheel-drive transmission which was developed from the 959's electronically controlled system. A five-speed synchromesh gearbox sits in front of the engine, with a planetary gear train to transmit drive to the front wheels. Although Porsche was claiming an attempt to tame the 911, they wanted to preserve a rear-drive feel, hence the torque split is 31/69 per cent front to rear. This ratio is fixed, but there are electronic locks controlled by wheel sensors which attempt to ensure that the power is distributed to the

most appropriate wheel, or wheels, capable of dealing with it. The same sensors also report to the ABS system, and the central electronics then process the information, take care of any speed differences caused by out-of-size or under inflated tyres and further adjust the amount of locking relative to the overall speed of the car.

Porsche insists that the Carrera 4 is not to be compared with previous models in the 911 range, but it is difficult not to do this. The same quality clunk is there when you shut the door – firmly, unless you open a window to let some air out as you do it – the same awful facia layout greets you, and the same awful offset pedals (but the clutch and brake are no longer hinged at the bottom), the same vertical steering wheel.

The same gruff instant hum from behind when you start the engine, soaring at a touch of the accelerator pedal. Same heavy clutch, but the gear change is meatier, going into a well-defined slot in the gate with a positive snick, and the steering is lighter – not Japanese twirly, but just right – back to how it was on the Carreras of the 1970s. Moreover, the wheel does not tug at the hands in motion. One of the most noticeable 911 traits has all but gone, and there are two likely reasons for this. One is the damping effect of power assistance, and second is the 'negative offset' geometry required to accommodate ABS brakes.

The centre point of the tyre's tread surface needs to be moved closer to the point at which the steering actually swivels, such that the wheel exerts less leverage back through the steering, should the braking effort vary (like when the ABS is pulsing away). The drawback for the enthusiast is that the road wheel sends less information back to the steering wheel, and the steering is generally not as sharp.

It does, however, understeer a lot more, or rather it seems to need a great deal more lock to get round a known corner. The steering is accurate and the car responds instantly and without any body lurch, but application of any serious amount of power seems to be sweeping you towards terminal understeer and yet the car still pulls itself round. Exit speed is dramatic, and largely gone is the 911's curious tail-bobbing tendency as you wallop out of a corner. Thus the second 911 trait has been ironed out. Porsche has done away with the torsion bars that provided the springing in previous models, and coil springs appear above the front end's MacPherson struts and the rear's semi-trailing arms. This is not really new – the RSR factory racers had coils *and* a 3.5-litre engine back in the 1970s. The engineers have also added a touch of passive toe-in response to sideways loads at the rear, which further helps to keep the tail stable under terrific provocation.

When decelerating hard in a corner, the tail will still step out in true 911 fashion, and if going too fast on a wet road it will still try to go straight

on. Engineers are not magicians, we should remember, and four tyre contact patches can only handle so much. The ride is more compliant, especially at low speeds where the jiggling on the Club Sport has gone, and yet body control is simply superb – especially over crests and hollows. The weight of the engine dips the tail more than the front, but it checks instantly without rebounding first. There is, too, that rare and delicious taut feeling about the car's responses, as if there is no inertia to the body and yet it still feels solid and substantial. There is none of the shuddering through the body which sharp road imperfections can produce in some cars.

Body roll is minimal, and part of the driving delight is that any movement of the steering is translated into pointing the nose without accuracy being lost to body roll. Unfortunately such precision leads to a fair degree of road harshness which tickles the feet and hands, and a lot of bump thump – heard rather than felt – through the shell. Brakes are superb, ideally weighted, with short pedal travel and lots of bite.

It is impossible to ignore the sound of an air-cooled, horizontally-opposed, six-cylinder engine, grumbling and humming away behind you, a strange, absolutely individual mixture of sounds, dominated by the cooling fan's circular saw whine which rises to a shriek at the 7,000 rpm maximum, and the transmission rattles away from rest at low rpm despite the presence of the voguish twin-mass flywheel; once again, the music is a delight to the enthusiast.

This latest version of the Porsche flat six is new to the car range, drawing on the technology of Porsche's *Flugmotor*, developed for the American Mooney light aircraft; hence the C4's engine has the aviation-mandatory twin plugs, although it manages with two valves per cylinder. Most of the internals are new, and it develops 250 bhp at 6,100 rpm with a peak 210 lb ft of torque at 4,800 rpm. Response to the pedal may be instant

PORSCHE 911 CARRERA 4

ENGINE

Cylinders: air-cooled flat 6, rear-mounted.
Capacity: 3,600 cc (216 cu in).
Bore/stroke: 100/76.4 mm (3.94/3.01 in).
Valve gear: sohc per bank, chain driven, two valves per cylinder.
Compression ratio: 11.3:1.
Fuel system: Bosch Motronic electronic digital injection.
Maximum power: 250 bhp/6,100 rpm.
Maximum torque: 210 lb ft (285 Nm)/4,800 rpm.

TRANSMISSION

Type: 5-speed manual, four-wheel drive.
Mph/kph per 1,000 rpm in top gear: 25.0/40.2.

SUSPENSION, WHEELS

Front: independent, by MacPherson struts, lower wishbones, coil springs, anti-roll bar.
Rear: independent, by semi-trailing arms, coil springs, anti-roll bar.
Steering: power-assisted rack and pinion.
Brakes: (Front) ventilated discs/(Rear) ventilated discs, servo assisted.
Tyres/wheels: front 205/55 ZR 16 -6J, rear 225/50 ZR 16 - 8J.

DIMENSIONS

Length: 167.3 in (425 cm).
Width: 65.0 in (165 cm).
Height: 52.0 in (132 cm).
Wheelbase: 89.4 in (227 cm).
Front/rear track: 54.3/54.0 in (138/137 cm).
Weight: 3,192 lbs (1,448 kg).
Fuel tank: 16.9 gallons (77 litres).

PERFORMANCE

Maximum speed: 155.1 mph (249.6 kph).
Acceleration: 0-60 mph (96.5 kph) 5.4 sec, 0-100 mph (161 kph) 13.6 sec.
Fourth gear: 30-50 mph (48-80.5 kph) 6.0 sec.
Fifth gear: 50-70mph (80.5-113 kph) 8.1 sec.
Fuel consumption (average): 24.3 mpg (11.6 litres/100 km).

and it pulls without protest or snatch from 1,000 rpm, but it does not *really* get going until the tacho reads 4,000, and for a big, unblown engine, it is in fact fairly cammy. Revving the C4's engine is fortunately a deeply joyful pastime, and there is never any harshness or vibration anywhere in the rev range.

The instant response and heavy clutch can occasionally make a learner out of an experienced driver, revs soaring while trembling foot tries to let the clutch up gently, then stalling because you have backed off the accelerator. Top speed is a substantial 155.1 mph, thanks in part to a reduction in drag coefficient from 0.395 to 0.32. Porsche claims that this could have been reduced even further but it preferred to trade a little slipperiness for reduced lift from the front and retractable rear spoiler. With a 0-60 mph figure of 5.4 sec, this statistic is down on Lotus Esprit SE and Ferrari 328, and down on Porsche's own Club Sport. More traction obviously does not overcome the extra 500 lbs of four-wheel-drive when it comes to drag racing.

Gears are well spaced, and the change positive and satisfying – more so than any 911 of recent memory. There is no wind-up or shunt in the transmission, and smooth, fast shifting is pleasurable and easy.

Returning to the interior, one can be nothing but disparaging about the layout of the minor controls – the scattering of switches dotted at random over and below the facia, or the offset pedals which are very uncomfortable on a long run, or the invisible speedometer, or why there is a separate control wheel to raise and lower the locking buttons in the tops of the doors, or why the headlamp wiper on the facia also operates the windscreen washers when that function is available on one of the excellent column stalks. Porsches have always been like this, so research must prove it makes no difference to sales. The heater no longer needs a knowledge of Cyrillic to operate, and there is a marginal increase in the trickle of fresh air supplied, accompanied by lots of electric fan noises.

If we comply with Porsche's wishes and compare the dynamics with the opposition rather than Porsches gone by, we can do it in two ways; price and performance or on overall specification, which must include a measure of the former. Only the Audi Quattro coupé can really claim to be a genuine all-wheel-drive supercar – and the Carrera is faster and more agile; but it is nothing like as docile and friendly when things go wrong. The Porsche cannot really live with a charge-cooled Lotus Esprit, or the Ferrari 328 for that matter anywhere except on top speed, but then neither of these has the benefit of four-wheel drive. It could, however, be argued that they do not need the all-wheel-drive to complete their particular performance equation whereas the Porsche does.

Porsche's all-drive metamorphosis is not unlike Lotus's chargecooled SE exercise. Each is probably the best of its type to emerge from the respective factory, but both are more money for less fun than their predecessors. But, 4 wd or not, there is still nothing that sounds or behaves quite like a 911, and until Porsche move the engine and cool it by water, there never will be.

PORSCHE 911 CARRERA CLUB SPORT

This could be seen as yet another version of the 911. In mid-1988 there were 11 variants and two years on there were even more, but the Club Sport was a very special 911. Porsche said that it was aimed at the true enthusiast (there was a time when all its cars were built with that type of customer in mind). There was no sunroof, electric windows or central locking – like the *real* 911s, the Carreras of the 1970s. But it cost nearly as much as the standard Carrera . . .

However, the customer was not really being asked to pay the same, for less. Consider this: the 911 has been in production since the mid-1960s without the shape or the concept altering significantly (until the arrival of the Carrera 4). How can the car be still so popular as to resist efforts by its own maker to lay it to rest? Could it be the lack of opposition at a similar price?

The engine has only six cylinders (most rivals have eight), displacing 3,164 cc, arranged in two horizontally opposed banks, and cooled by air rather than by water. Rather like a 1960s motorcycle engine, the cylinders are individual aluminium barrels mounted on an aluminium crankcase and topped with common cylinder heads. These have a single overhead camshaft per bank and two valves per cylinder.

Fuel and ignition are managed by a Bosch Digital Motor Electronics system. Unusual in a road car, the lubrication incorporates a dry sump, and the oil reservoir is a separate tank in the tail, rather than in the sump of the engine.

This aircraft-style power unit (it has been used for that purpose) delivers 231 bhp at 5,900 rpm and 210 lb ft of torque at 4,800 rpm. It is less powerful than many rivals but it has to propel less than 2,500 lbs, and the 911's good aerodynamics help its top speed. Timed at 152 mph at the Millbrook circuit, this is the fastest 911 we have tested.

Rear-engine traction allows a meteoric 2.0 sec to 30 mph and 60 takes 5.1 sec, with 100 coming up in 13.1 sec, which is outstanding among Division 2 supercars. In the mid-range, it loses out to some supercar rivals, but part of the joy of owning a 911 is zinging up and down the gears.

Porsche's flat-six is always utterly smooth mechanically, with barely a thrum through the car; yet the noises coming from the tail change constantly through the rev range. There are grumbles and zizzes at low rpm, then as the power starts to pour in earnest around 3,500 rpm, it takes on a hiss like a turbo-prop aircraft.

It revs instantly as if there were no flywheel, and the temptation to blip the throttle in neutral simply to savour the engine's electric response is all too tempting. Then you can hit the rev limiter at 6,800 rpm in the gears without even trying, so smooth is the engine, and the noise is never tooth-gritting.

The gear change on this Carrera was the best we have ever tried on a 911. Extremely light, it lacks the meaty finality of mid-engined cars but the throw is short and the syncro helpful. The clutch, too, is a smooth push now, rather than the springy over-centre action of 911s gone by. You need to match the revs on gear changing though, and move the lever swiftly because the engine's revs die away very quickly when the throttle is released. Failure greets the next ratio with a learner's shunt-and-lurch. The gate is a 'normal' H-pattern, with fifth to the right and forward.

We expected the Club Sport to be demanding

on the limit, with quirky controls, wriggly steering, and hideous understeer. Well, it *is* demanding on the limit, but it is restless, taut, and entertaining to be in. This lightweight Carrera has stiffer suspension than many of its predecessors, and wears 205 and 225/50 VR 16 tyres. Its feel is unlike that of other modern rear-engined Porsches of our acquaintance.

The steering has lost its writhing although it still tugs the hands a little, and sadly it has lost some of the telegraphic feel that was once a celebrated feature of the 911 range. It is still informative, but has gained weight at the expense of sharpness. The car feels rear-engined, too, by comparison with the mid-engined, kart-like sensitivity of some mid-engined cars: you can sense the weight out back, dipping the suspension and trying to pendulum the tail. Like all rear-engined cars, the CS displays that curious diagonal rocking sensation in response to road undulations or cornering forces. This one, though, does not understeer as the type once did. Exiting a corner, it takes the Porsche a moment to settle, for the expected swing of the tail not to take place. Despite this, it is absolutely alive all the time and, once the rhythm has been discovered, supremely rewarding.

On the safe confines of the test track, we explored the limits. It is now just possible to unstick the tail with power alone, whereas earlier Porsches would resolutely understeer when the right foot was extended. Lift off with lock

applied, though, and the tail swings out in an instant. This can be caught with the steering and then hold the balance with power but, held on opposite lock, the steering tries to centre with such a vengeance that two goes make the wrists ache. Lose commitment then, and even the sharpest reactions will not restrain the tail. Round it goes. There are two choices here: oversteer and more oversteer.

Of all high-performance sports cars, the 911 is one of the most accommodating to drivers of all sizes, offers excellent all-round visibility, and is also one of the easiest simply to get into and drive. It also has very grippy and comfortable seats. But the minor controls are scattered to the point of obscurity, and the essentially neat and simple facia has been spoiled by switches which have been stuffed in wherever they will fit.

Like the 2.7 RS of 1973, this will be looked back upon as one of the classic 911s.

PORSCHE 911 CLUB SPORT

ENGINE

Cylinders: air-cooled flat 6, rear-mounted.
Capacity: 3,164 cc (190 cu in).
Bore/stroke: 100/76.4 mm (3.94/3.01 in).
Valve gear: sohc per bank, chain driven, two valves per cylinder.
Compression ratio: 10.3:1.
Fuel system: Bosch L-Jetronic fuel injection.
Maximum power: 231 bhp/5,900 rpm.
Maximum torque: 210 lb ft (285 Nm)/4,800 rpm.

TRANSMISSION

Type: 5-speed manual, rear-wheel drive, limited-slip differential.
Mph/kph per 1,000 rpm in top gear: 25.0/40.2.

SUSPENSION, WHEELS

Front: independent, by MacPherson struts, lower wishbones, coil springs, anti-roll bar.
Rear: independent, by semi-trailing arms, coil springs, anti-roll bar.
Steering: unassisted rack and pinion.

Brakes: (Front) ventilated discs/(Rear) ventilated discs, servo assisted.
Tyres/wheels: front 205/55 ZR 16 -6J, rear 225/50 ZR 16 - 8J.

DIMENSIONS

Length: 169 in (429 cm).
Width: 64.0 in (163 cm).
Height: 51.9 in (132 cm).
Wheelbase: 89.4 in (227 cm).
Front/rear track: 55.0/55.3 in (140/140 cm).
Weight: 2,464 lbs (1,118 kg).
Fuel tank: 18.6 gallons (85 litres).

PERFORMANCE

Maximum speed: 152.1 mph (244.7 kph).
Acceleration: 0-60 mph (96.5 kph) 5.1 sec, 0-100 mph (161 kph) 13.1 sec.
Fourth gear: 40-60 mph (64-96.5 kph) 5.4 sec.
Fifth gear: 50-70mph (80.5-113 kph) 7.4 sec.
Fuel consumption (average): 26.0 mpg (10.9 litres/100 km).

PORSCHE 928 S4GT

T here is irony aplenty in the car which Porsche originally labelled the 928 S4 'with Sport Equipment'. Irony and a touch of desperation. For it seems that a major thrust of Porsche's recent marketing strategy is to keep pumping out muscled-up, limited edition models.

And, make no mistake, adding such a suffix to a Porsche is as incongruous as badging a few Ford Fiestas as Bravos or Festivals or Dashes; they may as well be labelled *new! exciting! buy me!*

Indeed Porsche seems to have realized the folly of this and have renamed the car 928 S4GT. This latest 928 S4GT is the second Porsche to have been smothered in the latest hi-tech glad-rags. The first was the 944 Turbo with Sport Equipment, the pastel-pink rocket which upped the ante with a bigger turbo, stiffer suspension, larger wheels and tyres, more capable brakes and a clutch of other, smaller changes. As a result the Porsche 944 Turbo moved from being simply very fast to a car that was very fast and endearingly responsive to drive. In short, then, the 944 Turbo could use a little sharpening to up its potential for down-the-road mayhem.

But the 928 S4GT? Is there a better long-distance grand tourer than the standard production car? Do you, as you step out of a 928 S4GT, automatically start to think that it might need a touch more power, a few centimetres more rubber on the road and a manual gear change to make it still faster accelerating away from the rest? No.

You leave a 928 S4GT secure in the knowledge that it always does the job well. You can cross Germany in a day or tootle down to the dry-cleaners with equal ease. There is an enormous capability built into the 928 S4GT – so much so that you tend to forget that this massive car is built just for two, with conceptual-joke rear seats and a luggage deck so shallow as to render it useless for anything more than an informal weekend away. Yet it is trustworthy, sturdy, not even particularly flamboyant in everyday use, and when the mood strikes and the roads are clear it can continue to shock with the breadth of its usable performance.

So Porsche decided to do a high-performance limited edition 928 S4GT. This seems to be an attempt to attract drivers who think the 928 is a shade old hat in these days of the 959 and F40. This is where Porsche begins to get a trifle silly. For example: the installation of a close-ratio five speed transaxle with a numerically longer final drive and limited-slip differential. It takes a couple of urban miles to see through this idea. When pottering around in first, second and third progress will be stuttery and jerky; this gear shift, with a dog-leg first, is a particularly ugly thing

to slide across the gate. First to second is laborious, and fourth to third disturbingly hit and miss. And then you will find yourself in the wrong gear at a set of traffic lights slipping to red and you will press the throttle at 800 rpm in fifth and the car drives softly and easily. And, later on, you will explore this further and discover that if, purely out of curiosity, you spool down to 500 rpm in fifth and then brush the rightmost pedal, the Porsche, with a mechanical servility which is almost touching, will accelerate away in top gear with not a whisper of complaint.

Which means that, on a major road, the 928 S4GT is a two-gear car: fourth and fifth. Third, shunting across the H-gate, becomes just an inconvenience, especially as the clutch is a mite sharp. The standard 928 S4GT has a four-speed automatic; with the autobox you lose the sternum-bending engine braking as you slip from fifth to fourth, but the automatic is the more genteel, easier-to-live-with alternative. But, of course, automatics are not macho and part of the 928 S4GT's reason-to-be is that Porsche claims it lops 0.6 sec from the 928 S4's

PORSCHE 928 S4GT

ENGINE

Cylinders: V8 (90-degree), in-line, front-mounted.
Capacity: 4,957 cc (297 cu in).
Bore/stroke: 100/78.9 mm (3.94/3.11 in).
Valve gear: dohc per bank, driven by toothed belt, four valves per cylinder.
Compression ratio: 10.0:1.
Fuel system: Bosch LH-Jetronic injection.
Maximum power: 320 bhp/6,000 rpm.
Maximum torque: 318 lb ft (430 Nm)/3,000 rpm.

TRANSMISSION

Type: 5-speed manual (automatic available), rear-wheel drive, limited-slip differential.
Mph/kph per 1,000 rpm in top gear: 27.0/43.5.

SUSPENSION, WHEELS

Front: independent, by double wishbones, coil springs, anti-roll bar.
Rear: independent, by semi-trailing arms, upper transverse links, coil springs, anti-roll bar, Porsche-Weissach geometry.
Steering: assisted rack and pinion.
Brakes: (Front) ventilated discs/(Rear) ventilated discs, servo-assisted, ABS.
Tyres/wheels: front 225/50 ZR 16 -8J, rear 245/45 ZR 16 - 9J.

DIMENSIONS

Length:: 175.1 in (445 cm).
Width:: 79.8 in (203 cm).
Height: 50.5 in (128 cm).
Wheelbase:: 98.4 in (250 cm).
Front/rear track: 61.1/60.8 in (155/154 cm).
Weight: 3,483 lbs (1,580 kg).
Fuel tank: 18.9 gallons (86 litres).

PERFORMANCE

Maximum speed: 163.5 mph (263.1 kph).
Acceleration: 0-60 mph (96.5 kph) 5.3 sec, 0-100 mph (161 kph) 12.7 sec.
Fourth gear: 30-50 mph (48-80.5 kph) 4.6 sec.
Fifth gear: 50-70mph (80.5-113 kph) 6.4 sec.
Fuel consumption (average): 20.3 mpg (13.9 litres/100 km).

usual 5.9 sec 0-60 mph sprint. (That, of course, is the difference between fast and exceedingly fast and therefore of absolutely no relevance in ordinary driving.)

So the Porsche gets a five-speed manual gear box. And huge – one inch wider at each end – 8J x 16 front wheels with 9J x 16 rears in that gloriously smooth-faced spoke pattern first seen on the 944TGT. And these are fitted with Japanese tyres, 225/50 front and 245/45 rear Bridgestone RE71 unidirectionals.

The one thing that the rear RE71s dislike is to tag a white line under acceleration. The whole rear end of the car snakes and darts and becomes very obstreperous. That quirk is not what you expect in a car as thoroughly developed as the 928 S4GT.

Neither is the constant hint of power oversteer. The usual 928 S4 is easy-on-the-arms neutral; the GT has a dash of tail-happiness plumbed into its underpinnings. The driver is made aware of the fact that the rear end is just a fraction loose – it is not a gigantic handling problem, more an ever-present reminder that more throttle is always an option to dampen the reassuring initial hint of understeer that marks the way the Porsche turns into a bend. In the tried-and-trusted 928 S4 more power through a turn simply means greater exit speed – it takes great stupidity even to think about getting the tail out of the public highway. Yet the Bridge-stones are predictable enough and, despite their greater width, seem quieter on tarmac surfaces than the narrower, standard rubber – on concrete, however, they sing and hum with an off-key cheek.

As well as the new tyres, the Porsche 928 S4GT gets 10 per cent stiffer front springs, sport shock absorbers and 17 mm wider rear track. The result is a ride that is firm but rarely ragged. Around town, amid the patchwork potholes, the Porsche's ride is positively chunky, but the pay-off is glorious high-speed stability and the ability to place the car on the road accurately. In other words, the beefed-up suspension is worth having: but taken in context with the subtle aroma of oversteer, the manly gear change quality and largely unnecessary close-ratio gear-box and one gets the feeling that this car is simple-mindedly and needlessly muscular. Which is unfair. The 4,957 cc, all-alloy, 32-valve V8 is already one of the world's great engines – but in GT guise it gets even better. The changes are so small as to be practically invisible – higher profile cams, modified engine management unit and new exhaust with twin tailpipes – and leave the specification figures unchanged. This car, like any other S4, produces 320 bhp at 6,000 rpm and 318 lb ft torque at 3,000 – but something wild comes on strong at 4,000 rpm.

Smoothness is this engine's forte, and a feeling of sheer unburstability. Apparently the GT has less torque than the standard alternative below 3,000 rpm – you would not notice – and then flattens out at around 4,000. Which means that this car is stupendously quick, but docile. It dawdles around town, and the throttle action is friendly bordering on obsequious. But show it 3,500 rpm and there is the most glorious bark from the engine and the horizon approaches very rapidly up to the rev cut-out at 6,750 rpm. And, remember, this car will pull from 500 rpm in fifth right the way up to the no-go zone without a mechanical grimace.

Fast Lane took the 928 S4GT to the Millbrook speed bowl for quantitative performance testing. Mark Hales was behind the wheel, and was filled with the feeling of awe that comes with running this car to the maximum. Its top speed is a mean 163.5 mph, a one-way best of 166 mph, with a quarter-turn of lock on around the high-banked oval; on the straight and level, says Hales, 170 mph is easy. The car felt stable and composed as it travelled at almost three miles a minute, with the stamina to do that speed all year. The acceleration was better than claimed. The sprint to 60 mph takes just 5.3 sec, including hooking that dog-leg first-second change; 100 mph comes up in 12.7 sec, with all the fourth gear 20 mph increments up to 120 mph taking around four seconds. An average speed of 55.5 mph at 19.1 mpg point-and-squirting just for fun is an impressive display of Porsche engine efficiency.

The 928 S4GT features some simplification of its interior equipment – seat adjustment is by a combination of electrics and lever-yanking, whereas the base S4 is all electric – but it has air-conditioning and sports seats with generous side bolsters. The superb instrument binnacle and neat interior layout remains untouched; this is a good car for long-distance work.

But there remains the irony of a close-ratio transmission in what is, effectively, a two-gear car, the fatter tyres and stiffer springs leading to more oversteer, not less; the irony – if that is what it is – of Porsche applying the same marketing tactic on the 928 S4 as on the 944T, when the 944T needs it and the 928 S4 does not. There's the rub. The 928 S4 is about as good as a grand

tourer gets. The impetus for the GT model came, not from Germany, but from Porsche GB; management there thought that, perhaps, the 928 S4 was perceived as a touch soft, a shade on the plump and dainty side. Raunch, they said, was required. This is the result, for the British market at least; in Germany, there is a model available called the Club Sport, which offers less sound-proofing, the stripping out of various creature comforts, even the fitment of a simpler, lighter air conditioning unit. The result is a perceptibly slimmer 928 S4 aimed at deaf speedfreaks. The British GT model is more of a compromise: greater grunt with little reduction in comfort.

But why should one buy a 928 S4GT instead of the standard version? Perhaps only because GTs have a rarity value and would therefore perhaps hold their value slightly better, so what the hell? That is a true sign of the times. To buy this car is not because it is the zenith of 928 S4 performance but because it makes greater financial sense is, of course, the ultimate irony.

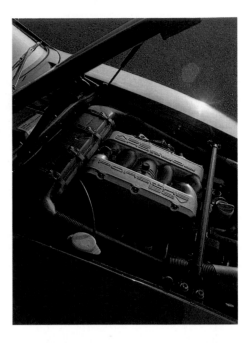

PORSCHE 944 TURBO

Ask the absurd saloon-bar question: 'What is the best car in the world?' and you will get a wide variety of answers, even from those who have driven most or all of the potential candidates. Narrow your parameters and ask: 'What is the best high-performance coupé?' There can be only one answer: the 944 Turbo.

Perhaps in the second half of the 1980s, when we tested it, the 944 Turbo was not as quick as some Ferraris, the Lamborghini Countach and one or two other supercars, but it was a sports car which combined excellent handling with a top speed of well over 150 mph, 0-60 mph acceleration in around six seconds, fuel consumption during hard driving better than 20 mpg, with a high level of comfort for two people and their luggage, *and* reliability and build quality which are justly renowned.

Arguments against the 944 Turbo are few and easily demolished. Should a car with an engine of only four cylinders should be so highly rated? It could be fancifully argued that having six, eight or 12 cylinders is good for the soul. But look at what this particular four-cylinder engine can do, and you will have to agree, once again, that logic supports its case.

To our eyes, the styling of the 944 is very attractive, and that of the Turbo even more so, with its all-round deformable polyurethane and glass fibre nose section giving it a similar sensuous yet aggressive look to that of the 959. This and other modifications are dynamically effective too, not only giving a marginal reduction of drag coefficient, but also reducing front and rear lift: the rear spoiler has been gently altered, there is a rear under-spoiler, which also cools the transmission, exhaust and petrol tank, and vestigial side 'skirts'.

The modifications by which the respectable power (163 bhp/5,800 rpm) and torque (151 lb ft/3,000 rpm) of the normally aspirated 944 are raised to mini-supercar levels (220 bhp/5,800 rpm and 243 lb ft/3,500 rpm) do not simply consist of sticking turbocharger and intercooler on to the harmonically balanced 2,479 cc engine, which has one of the highest bore/stroke ratios of any type of production engine.

It has forged pistons instead of the usual cast aluminium type, reinforced valve guides, valve seat rings and inlet valves, stronger valve springs, and sodium-filled exhaust valves with Nimonic heads. 'TOP' (Thermo-dynamically Optimized Porsche), a fancy acronym for combustion chambers designed to cause high turbulence and to lead to excellent thermal efficiency, is retained from the standard engine, which has allowed the compression ratio to be 8.0:1.

A knock sensor is fitted so that the engine will be less prone to damage if low-grade fuel has to be used. This retards ignition in any cylinder by three degrees, and if further knocking is sensed, by up to six degrees; if knocking still persists, the boost pressure can be lowered electronically right down to basic charge pressure.

Bosch's 'black-box' computer operates both the Motronic ignition (with a memory covering 256 fixed points in the engine 'map') and fuel injection, of the L-jetronic type.

The turbocharger itself is a K K K unit, with water cooling. It is mounted on the left flank of the engine, opposite the exhaust manifold, which apparently reduces maximum gas entry temperatures by 90°C. A secondary cooling circuit in the turbo housing switches on automatically to prevent excessive 'heat soak' when the engine is turned off.

Around Millbrook's banked circuit, in poor conditions we recorded a lap at 150.8 mph. With tyre scrub and wind effects removed, the true figure of our test car would most likely be well above 155 mph.

We got within 0.1 sec of the claimed 0-100 kph time of 6.3 sec, which gave us a 0-60 mph time of 6.1 sec. The car went on to do 0-100 mph in 16.4 sec. Although this makes the 944 Turbo slower than the 911 it is not to the extent that the rear-engined car will disappear into the distance.

Turbo effects show up clearly in top gear acceleration, 20-40 mph taking 13.6 sec, (the starting point is well under 800 rpm), but 70-90 mph occupying only 7.5 sec. Fourth gear gives a broad band of acceleration, all the 20 mph increments between 40-60 mph and 80-100 mph taking 6.1 sec or less.

We averaged 19.9 mpg, a very respectable figure in view of the performance. We would expect most owners to achieve more than 22 mpg

in their normal driving. The big fuel tank (with a 17.6-gallon capacity) gives a range during fast motoring of over 330 miles, and more than 500 'touring' miles can be squeezed out of it.

Although the gearbox has been strengthened, the quality of the change remains the same, which means that while possibly not as slick as that of some lesser-powered cars, it is the equal at least of any of the 150 mph plus cars with the exception of the BMW M635/M5. It may feel a little ponderous at first, but it certainly is not vague, and it can accept changes just about as quickly as the human hand can move, aided by a lightly-weighted and progressive clutch. The gearbox, like that of the racers derived from the

924 and 944, has an external oil cooler.

The final drive has been raised (numerically lowered) to 3.37:1 and with an identical top gear ratio this gives 25.8 mph per 1,000 rpm.

With suspension (MacPherson struts and coils at the front: semi-trailing arms and transverse torsion bars at the rear) unchanged from standard, but wider, lower-profile tyres (205/55 VR 16 front, 225/50 VR 16 rear), it is not surprising that the Turbo gives the same general feel as the standard 944. As might be expected, the road-holding has a more adhesive quality, at least on dry roads.

Those who remember the awkward tendencies of the 924 Turbo and Carrera will be pleased to

learn that the 944T is a considerably easier car to drive quickly, and it does not present the unwary driver with a sudden and massive increase of power just as the apex of a slippery bend is reached. Though not much happens below about 2,500 rpm, the onset of full boost is not like lighting the afterburner in a jet engine, but simply a steady though substantial increase in the rate of acceleration. In any case it is rare that a competent driver, hustling along even unknown roads, will need to drop below that engine speed.

Initial understeer is slightly stronger than in the latest standard 944, but once settled into a bend, the 944T is more neutral and unlikely to run wide on the exit. More important than that,

PORSCHE 944 TURBO

ENGINE

Cylinders: harmonically-balanced straight four, in-line, front-mounted.

Capacity: 2,479 cc (149 cu in).

Bore/stroke: 100/78.9 mm (3.94/3.11 in).

Valve gear: sohc, driven by toothed belt, two valves per cylinder.

Compression ratio: 8.0:1.

Fuel system: Bosch L-jetronic injection, KKK K26/70 turbocharger.

Maximum power: 220 bhp/5,800 rpm.

Maximum torque: 243 lb ft (329 Nm)/3,500 rpm.

TRANSMISSION

Type: 5-speed manual, rear-wheel drive, limited-slip differential.

Mph/kph per 1,000 rpm in top gear: 25.8/41.5.

SUSPENSION, WHEELS

Front: independent, by MacPherson struts, lower wishbones, coil springs, anti-roll bar.

Rear: independent, by semi-trailing arms, transverse torsion bars, anti-roll bar.

Steering: power-assisted rack and pinion.

Brakes: (Front) ventilated discs/(Rear) plain discs, servo assisted, ABS.

Tyres/wheels: front 205/55 VR 16 -7J, rear 225/50 VR 16 - 8J.

DIMENSIONS

Length: 166.5 in (423 cm).

Width: 68.3 in (173.5 cm).

Height: 50.2 in (127.5 cm).

Wheelbase: 94.5 in (240 cm).

Front/rear track: 58.1/57.1 in (147.5/145 cm).

Weight: 2,778 lbs (1,260 kg).

Fuel tank: 17.6 gallons (80 litres).

PERFORMANCE

Maximum speed: 150.8 mph (242.6 kph).

Acceleration: 0–60 mph (96.5 kph) 5.9 sec, 0–100 mph (161 kph) 14.9 sec.

Fourth gear: 30–50 mph (48-80.5 kph) 7.8 sec.

Fifth gear: 50-70mph (80.5-113 kph) 9.2 sec.

Fuel consumption (average): 30.2 mpg (9.4 litres/100 km).

it does not swing into vicious oversteer if the throttle is closed suddenly with a significant cornering load building up. Instead it simply resumes the chosen line, and if the tail does slide out, it does so smoothly and progressively.

Even so, it cannot be 'sent' into bends with quite the controlled aggression that may be used in the normally aspirated model; this is partly a function of the fatter tyres, and partly because of the turbo. The car responds much better to a neat style.

With its bigger tyres, as might be expected, there is rather more road noise, both bump thump and roar over coarse surfaces, than in the slimmer-tyred standard 944. However, this is heard more than felt, and we cannot think of a sports car (even those of significantly lower performance) with a more supple overall ride quality.

Damping control at high speed cannot be faulted. The 944T's rack-and-pinion steering seems rather light and lacking in feel for the first few miles. However, one soon becomes accustomed to it, and we found that after a while we forgot entirely that it was assisted except at the important times that it is needed – during low-speed manoeuvres.

On the basis of our experiences with this test car in a wide range of conditions, we would say that paying extra for the optional limited-slip differential would be money unwisely spent, since traction without it is outstandingly good. The same applies to the 'sports dampers'.

One of the reasons why the Turbo is so quick despite its relatively small engine is its aerodynamic efficiency, a claimed drag coefficient factor of 0.33 being combined with a fairly small frontal area. However, a price that is sometimes paid for good air penetration is some loss of stability, and we did find the car to be slightly wayward (though not to an alarming extent) in crosswinds when moving up into the higher speed ranges, despite the claimed reductions in lift.

After about three-quarters of an inch of soft free play, the brake pedal has a good, solid feel and the uprated system (with enlarged, internally ventilated front discs with four-piston fixed calipers, and forced-air cooling) performs exceptionally well, being both progressive and powerful. We experienced none of the fade which can afflict the less powerful normally-aspirated car, despite trying our level best. However, although the suspension has been modified to accept ABS the system was not yet available when we tested the car.

The Turbo shares the basic overall interior design, with only detail changes, and it does not look out of place in a car of this price. The strengths of the new design are a vastly improved driving position, the relationship of the major controls and the impression of quality. The weakness is the siting (and lack of illumination) of the minor switches.

The only differences inside the Turbo from the basic model are that it has one unnecessary and virtually meaningless gauge for turbo boost instead of another (an 'econometer'), it has air conditioning as standard instead of as an option and the partial leather front seats (with electric adjustment fore/aft and for backrest angle and tilt) are standard, as is the electrically operated tiltable and removable sunroof. The optional 'Sports' seats were fitted to our test car, and we found them exceptionally comfortable. As in all 944s, the fitting of a clutch-foot rest and the proximity of the throttle pedal to the carpeted panel covering the front wheelarch bulge lessens the strain on the ankles during long journeys.

Immensely powerful on main beam, the headlights seem rather ineffective on dip for a car as fast as this.

In all other respects, the all-round visibility is excellent, the three mirrors together giving a comprehensive view of the road behind. The windscreen wipers are much improved not only because of their resiting to give a proper sweep for right-hand drive cars, but also because they now have three speeds and an intermittent setting. In operation they are pleasantly quiet too, but it is a pity the same cannot be said of the rear-screen wiper, which emits a creaky whining noise reminiscent of cars of 30 years ago. For the price of the car, Porsche could surely have added an intermittent setting and a washer.

The air conditioning is simple to operate, with rotary dials for the four-speed fan (almost silent as it squeezes out a gently breeze on its lowest setting) and the temperature setting, two volume slides, one for the upper half of the car and the other for the footwells, and two buttons: one operates a very efficient demister, and the other is for recirculation. The centre vents are individually adjustable for direction in two planes, but cannot individually be closed; the outer ones on the facia can be.

Although all this works very well to cool the interior on a very hot day, and also churns out plenty of warm air very soon after starting up on a frosty morning, it cannot cope very well with the muggy winter day when you want warm toes and cool air to the face simultaneously. There is a solution – open the tilting sunroof; this should not be necessary.

This is a stylish and beautifully executed car with only minor flaws which, added together, do not mount up even to an irritant. Porsche's problem with the car is that it resembles too closely the lesser cars in its range. These enabled the company to become a relatively high volume manufacturer, but at some cost to its image: that has cost Porsche two bosses, and repair work is still in process.

PORSCHE 959

O ne moment, we had been hurtling down a hedge-lined secondary road at speeds liable to invoke local hysteria. The next, we were faced with a torrential wall of water: the flat-six engine's second turbo had *burst* into action, in fifth gear, at precisely the same moment as the heavens above.

But still we could see no reason for lifting from the throttle pedal. Not yet. Not in a Porsche 959, on a traffic-free road and several hundred more engine revs tempting exploitation and another, higher gear to enjoy after that. With the tachometer needle continuing to move, we had soon shifted up to sixth.

This is not meant to be paean of praise to the road tester's driving skills; all the driver had to do, apart from hold the steering wheel straight and press the throttle to the floor, was flick two cockpit control stalks. One sent into action the peculiarly old-fashioned windscreen wipers. The other relayed a message to the uniquely advanced transmission system. Instead of adjusting, through the accelerator pedal, the throttle opening of the engine, we had altered, through a magic wand attached to the steering column, the programme setting of the four-wheel-drive torque split. It kept raining just as hard. We kept driving just as hard. In a Porsche 959, it is as simple as that. Faced with this sort of rain in any other supercar, our enthusiasm would quickly have dissolved.

But, as one appreciates within minutes of driving it, the Porsche 959 is not much like any other supercar. It is more than the most sophisticated supercar ever built. It is technologically the most advanced 'production' car (of any kind) on the planet.

Originally, Porsche limited production to 200, chiefly to satisfy FISA eligibility rules. It was an immediate sell-out. Under pressure from a frustrated client list Porsche later consented to build a further 50 copies of the car.

This is the most significant supercar of the 1980s. It will catapult from a standstill to 60 mph in 4.2 sec and to 100 in 9.7, and its top speed is, depending upon which factory source you listen to, somewhere between 196 and 198.9 mph. Its 2,936 cc powerplant is of the finest pedigree, an offspring of the engine which has propelled Porsche's type 956 and 962 Group C sports prototype racing cars to victories all over the world. This marvellously sophisticated, 24-valve, quad-cam, flat-six engine, with its air-cooled cylinder barrels and water-cooled aluminium heads, has sequential, two-stage, intercooled turbocharging. At 6,500 rpm, it lets loose 450 stampeding horses, as many as an early 1970s Formula One engine strained to produce at 10,000 rpm. Its four-wheel-drive system is blessed with automatically variable torque split, and dry weather/rain/snow/rough-terrain programmes which can be selected in the cockpit. It has a close ratio six-speed gearbox, and automatically adjustable Bilstein dampers, and ride height that is adjustable too, and brakes with ABS, and tyres with run-flat capability, and . . . the list goes on. In spite of its awesome potential, this car is astonishingly easy to tame. It is not – unlike too many exotic cars – prone to the unsettling nervousness or embarrassing tantrums of a spoiled and precocious thoroughbred. There were no rude retorts from the exhaust system; there was no oiling of the plugs, no juddering of the stressed clutch, no gnashing of teeth within the gearbox, no temperature needles crawling inexorably towards the edge of the scale. From the inside, with the electric windows raised, there was not even the intrusive low-speed whine which you would find in a standard 911: just a contented, muted hum, a strangely restrained hint of latent power.

Indeed, when you first settle into the high-backed seat of the 959, you could be forgiven for wondering what all the fuss is about. Drivers who are familiar with a 911's cockpit and controls will immediately enjoy commanding a 959. This car is 168 inches long and 72 inches wide (about seven inches fatter than a typical saloon), but beneath the traditional 911-style bubble top the cockpit is narrow enough somehow to make the whole car feel small. You cannot see the extremities of the bulbous nose from the left-hand driver's seat. You cannot see, in the interior mirror, the beautifully integrated tail spoiler. Certainly, each of the external rear-view mirrors catches a glimpse of a wide rear wheel arch and an air scoop and a spoiler endplate. Otherwise, within seconds of strapping himself in, the driver could think he was about to turn the key of an ordinary 911.

The only difference is that first one must clamber in over a fairly wide sill, and *slam* shut

the door. On top of a galvanized steel shell, the 959's body is mostly a combination of Aramid and Kevlar, with aluminium for the two doors and rear lid, and the owner's handbook makes a ready confession: the door fits will not meet the precise standards to which the owners of other Porsches might be accustomed.

The Sport version of the 959, stripped of such niceties as electric windows, electrically adjustable front seats, and air conditioning, tips the scales at 2,970 lb. The 'Comfort' version carried 530 lb more. Both, of course, have to accommodate an all-wheel-drive system whose inherent bulk (like that of the enlarged 18.8 gallon fuel tank) is most obvious when you open up the luggage space to find that most of its stowage area has gone.

With the door slammed shut, it is soon noticeable that every other aspect of build quality is predictably Porsche, predictably perfect. The handbrake pulls up through the shortest, firmest arc. The seatbelts slip through their rollers smoothly and quietly. The interior leather is joined with arrow-straight seams and impossibly tidy stitches. The stalk controls all move crisply. There are the clearest conceivable white–on-black instruments. The gear lever feels naturally placed. Even the tachometer needle is rock steady. With the engine ticking over it points precisely at 750 rpm and resolutely stays there.

its pilot. It could, of course.

It seems tame enough at first. The 959's throttle response at low revs is certainly adequate, and by ordinary standards it might even be called vigorous.

Then the polite deception ends. The first of the two turbos goes silently to work, the rate of acceleration smartly hastens, the tacho needle ascends like a military jet, the four fat tyres begin to feel as if they are clawing greedily at the tarmac, and suddenly you find yourself breezing past slower traffic (which is all of it), and then, at about 4,400 rpm, there is the violent explosion. The second turbo *erupts* into action; the previously refined engine note is swept away by a hard, guttural bellow, the whole car tilts back on its fat haunches and, apparently disregarding the velocity it has already amassed, launches itself down the road like a torpedo out of a tube.

The 959 accomplishes all of this with so little drama or fuss. The suspension is so good it sets entirely new standards among supercars. It does not bump or thump, it does not crash dramatically down potholes, it doesn't transmit bucketfuls of road or tyre noise into the cabin. The ride really is absorbent yet firm, rigid when it needs to be yet supple whenever you are travelling slowly. True, there are two big rotary switches in the centre console, one for the adjustable dampers (offering soft, normal and hard settings), and the other for the hydropneumatically adjustable ride height. But these can be ignored. The car does it all for you. The Bilsteins firm up automatically at speed, regardless of manual setting, and the ride height drops automatically at 94 mph.

Complementing the virtuous ride, the Porsche's steering is sharp and accurate (though a little lacking in feel); the gear change is crisp and light (though with a very definite notch marking the entrance to each leg of its gate); the brakes are progressive and stunningly powerful

Like almost everything else about the car, it is so orderly, so exact, so *right*.

There are a couple of quirks, though, which take a bit of getting used to. For one, there is the switchgear. In worst 911 fashion, it could have been shaken out of a great big cardboard box and glued down at random. For another, there are the foot controls. Both the brake and the clutch pedals ae slightly offset to the left, and the accelerator is an inch or more lower than the brake pedal.

There is nothing wrong with the way the controls do their work: the first part of their travel is deceptively light, but the required effort loads up very positively over centre. The single-plate clutch can be moved in and out with surprising progression and ease. The brake pedal, too, is fairly light of feel: no grab or snatch, no indication that pressure is being applied to four ventilated discs the size of dustbin lids. Even the throttle pedal, which is sharply responsive to the most delicate of inputs at the top of its travel, is charmingly deceptive: it never allows the terrifying impression that this car could run away with (if deceleration exceeds 1.2 g, they are helped out by a Wabco anti-lock system); the roadholding is fantastic, from the big Bridgestone RE71s.

Apart from the obvious need to be judicious in the lower gears when the second turbo comes alive, there is always traction when required, even in the pouring rain. Once or twice, through an ever-tightening sequence of twists and turns, we did find that we were getting off the brakes, and back on to the power, rather too late; we did feel that the Porsche was too deep into the bend before we achieved a balanced throttle; but we had to admit, later, that we were headed for the apex far too fast anyway. But it mattered not: back on to the gas and turn harder at the steering wheel and, no matter how optimistic it seemed, forcibly *power* the car round.

We would like to say we pushed so hard, grew so adventurous, became so demanding, that we had manfully to battle with understeer and oversteer and sometimes a combination of both. The truth is, we did push hard, and we did grow adventurous, and we did become demanding, and the Porsche obediently satisfied every unreasonable request made of it. Sure, the tail once or twice hinted vaguely at lightness, on the exit of damp roundabouts, and the steering once or twice loaded up very heavily indeed, ploughing at great speed into corners. Free of body roll, or squat, or dive, this remarkable car obsequiously goes wherever it is pointed.

After 400 miles of hammering hard, this writer has reluctantly to conclude that we ordinary mortals reach *our* limits long before the Porsche 959 does.

PORSCHE 959

ENGINE

Cylinders: air-cooled flat 6, rear-mounted.
Capacity: 2,936 cc (176 cu in).
Bore/stroke: 82/69.5 mm (3.23/2.74 in).
Valve gear: dohc per bank, driven by toothed belt, four valves per cylinder.
Compression ratio: 8.3:1.
Fuel system: electronic fuel injection integrated with engine management system, twin KKK turbochargers.
Maximum power: 450 bhp/6,500 rpm.
Maximum torque: 369 lb ft (500 Nm)/5,500 rpm.

TRANSMISSION

Type: 6-speed manual, four-wheel drive, electronically-controlled differentials.
Mph/kph per 1,000 rpm in top gear: 27.3 44.0.

SUSPENSION, WHEELS

Front: independent, by transverse upper and lower links with angled radius rods, forming top and bottom wishbones, coil springs, anti-roll bar.
Rear: independent, by transverse upper and lower links with angled radius rods, forming top and bottom wishbones, coil springs, anti-roll bar.
Steering: power-assisted rack and pinion.
Brakes: (Front) ventilated discs/(Rear) ventilated discs, servo-assisted, ABS.
Tyres/wheels: front 235/45 ZR 17 –8J, rear 255/45 ZR 17 – 10J.

DIMENSIONS

Length: 167.7 in (426 cm).
Width: 72.4 in (184 cm).
Height: 50.3 in (128 cm).
Wheelbase: 89.4 in (227 cm).
Front/rear track: 59.3/61.0 in (150.5/155 cm).
Weight: 3,192 lbs (1,448 kg).
Fuel tank: 18.7 gallons (85 litres).

PERFORMANCE

Maximum speed: over 196 mph (315 kph).
Acceleration: 0-60 mph (96.5 kph) 4.2 sec, 0-100 mph (161 kph) 9.7 sec.
Fuel consumption (average): n/a.

RENAULT GTA V6 TURBO

This car is known in most countries as an Alpine, in a few such as the UK as the Renault GTA. It has altered little since its introduction, save for a few minor cosmetic changes. Made under Renault guidance by the Alpine factory in Dieppe, in specification at least it is similar to the Lotus Esprit Turbo. Both are plastic coupés with backbone chassis and both claim around 200 bhp, although the GTA's all aluminium 2.5-litre single overhead cam single turbo V6 – borrowed from the 25 – is mounted aft of the gearbox rather than amidships as in the Lotus. In the original comparison, the

Renault lacked the consistent dynamic class of the Lotus. Its handling was decidedly more tricky thanks to the rear-mounted engine, and the single turbo took ages to spin up. The interior was a shade gimmicky too, but on the plus side there was the added advantage of two, albeit vestigial, seats in the rear, and a slightly lower price tag. This has risen.

The Renault has a spiky grey plastic facia exactly like a downmarket Renault 5, with toothy vents spattered liberally across its width. It is smooth like a plastic model and leaves fingerprints when you touch the surface. Span-

ning the gap between floor and facia is a binnacle containing the best studio impression of a WW3 fighter – actually a Philips stereo radio/cassette and graphic equalizer, with remote controls for volume and station selection on the steering column. You don't have to take your eyes from the road in order to change stations. Then, the seats are covered in fuzzy black velour, although there is a leather option, and you sit on, rather than in them. An easy win for the Lotus then... In fact, the Renault instruments are bold and easy to read. The stereo may be complicated to drive but it is excellent to listen to; the vents dispel

plenty of cool air wherever you want – especially to the face – and the seats adjust up, down, and far enough back to accommodate even the tallest of drivers. They also offer plenty of side support.

Smooth and six-like at low rpm, GTA's engine begins to thrum a little towards its 6,000 rpm limit, and although quick by any other yardstick, it cannot compete with the Lotus Esprit Turbo for acceleration through the gears. Only in fifth does the GTA's extra capacity tell, and here it can all but match the Lotus's lugging ability. Both turbocars will comprehensively shut down both the Ferrari 328 and the Porsche Carrera CS, if you can't be bothered to shift out of top gear.

The French car's top speed of 151.4 mph probably reflects its slippery 0.30 Cd shape, but the turbo lag which has blighted the car for many is still there. You can adapt your driving round it, of course, and the traction from the rear 255/45 Pirellis is predictably excellent so a sudden rush of power rarely causes any embarrassment unless there is water about. The Renix electronic fuel injection ensures that starting is always instant, and there are no hiccups to the power delivery.

The gearbox is now a common item between the GTA and Esprit and, for the Lotus, it represents a vast improvement in the shift quality. Lotus describes the new change as 'low inertia' which means that the wrestle of a stubby lever over long twanging steel tubes running the length of the chassis to the gearbox has been replaced by cables. It also means you are less likely to change the radio station with your knuckles every time you select third gear. Oddly perhaps, the change feels more positive and less rubbery in the Renault, which could well be down to the siting of the lever, lower down on the floor. Neither car has the meaty precision of the Ferrari's gear shift.

The Renault has soft suspension. It soaks up bumps with great ease and yet it rolls very little. Steering is light but the front end does lack bite and the car understeers considerably. Sudden

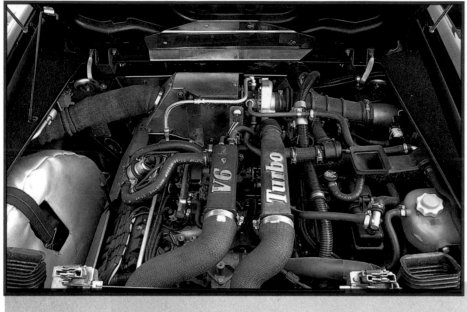

arrival of boost at low speeds will push the nose almost straight on. It is, however, quite easy to drive and place on the road, because the controls are light. It does not have vast outright grip but it shows a surprising unwillingness to wag its tail. Renault says that there have been no changes to the suspension, but from our experiences with this car we do know that on a wet road the Renault GTA can be *extremely*, irrecoverably wayward, particularly when the power is cut in mid-corner. You would not suspect that from its dry road performance though.

Finish is good and there is an impressive feel of tautness about the structure though it is noisy to ride in, largely because of the constant booming which fills the cabin. Heating and ventilation is well organized in the GTA. Rearward visibility is minimal.

We are here to nitpick. When you are being asked to spend so much money (leather, radio, metallic paint are extras) on a car that will seat just two people there has to be plenty of compensation.

The Renault has emerged as more attractive in the light of the Lotus Esprit's sanitization. It costs less, has two more seats and is easier to drive. The shape, which once looked almost prosaic, now looks less so by comparison. For those people seeking a fast car with just a dash of practicality, France may have the answer.

RENAULT GTA V6 TURBO

ENGINE

Cylinders: V6 (90-degree), in-line, mid-mounted.

Capacity: 2,458 cc (147.5 cu in).

Bore/stroke: 91/63 mm (3.58/2.48 in).

Valve gear: sohc per bank, chain-driven, two valves per cylinder.

Compression ratio: 8.6:1.

Fuel system: A.E.I. Renix electronic injection, Garrett T3 turbocharger.

Maximum power: 200 bhp/5,750 rpm.

Maximum torque: 214 lb ft (290 Nm)/2,500 rpm.

TRANSMISSION

Type: 5-speed manual, rear-wheel drive.

Mph/kph per 1,000 rpm in top gear: 26.5/42.6.

SUSPENSION, WHEELS

Front: independent, by double wishbones, coil springs, anti-roll bar.

Rear: independent, by double wishbones, coil springs, anti-roll bar.

Steering: unassisted rack and pinion.

Brakes: (Front) ventilated discs/(Rear) ventilated discs, servo assisted, ABS.

Tyres/wheels: front 195/50 VR 15 -6J, rear 255/45 VR 16 - 8.5J.

DIMENSIONS

Length: 170.5 in (433 cm).

Width: 69.1 in (175.5 cm).

Height: 47.1 in (120 cm).

Wheelbase: 92.1 in (234 cm).

Front/rear track: 58.8/57.6 in (149/146 cm).

Weight: 2,598 lbs (1,179 kg).

Fuel tank: 15.8 gallons (72 litres).

PERFORMANCE

Maximum speed: 151.4 mph (243.6 kph).

Acceleration: 0-60 mph (96.5 kph) 6.0 sec, 0-100 mph (161 kph) 16.0 sec.

Fourth gear: 30-50 mph (48-80.5 kph) 5.7 sec.

Fifth gear: 50-70mph (80.5-113 kph) 6.8 sec.

Fuel consumption (average): 30.8 mpg (9.2 litres/100 km).

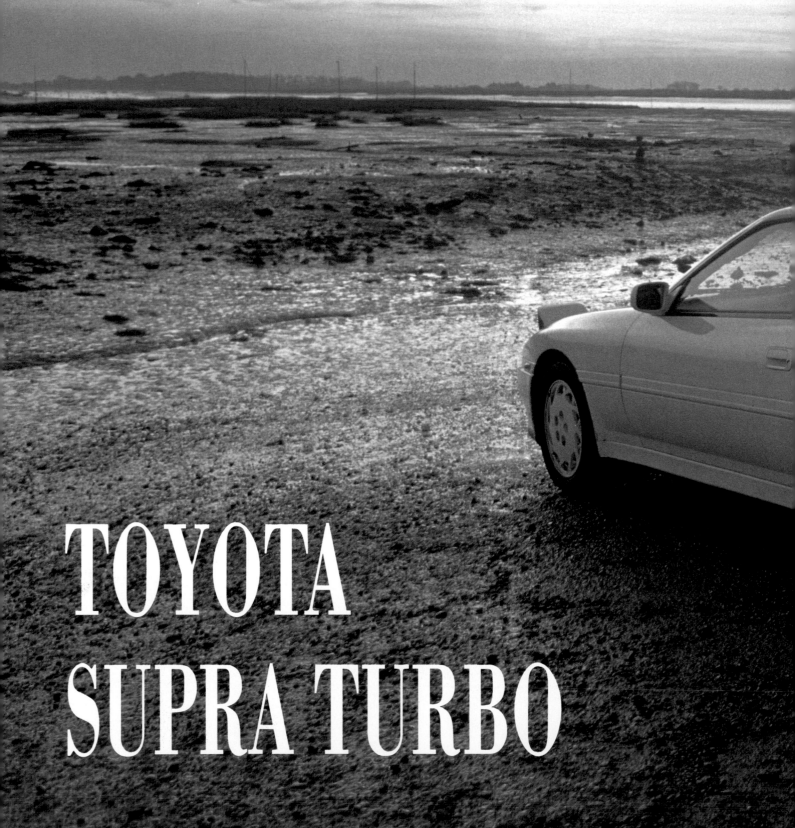

Examine the price, the performance and the specification. Drivers in the market for a comfortable but very fast two-plus-two will find that the new Toyota Supra Turbo is very enticing. Most people will find its appearance attractive, even if derivative.

There was a time when Porsche had variants of the 924/944 range down in this 'cheap' sector of the sports car market, but since the demise of the 924S, the starting price for a 944 became substantially higher. For that, you get the Porsche badge, undeniably excellent dynamic behaviour, the Porsche badge, considerably less 'grunt', and the Porsche badge . . .

However, there is one car that we regard as a serious rival to the Toyota in both price and performance: even in non-turbo form, the Renault GTA V6 is in the same league in a straight line, much easier to drive quickly but safely (despite the 'incorrect' situation of the engine overhanging the rear wheels), considerably more stylish and almost as well equipped. Also, what a Lotus Excel SE loses on the straights, it will more than make up through the twisty bits, while the slightly cheaper Cosworth Sapphire, even if its is 'only a Ford', is the winner in both departments and also has four doors.

So although the Supra Turbo ostensibly has a lot to offer, it does not lack some fairly serious rivals, even if some of them are significantly different in character.

It certainly is a very fast car. Toyota claims a top speed of 153 mph, and our fastest lap of Millbrook's banked bowl (where tyre scrub can easily remove up to 10 mph at such speeds) at a shade above 146 mph suggests that this is no exaggeration.

It is rather heavy, however, at 3,540 lbs (more than a Ford Scorpio 4x4!), which makes its standing-start acceleration times impressive rather than outstanding: on the test track we

TOYOTA SUPRA TURBO

achieved 0-60 mph in 6.6 sec (Toyota's possibly optimistic claim is 6.1 sec) and 0-100 in 17.2.

Mid-range figures are very good, despite the high gearing, and on the road, the performance is really excellent. This is possibly the best turbocharger installation we have ever tested, as the engine will pull strongly from below 1,000 rpm in any gear, with no hesitation and no noticeable 'step' as maximum boost is achieved. From only 1,000 rpm the needle on the turbo boost gauge begins to haul itself upwards, and by 2,000 rpm it is already at its peak, with another 5,000 rpm to spare before the red line is reached.

It is because of this absence of detectable lag, coupled with supreme flexibility, that the Supra Turbo's figures in fourth and top gear are as impressive on the road as they are on paper: for example, 30-50 mph in fourth in 5.6 sec, and 50-70 mph in top in 7.6 sec,

A second factor acting as a drag on the standing-start figures is the gear change, which is just a bit slow and baulky when subjected to the absolute required on the test track. In normal use on the road, however, the change is light, quick and precise, and is matched by a pleasant clutch action. The ratios are nicely spaced, with 41, 69, 103 and 135 mph attainable in the intermediates, and fifth geared to give 25.6 mph/1,000 rpm. A four-speed automatic is also available.

Due to a problem beyond our control we were unable to conduct a proper fuel check on the car, but the indications we have are that hard use will drop it to around 19 mpg, and that up to 25 may be achieved with a measure of restraint. The tank takes 15.4 gallons (70 litres), which is not a lot

these days for a car of this size and performance, meaning that it has a range of less than 300 miles. That should be enough, though, to get you to an unleaded pump, essential to this environmentally acceptable catalyzed engine.

The Supra Turbo has ventilated disc brakes on all four wheels, and although it is possible to get the pads hot enough to produce an acrid smell, they never seem to fade, and instead provide outstandingly good stopping power with well-engineered progression. The anti-lock system is discreet yet effective.

While the performance and refinement of its engine, the quality of its gear change, and the progression and power of its brakes are in the supercar class, and worthy of a far higher price tag, the Supra Turbo is let down by its dynamic behaviour in an area of fundamental importance in a sports car: its handling.

There is not much wrong with its roadholding, as the 225/50 VR 16 Goodyear Eagles (on 7J rims) give good reserves of grip on dry surfaces and remain fairly sure-footed when the going becomes wet or greasy. Thanks to a standard issue limited-slip differential, traction is very good. The problem occurs when the limit of those reserves is approached.

The suspension's specification promises much: double wishbones with double-acting dampers on each corner, and an anti-roll bar at each end, while the steering is by power-assisted rack and pinion. Springs, dampers and anti-roll bars have all been uprated from those in the normally aspirated Supra, and something seems to have been overlooked in that process.

The first sensation when driving the car is that its spring and damper rates are imperfectly sorted, as the body (especially the front end) jiggles uncomfortably over apparently smooth surfaces at low speeds, and when travelling faster, suspension control is excessive.

On the entry to a curve, the Supra initially feels stable, turning in well and settling into gentle understeer. However, it then becomes untidy (again, even on ostensibly bump-free roads) and moves into a series of minor lurching motions, any one of which can result in a vicious tail slide.

If this occurs it needs to be dealt with instantly, and with finesse, because anything less can cause unpleasantly abrupt weight transfer, itself leading to fishtail movements which could all too easily end in a spin.

The steering does not help the driver to control all this, for it lacks sufficient sensitivity to give a true picture of what is happening to the front wheels. Its assistance varies in inverse proportion to road speed, and at low speeds it is excessively light, which adds to the problems of negotiating tight bends. When the car is travelling faster, the resistance increases and straight-line stability is good, but there is still no real 'feel'.

The Supra is a big car, but like most sports

coupés, not much of its bulk is converted into accommodation. There is plenty of room for two people, though, and the very long doors allow them to get in and out easily, but the rear seats are designed either for children or for very short journeys. Luggage space is limited by the rear

suspension design and by intrusion into the rear deck of the spare wheel, but there is a spring-loaded tonneau to hide it from prying eyes, and the space may be increased considerably by folding one or both of the rear seats.

The adjustability of both the steering wheel (for reach as well as angle) and the driver's seat ensures that drivers of most sizes will be comfortable in the Supra. There is more than enough legroom, and plenty of headroom. The pedals are well spaced, and there is a rest for the clutch foot. The seat is trimmed in leather as standard (as also, at last, are the steering wheel and gear lever knob), and is well shaped and padded, with adjustable torso wings and lumbar support. All seat adjustments are carried out electrically. Many cars costing two or three times as much are not as comfortable.

The stalks and switches are generally well designed, and the instruments, of conventional design with large majors and minors angled towards the driver, are excellent. The whole interior combines luxury with attention to functional detail, and the result is more aesthetically pleasing than in most Japanese cars.

A complex air conditioning system is among the wide selection of standard equipment with which Toyota supplies the Supra Turbo. The controls are self-explanatory, and the system operates well, even to the extent of providing an effective division between the functions of heating the footwells and providing cooling air

TOYOTA SUPRA TURBO

ENGINE

Cylinders: straight six, in-line, front-mounted.

Capacity: 2,954 cc (177.2 cu in).

Bore/stroke: 83/91 mm (3.27/3.58 in).

Valve gear: dohc, driven by toothed belt, four valves per cylinder.

Compression ratio: 8.4:1.

Fuel system: electronic injection, turbocharger.

Maximum power: 232 bhp/5,600 rpm.

Maximum torque: 254 lb ft (187 Nm)/3,200 rpm.

TRANSMISSION

Type: 5-speed manual (4-speed auto available), rear-wheel drive, limited-slip differential.

Mph/kph per 1,000 rpm in top gear: 25.6/41.2.

SUSPENSION, WHEELS

Front: independent, by double wishbones, coil springs, anti-roll bar.

Rear: independent, by double wishbones, coil springs, anti-roll bar.

Steering: Assisted rack and pinion.

Brakes: (Front) ventilated discs/(Rear) ventilated discs, servo assisted, ABS.

Tyres/wheels: front and rear 225/50 VR 16 -7J.

DIMENSIONS

Length: 182.3 in (463 cm).

Width: 68.7 in (174.5 cm).

Height: 51.2 in (130 cm).

Wheelbase: 102.2 in (260 cm).

Front/rear track: 58.5/58.3 in (149/148 cm).

Weight: 3,539 lbs (1,605 kg).

Fuel tank: 15.4 gallons (70 litres).

PERFORMANCE

Maximum speed: 146.3 mph (235.4 kph).

Acceleration: 0-60 mph (96.5 kph) 6.6 sec, 0-100 mph (161 kph) 17.2 sec.

Standing km 27.3 sec.

Fourth gear: 30-50 mph (48-80.5 kph) 5.6 sec.

Fifth gear: 50-70mph (80.5-113 kph) 7.6 sec.

Fuel consumption (average): 25.5 mpg (11.1 litres/100 km).

at face level, which is increasingly rare these days.

Included in the basic price, apart from items already mentioned, are the following: electrically adjustable, automatically heated door mirrors, heated rear window with timer, electric windows with one-push opening function, cruise control, central locking, rear wash/wipe, headlamp wipe/wash and a very good radio/cassette player with automatic electrical aerial.

In this new version of the Supra, a potentially satisfying driving experience is reduced to being merely a difficult one, and there can be no adequate excuse: this car has a sophisticated chassis design, yet it is really not much better in overall handling, and in some areas worse than, the sharp-edged Supra of a few years ago. Toyota's smaller cars handle and ride very well, and the company's suspension engineers really ought by now to have sorted this, the high performance sporting flagship. It is a far better car than Nissan's old 300ZX Turbo (though annihilated by the new one). It is frustrating that it is still so far from realizing its full potential.

It is difficult to imagine that those who buy sporty cars for their image will enjoy the knobbly ride quality, while true enthusiasts will generally dislike the suspension settings. If Toyota were able to supply more than a very limited number of these cars, they might find that even a combination of keen pricing, a sexy appearance, near-supercar performance and loads of equipment is insufficient for success in today's competitive market.

TVR 420 SEAC

This is an exclusive club: the 150 mph club. But there is another condition: that the car must be in series production, and made in Britain. In addition the speed should, if possible, have been verified by us. For a moment though, let us ignore the made in Britain proviso, and take a look at the speed tables.

The 150 mph list is short enough to examine here and it even begins in Britain, because Newport Pagnell's finest begins with the letter 'A'. Aston's 5.3-litre V8 Vantage has a claimed top speed of over 180 mph; this for the moment

155 mph. Ferrari is there of course – a 328 to 161 mph, with a mean lap of 158.5 – and there's also the Testarossa and the F40. Lamborghini has the Countach in which the author touched 190 mph, but not at Millbrook. Renault's slippery GTA is the sole French representative with 151 mph and we must not forget Lotus's latest Esprit turbo (153 mph) or the XJ-S Jaguar V12 which managed 151 mph as long ago as 1981. There are some more, which might have done it given a different day – the Mercedes 560 probably (149.3 mph), and the BMW again, the M635 fell only just short.

remains a manufacturer's boast, simply because Millbrook's two mile bowl is too tight to contain any road car at that sort of gait. Even 160 mph needs nearly a quarter of a turn of lock in anything, and you begin to fear for the tyres after two laps.

There's absolutely no doubt that the Vantage Aston will easily exceed 150 mph though – the basic standard V8 managed that some years back. Further down the list, Germany sneaks in by courtesy of BMW and Porsche; the 944 turbo, the 928, and all the 911s will quite comfortably put away the 150 break, never mind the 959.

Back to Germany and the world's fastest five-seater saloon qualifies (at Millbrook) by 0.1 mph, without needing to test out BMW's claims that the 750 is electronically restricted to

More members perhaps than might have been thought at first, but it nevertheless remains an exclusive club, and the dynamic demands required to push a ton of machinery through the air at that speed are substantial. To add 10 mph to the top speed of a car with a drag coefficient of around 0.35 requires about half as much power again.

Unsurprisingly this is not a gathering for the down at heel either. These are all expensive cars. Thanks to Aston, Lotus and Jaguar, Britain is well represented in this exclusive company, despite its declining car industry.

There is, however, a new name to add to the list. The Blackpool sports car specialist TVR has finally done it. We took a standard production 420 SEAC to the magic 150 mph mark, at which speed it felt utterly stable and understeered less than most round the diameter of the bowl. Not only that, we also recorded 0-60 mph in 4.7 seconds and this with two up as always and without resort to special grippy tyres. This is 0.1 sec quicker than Lamborghini's Countach.

The 420 SEAC's price is cheap given what it does, but risks comparison with some classy products, and for attributes other than sheer speed. But the TVR is also a convertible, and there they have it. There simply is nothing else which is roofless, and goes as fast for the money.

The recipe is simple. The basis of the car is the now familiar 390 wedge, with an aggressively restyled body, and a larger capacity development of the Rover V8. The trusty, all-aluminium, Buick-derived Range Rover engine (produced by Land Rover to Vitesse specification especially for TVR) receives larger (93.5 mm) diameter Cosworth pistons, and a specially made steel crankshaft to expand the stroke to 77 mm. This gives a total swept volume of 4,228 cc, and there are also gas-flowed heads with bigger valves operated by a different camshaft via a set of solid lifters. These are an option over the standard hydraulic items, and are more efficient at high rpm but they do clatter. Maximum power varies slightly as each engine is hand-built and dyno-tested, but a representative figure is our test car's 304 bhp at 5,750 rpm. Torque is quoted as 290 lb ft at about 4,500 rpm. The whole engine is built and prepared with the care and time normally reserved for a racing engine, and it shows. Not only that, but just over 12 seconds to reach 100 mph says most things about a power unit's effectiveness.

The figures, however, cannot convey the sheer sweetness of the power unit, combined with a free-revving urgency and a high rpm bark that sets the senses tingling. It is better if it is revved too, although the SEAC's five and a half second average to gobble up any of the 20 mph gaps up to 110 mph can hardly be described as a disappointment.

Stir the gear lever, though, and the 420 really wakes up. From a slightly nervous idle the power begins to pour from 2,000 rpm. Add another 2,000, and the exhaust note, booming from the single stainless steel drainpipe poking through the rear skirt, takes on a harder edge. It is not a heavy, uneven throb like a Chevrolet, nor the demonic scream of a Ferrari, but somewhere in-between. It feels much classier than it should, given the commercial vehicle origins of the engine, and it is smooth, devoid of any mechanical harshness or the thrumming that sets the panels of a Range Rover shimmying in sympathy when it is revved. There's no red sector on the TVR's tacho – Lotus

style – but we were told that 6,200 rpm was the advisable limit, although there is rarely any need to venture into those areas in everyday use.

The gearbox is the Rover Vitesse manual item, and if the change is not up to the standard of the best modern Japanese units, it is light and quite pleasant to use although the spring biasing between planes can be rather vague. This really only causes problems while performance testing, not in everyday use. The lever is sited too far back on the transmission tunnel, though.

The body is different in construction as well as style from those of ordinary 390 TVRs. The nose is sleeker and lower (an improvement), and there are blended-in side skirts and a beaver-tail rear spoiler atop the boot surface which is a matter of taste. The car's dimensions are possibly a little bluff for this sort of treatment, and the side skirts and spoiler tend to accentuate the truncated rear. It is undeniably purposeful, and in fact TVR could easily sell more than the 20 or so cars that they can build every year.

The body is hand-laid in a lightweight composite fibre material (hence the acronym Special Equipment Aramid Composite), and is

some 200 lb lighter than the 350/390 with no loss of strength. Mounted on the rugged, square-tube spaceframe chassis by silent-bloc rubber sandwiches, the structure feels rigid, and as shake-free as can be expected in a roofless vehicle.

Suspension is the 390 twin wishbone front, lower wishbone with driveshaft as upper link rear, arrangement, and the car sports 225/50 x 15 Bridgestone RE71 tyres on 8.5 in TVR pattern aluminium wheels – 245/45 x 16 on 9 in wheels are an option for the rear. On the road, the SEAC has all the traditional TVR virtues: super-sharp, accurate turn-in, gentle understeer which can be banished then converted to a gentle power slide by pressure of the right foot, superb balance and absolutely enormous grip. The ride, however, is less satisfactory, and dampers are currently an area of great concern to TVR. The test car had Bilstein at the rear, Spax at the front, and the compromise between taut body control over crests at the expense of much jiggling at low speeds – or a wallowing of the front – has yet to be discovered. At the time of writing (1988) it seems that Koni may provide the long-term answer. Like Ferrari's 328, the steering, which

is subtly power assisted, may have excellent feel, but there is wrist-jarring kickback over large potholes.

Interior finish is traditionally-styled walnut veneer and leather, and is nicely executed. Heating and ventilation are fairly primitive, especially the cool air supply, but then the roof can always be taken off – something which needs barely 30 seconds thanks to TVR's award-winning hood design. Wind buffeting is minimal.

Summing up the 420 SEAC is difficult. The problem, as always, is what else you can buy for the money, but then as we discovered while assessing the 390, there is really nothing directly comparable. Ironically perhaps, the major opposition comes from TVR itself. The 390 is almost as quick, and is substantially cheaper. Cheaper still is the 350. None of them has the class of a Ferrari, or is as well made as a Jaguar XJ-S, but then the TVR is different. It has a supremely muscular charm, is devoid of temperament, and with the roof off on a sunny day, makes all the sense in the world.

TVR 420 SEAC

ENGINE

Cylinders: V8 (90-degree), in-line, front-mounted.
Capacity: 4,230 cc (254 cu in).
Bore/stroke: 93.5/77 mm (3.68/3.03 in).
Valve gear: single central camshaft, chain driven, pushrod ohv, two valves per cylinder.
Compression ratio: 9.75:1.
Fuel system: electronic injection.
Maximum power: 304 bhp/5,750 rpm.
Maximum torque: 290 lb ft/4,500 rpm.

TRANSMISSION

Type: 5-speed manual, rear-wheel drive.
Mph/kph per 1,000 rpm in top gear: 28.5/45.8.

SUSPENSION, WHEELS

Front: independent, by double wishbones, coil springs, anti-roll bar.
Rear: trailing arms, lateral links (driveshafts acting as stressed members), coil springs, anti-roll bar.
Steering: assisted rack and pinion .
Brakes: (Front) ventilated discs/(Rear) plain discs, servo assisted.
Tyres/wheels: front and rear 225/50 VR 15 -8.5J (or 245/45 VR 16 -9J).

DIMENSIONS

Length: 153.0 in (389 cm).
Width: 68.0 in (170 cm).
Height: 47.4 in (120.5 cm).
Wheelbase: 93.8 in (238.5 cm).
Front/rear track: 57.9/58.3 in (147/148 cm).
Weight: 2,486 lbs (1,130 kg).
Fuel tank: 13.4 gallons (61 litres).

PERFORMANCE*

Maximum speed: 155 mph (248 kph).
Acceleration: 0-60 mph (96.5 kph) 5 sec.
Fuel consumption (average): 22.6 mpg (12.5 litres/100 km).

*Estimated

VECTOR W-2

Finally, a real dream car that has yet to become a reality. A lot of names have been thrown into the lexicon of supercar possibilities in recent years, some of them known, some of them unknown. The Vector W-2 was one of the early names, as in the early 1980s it came into being with quite a bang and then went silent until early 1989. In that time a small miracle took place.

The vision of Gerald Wiegert (now CEO and Chairman of Vector Aeromotive Corporation, the heir to the Vector Cars Limited partnership he first formed in 1978), Vector underwent extensive financial planning and marketing studies for several years and is now the foremost product of a publicly traded company with an extremely well-planned board of advisors and a verified order list of 10 very wealthy customers who have advanced deposits on their hi-tech, hand-built, Vector Twin Turbos. Amongst the advisors is Peter W Schutz, former CEO and Chairman of Porsche AG and Ron Tonkin, President of the US National Automobile Dealers Association.

Vector plans on delivering several of its current orders in time for owners to be driving them

not long into the 1990s. The list of owners reads like a who's who of automotive executives and world-wide wealth. Having gained the necessary funding through public status (that took place in November 1988), Vector has done something several other companies are rumoured to be considering: it has designed and produced a proprietary all-aluminium V-8. Like the original W-2 engine, it uses the standard American prescription of stump-pulling torque (allegedly 700-plus lb ft!) at low rpm gained from a two-valves-per-cylinder design. Electronic fuel injection and twin turbochargers add the icing to this engine that carries a dyno-certified figure of 600-plus bhp from a mere 8psi of boost, and using 92-octane unleaded petrol.

Dyno figures have shown that 725 bhp is available but production 6.0 litre Vectors will be delivered with the 600-plus bhp as Vector wants a dependable, 'turn-key' engine that is emissions-legal under strict California standards.

The 6.0 litre alloy engine uses the latest digital electronic ignition, EFI, twin intercoolers, dry sump oiling, a high capacity water pump, stainless exhaust and even dual catalytic exhaust system to extract emissions-legal power from what is really an aluminium racing block and heads design detuned for road use.

True to the original design of over a decade ago, the radical

wedge shape and steeply raked cab section have not changed much, as the technology of manufacturing now matches the technology of composite body materials. Although Kevlar and carbon fibre are not new words to racing structure, the Vector may well be the first to use these materials over a semi-monocoque aluminium honeycomb built for street-legal vehicles.

Using nothing but the finest aerospace fastening hardware of 6,000 50,000 lb rivets, a bonding agent named Redux 410 and Grade 8 and 12 fasteners to hold the various aluminium panels and steel surrounds, they recently passed the Federal standards for roof crush, seat and seat belt and door entry standards with a margin of two to three times the government requirement.

Possessing the aerodynamics to break the 200 mph barrier, they have also made sure the Vector will stop and turn when required. The brakes are actually Formula One Alcon four-piston calipers holding 13 x 1.1 in ventilated discs. Front suspension is a simple adjustable upper and lower A-arm derivative with Vector designed de Dion-style rear suspension, using Koni coil spring/dampers and anti-roll bars.

Although the drag coefficient of the heavily wedge-shaped body is not discussed, the road-holding figures should be impressive with the use of Michelin P255/ 45ZR16 front and P315/40ZR16 rear tyres mounted

on Vector proprietary billet aluminium wheels.

Vector Vice President of manufacturing, Mark Bailey, a 15-year aerospace veteran, sees the Vector as a synthesis of team work, many of the staff having joined Vector with not only his own high degree of speciality, but a yearning to complete a once-in-a-lifetime project. On the comparison between the established names and Vector... 'We use the best American technology we can, apply it where it makes sense and build the best product possible... We really have no limits on the quality, the materials and the type of components we use here. The intent is to build the finest automotive product possible.'